ROWS OF MEMORY

ROWS OF MEMORY

JOURNEYS OF A MIGRANT SUGAR-BEET WORKER

||||||||||||||||||||||||||||||||||||||||||||||||||||||||||||||||||||||

SAÚL SÁNCHEZ

UNIVERSITY OF IOWA PRESS | IOWA CITY

University of Iowa Press, Iowa City 52242
Copyright © 2014 by the University of Iowa Press
www.uiowapress.org
Printed in the United States of America

Design by April Leidig

The University of Iowa Press is a member of Green Press Initiative
and is committed to preserving natural resources.

Printed on acid-free paper

ISBN-13: 978-1-60938-233-9
ISBN-10: 1-60938-233-1
LCCN: 2013952704

To my parents, children, and grandchildren:
Gabriel, Alejandro, Isabel, Alexandria, and Jasmine.

ıııııııııııııııııııııııııııı

To live is to create; to create is to love; to love is to live.

Contents

Acknowledgments

Thanks to Charlotte M. Wright, Managing Editor, University of Iowa Press, for her editorial comments and technical support on this project. I thank also Norma R. Salinas for providing valuable advice and technical expertise. To my *compadre* Oscar Pérez I convey my heartfelt gratitude for his generosity of spirit, and likewise my gratitude to Kyle D. Olson of Texas Lutheran University for reproducing admirable photocopies. I also appreciate the many contributions of my family: sisters, brother, cousins, aunts and uncles. Lastly, to Catherine C. Cocks, Acquisitions Editor of the University of Iowa Press, I am grateful for the opportunity to publish this memoir.

This story is a personal account of one individual's experience, but my hope is that it mirrors the broader reality of that vast underclass of humanity known as migrant workers. It is intended to pay homage to their resourcefulness and integrity. My efforts, however flawed, were nonetheless guided by Abelard's dictum: "By doubting we come to inquiry, by inquiring we come to perceive the truth."

OMAR VALERIO-JIMÉNEZ

||||||||||||||||||||||||||||||||||||||||||||||||||||||||||||||||||||||||||||||||||||||||||||||||||||

Rows of Memory as an Exemplary Migrant Experience

Rows of Memory offers a revealing look at the life of a Mexican American migrant worker from childhood to young adulthood as he traveled with his extended family from their home in Texas to various sites in the Midwest. The significance of Saúl Sánchez's memoir lies not only in his detailed descriptions of farmworkers' experiences, but also in his documentation of his family's persistence as migrant workers over five decades, his own eventual educational attainment, and his analytical insights into migrant life.

Born in California, Sánchez grew up in a migrant family from the Texas border region. Despite frequent interruptions in his elementary and secondary schooling due to his family's yearly migrations north, the author succeeded academically and eventually left the migrant circuit in order to obtain a university education. Although Sánchez became a socially mobile college professor, he never forgot his migrant roots. *Rows of Memory* is a touching testimony of his admiration for his family and the pride he still maintains for his working-class origins.

Among the strengths of this memoir are the detailed descriptions of migrant life that most readers know about only in the abstract. *Rows of Memory* provides specific examples of seasonal (or circular) migration, the creation of migration routes, the influence of labor recruiters on migration, and the use of the Border Patrol to target workers while ignoring employers. The text also describes the tools and techniques employed by agricultural workers, the working conditions they endured, and the difficult decisions they had to make about migrating. Sánchez provides vivid examples of how his social networks enabled him and his family to overcome many obstacles. The author invokes the collective memory of three generations to describe migrant family life during a time when his family was expanding the geographic scope of its seasonal sojourns. This allows Sánchez to describe events that he did not actually witness, but that are nonetheless part of his family's oral tradition.

Central Themes

Some of the most captivating sections in the book deal with the tensions between the author's need for an education and his responsibilities to his family, tensions that many students (especially those from immigrant backgrounds) continue to face. Like several other recent memoirs, *Rows of Memory* is a gripping and honest portrayal of the struggles, disappointments, and triumphs of Mexican migrants. In a narrative similar to Francisco Jiménez's account of migrant life in California in *Breaking Through*, Sánchez's memoir describes the struggle that young migrant students experience while trying to balance family responsibilities and traditions with their education and other aspects of life in U.S. society. By examining the migrant experience in the Midwest, *Rows of Memory* makes an important contribution to a common topic in Latino coming-of-age memoirs.[1] The author's frank description of this tension will appeal to various readers, including those currently in school (and not just those who have immigrant backgrounds). It is rare to read such a detailed exploration of this issue from a migrant worker's perspective. Like Elva Treviño Hart in *Barefoot Heart*, Sánchez finds education to be a refuge from the poverty and the harsh labor conditions endured by his family. Although faced with numerous educational obstacles as a migrant student, Sánchez (like Jiménez and Treviño Hart) perseveres after realizing that a college education provides the types of opportunities that remain out of reach for many of his migrant peers.[2]

This memoir illuminates language issues for a migrant youth who grows up bilingual. Because several family members are monolingual Spanish speakers living within a monolingual English-speaking society, Sánchez often has to interpret between these two groups. Translating between English and Spanish is a common skill for children of immigrants, placing the child in a role where his double identity (one in Spanish and the other in English) is not just emphasized, but relied upon by both family and society. Sánchez's descriptions of these distinct linguistic worlds recall those in Richard Rodriguez's memoir, *Hunger of Memory*.[3] Like Rodriguez, Sánchez describes going through periods of feeling ashamed of his family's Mexican heritage and their Spanish language use in the home, while he enjoys increasing educational opportunities resulting from his command of the English language. In contrast to Rodriguez, however, who attempts to flee from his ancestral roots and becomes an opponent of affirmative action programs, Sánchez follows an educational trajectory in which he excels in school, recognizes the distinct disadvantages of his migrant education, and remains proud of his ancestral roots. The author's experience of living in these two worlds also recalls the memoir of Frances Esquibel Tywoniak, who, in *Migrant Daughter*, describes a farmworker experience similar to Sánchez's account of growing up in two distinct cultures. As historian Mario García has observed, Tywoniak occupies "multiple positions of identity" as she negotiates various social worlds that often overlap.[4] Similarly, Sánchez assumes multiple identities in his memoir: a child of immigrants, a migrant worker, a student striving to succeed in segregated schools, a teenage boy exploring romantic love, a youth enthralled by American popular culture, and a college student. In addition to his academic studies, sports and U.S. popular culture provided a refuge for Sánchez as he struggled with feelings of guilt for abandoning the migrant circuit and interrupting his contributions to his family's income by pursuing a university education.

Historical Context

Rows of Memory covers approximately the first twenty-five years of Sánchez's life. By invoking collective memory, the author also explores his family's history beginning in the 1910s, when some of his grandparents arrived in Texas as immigrants. The memoir's twenty chapters follow a general chronological order that explains his family's origins in the Texas-Mexico border region and their migrations to various agricultural regions in the Midwest and West from grade school through college. Sánchez's individual recollections are interspersed with his family's collective memories in a way that complement one another and give a richer account of migrant agricultural life than if he had relied only on his own memory. The photographs in *Rows of Memory*, from the author's personal collection, are a valuable addition to his written account, and help readers understand the conditions under which migrant laborers toiled.

Through the experiences of his extended family, Saúl Sánchez is able to illustrate larger patterns of migration. Mexican immigration into the United States began shortly after the U.S.-Mexican War (1846–1848), when indebted laborers fled across the Rio Grande to escape their debts and obtain higher paying jobs. Racked by political instability in the mid-nineteenth century, Mexico witnessed crippling losses of laborers from its northeastern states. Arriving throughout southern Texas, these immigrants joined long-standing Tejano (Texas Mexican) communities with roots in colonial-era settlements. Many of the immigrants found employment in ranching, domestic service, and agriculture in southern Texas. This flow of migrants accelerated during the last two decades of the nineteenth century, as the economic policies of Mexico's dictator Porfirio Díaz increased landlessness and unemployment.[5] By the late nineteenth century, some Mexican workers had begun participating in a pattern of circular migration in which they worked in Texas for a season, then returned to Mexico and repeated the process in subsequent years.

The turmoil of the Mexican Revolution provided the motivation for several of the author's grandparents to move to the United States. Sánchez's maternal grandfather joined this exodus during the early part of the Mexican Revolution (1910–1920) and found work in Uvalde County, Texas, as a sheepherder and sharecropper. In general, Sánchez's grandparents formed part of a larger stream of immigrants who left Mexico to escape the military conflicts, forced enlistments, and devastation caused by its civil war. These push factors led Mexico to lose a tenth of its population. In turn, the Mexican immigrant population in the U.S. surged, as some 119,000 entered between 1900 and 1910, while at least 206,000 immigrants immigrated legally between 1910 and 1920. Thousands more arrived as undocumented workers and refugees.[6] Among the pull factors attracting these immigrants were social stability, political refuge, and most importantly, economic opportunities. The need for labor in the U.S. Southwest continued to increase as railroad development and irrigation projects made farming possible throughout the region. In southern Texas, these developments led to a large-scale conversion of ranch property into farming lands.[7]

Foreword

The arrival of Sánchez's grandparents in the U.S. fits a larger pattern of Mexicans' chain migration and integration into existing Mexican American communities. Like that of many other immigrant families, the Sánchezes' journey began with the arrival of an unaccompanied male who found work, sent remittances to his family, and eventually paid for one sibling after another to join him. A variation in this pattern would involve a husband arriving first, and then sending for his wife, children, and extended family. This process of chain migration repeated itself multiple times, allowing communities of family and friends to reestablish themselves in the United States. Such chain migration explains the phenomenon found throughout the nation in which neighborhoods in San Antonio, Texas, or West Liberty, Iowa, are made up of immigrants from the same towns in Coahuila and Durango, Mexico, respectively. Because Mexican immigrants often settle in regions that have existing Mexican American communities, their arrival helps both Mexican immigrants and Mexican Americans create new social ties based on shared work and living experiences. Like many other ethnic Mexican families, Sánchez's grandparents included a Mexican immigrant who married a Mexican American, as well as Mexican Americans who had lived on both sides of the border. Historically, the arrival of new Mexican immigrants in established Mexican American communities helped to renew cultural traditions, reinforce the Spanish language, and diversify its regional origins.[8] In Texas, Sánchez's family contributed to this reinvigoration of Mexican cultural practices, while their journeys to the Midwest, in some cases, led to the introduction of Mexican influences in communities without a previous Mexican American presence.

The Sánchez family's immigration experience illustrates the multiple crossings of the U.S.-Mexico border experienced by so many Mexican and Mexican American families. This international boundary has symbolized various opportunities to residents of both sides, including political refuge, jobs, and social stability. While the flow of immigration was mainly northward during the reign of Díaz and the Mexican Revolution, in subsequent years, large numbers of former immigrants returned south to escape the increased racial hostility in the United States during the Great Depression. Many people found it beneficial to migrate back and forth as their personal situations changed—in response to divorces, personal disagreements, and the need for family reunification. As a result of these migrations, families often included some members born in Mexico and others born in the United States. Several members of the Sánchez family also followed this pattern, including Saúl's paternal grandparents, who were born in the United States but later returned to Mexico, where their children were born. Thus the Sánchez family is an example of the many generational and social ties that develop within families and that create extensive links across the border.[9]

Arriving in the Winter Garden area in Zavala County, Sánchez's grandparents were part of a larger pattern of migration to a region that underwent tremendous change during the first three decades of the twentieth century. The area's development and population boomed after the railroad's arrival linked it to San Antonio in 1909. Developers had given the area its name in an effort to promote an image of agricultural abundance and a temperate climate. Encompassing Dimmitt, Maverick, Zavala, and a portion of La Salle counties, the Winter Garden area developed as a commercial farming region in the first decade of the twentieth century. Encouraged by the arrival of the railroad, developers began subdividing ranch properties into farm tracts and towns, establishing irrigation companies to provide water for farms that were sold to European American newcomers from midwestern states.[10]

This agricultural development created a demand for labor that could not be met by the existing resident Tejano population alone. Agricultural jobs attracted Mexican immigrants (like the Sánchezes) from Coahuila, Nuevo León, and Tamaulipas in particular.[11] Spinach and onions became the primary crops in the region, whose population boomed in the 1920s. Crystal City, where the Sánchez family settled, grew into the main commercial and population hub of the area.[12] Then, during the 1930s, Tejano agricultural workers began experiencing underemployment due both to a precipitous decline in spinach and onion production and to an increase in competition for jobs. To lower their production costs, agricultural employers had resumed labor recruitment from Mexico. In addition, the arrival of white Dust Bowl migrants displaced local Tejano workers from higher-paying jobs in packinghouses. As they faced increasing underemployment, the Tejano workers increasingly looked toward the Midwest as a region with better employment opportunities.[13]

The Midwest as Destination

Rows of Memory powerfully demonstrates the varied experiences of Tejano agricultural workers who followed interstate migrant circuits and began the gradual process of settlement in the Midwest. After following seasonal migration routes within Texas, the Sánchez family eventually began participating in circular migration between Texas and the Midwest. Agricultural work drew migrant laborers to various regions of the nation's heartland as Mexicans started harvesting sugar beets in Iowa, onions in Minnesota, cucumbers in Michigan, and potatoes in Wisconsin. Labor agents played an influential role in recruiting families like the Sánchezes to travel to the Midwest. Although ethnic Mexicans had been arriving there since the late nineteenth century to work in the agricultural fields and railroad yards, these early migrants had mostly migrated with the seasons. Few stayed there throughout the year, preferring instead to return to Texas or Mexico after a period of work. These early arrivals were also mostly unaccompanied males— either single men or married men who migrated without their wives or children.

Recruiting unaccompanied males was a purposeful strategy by the agricultural employers to depress wages, giving them an excuse not to provide the workers with a family wage. According to historian Dennis Valdés, this strategy also appeased local white residents' fears that Mexicans would form permanent settlements in regions where these workers were considered non-white, and therefore not welcomed. Agricultural employers gradually began hiring Mexicans for jobs previously performed by European immigrants such as Russian Germans, Slovakians, and Bohemians.[14] The European immigrants had settled in the Midwest during an earlier period, when they were able to work toward becoming farmers after saving money or obtaining loans to purchase land. As Sánchez explains in his memoir, the sugar beet companies initially began recruiting Japanese laborers from California to offset the loss of European immigrants, but this source was not enough to fill demand. Subsequently, employers turned to Mexican immigrants to fill a labor need aggravated by a change in the nation's immigration laws in the 1920s. The arrival of European immigrants decreased after the U.S passed the so-called "quota laws" (1921 and 1924), which sharply curtailed the number of people who could legally migrate to the U.S. from southern and eastern Europe. By the 1920s, agricultural wages had also dropped precipitously, leaving Mexican immigrants unable to save enough money to purchase farms or even to obtain equipment so that they could work as tenant farmers.[15]

At the same time, companies such as the Great Western Sugar Company and the American Beet Sugar Company changed their recruiting methods in an attempt to resolve the problem of an unstable workforce. They reasoned that men with families were more stable than single males, who often abandoned their contracts to switch employers. Agricultural companies also wanted to take advantage of the extra workers provided by the use of family labor.[16] The new strategy proved successful because laborers were more likely to remain with an employer when their families accompanied them.

The migration of families led to the gradual creation of new Mexican settlements throughout the Midwest, including Iowa, because laborers found they could remain in the region after the agricultural harvests, working in nonagricultural jobs during the off-season. While some migrants continued to participate in circular migration, others found more stable jobs in railroad maintenance, industrial factories, and packinghouses. The Mexican population in the Midwest increased dramatically during the 1920s. In 1900, Mexicans barely registered in the census totals for Kansas (71) and Illinois (156). By 1927, the Mexican population in the Midwest stood at 63,700.[17] Iowa saw a corresponding rapid growth in its Mexican population. Approximately 2,720 Mexicans lived in the state by the mid-1920s. They lived in various towns, with approximately 544 in the Manly and Mason City area, but the largest concentration (1,055) resided in the Mississippi River towns of Bettendorf, Davenport, and Fort Madison.[18]

Several of the Mexican settlements in Iowa began as company towns. Agricultural concerns, railroad companies, and industrial factories established rental housing for their workers on company-owned land. The Bettendorf Company, for example, constructed housing in Holy City to rent to its laborers, while the Lehigh Portland Company did the same for its workers in Mason City, although the housing ordinarily consisted mostly of shacks, flats, cottages, and old railroad boxcars. Some enclaves, like Cook's Point in Davenport, were prone to flooding. Living conditions were rudimentary, as most houses lacked electricity and running water.[19] Among the company towns were some, like Cook's Point, that housed mostly Mexicans, while others, like Lehigh Row in Mason City, were home to a mix of southern and eastern Europeans in addition to Mexicans and Mexican Americans. Like many other migrant families, the Sánchez family lived in railroad boxcars, shacks, and makeshift labor camps. In addition to relying on their employers for housing, laborers also had to depend on them for medical care, transportation, and food. As Sánchez explains in chapter 2, Mexican immigrants obtained credit at company stores to buy food and supplies. A distinguishing characteristic that set these Mexican workers apart from their counterparts in larger midwestern cities was the high level of control exerted by their employers.

Educational and Occupational Challenges

As a native Spanish speaker in a migrant family, Saúl Sánchez faced significant educational challenges. By the time he began primary school in Texas, the state had replaced "additive" Americanization in its public school curriculum with "subtractive" Americanization. With the additive model, teachers introduced English-language instruction in core subjects but respected and even nurtured a student's native culture and language. By contrast, the subtractive Americanization model featured English-only instruction, punishments for children who spoke their native language, and the belief that the maintenance of ethnic differences was un-American.[20] Like other schoolchildren of his generation, Sánchez endured emotional trauma from the punishments administered by school officials whenever he spoke Spanish. He describes the humiliations and feelings of being rejected by his teachers, who enforced the prohibition against Spanish even on school playgrounds. In addition to reprimands, school children guilty of infractions incurred spankings, ear pinchings, and even expulsions.[21]

The most significant outcome of the state's English-only instruction was the convenient rationale for maintaining segregated schools. Because Mexicans were legally classified as white, they were entitled to the same educational rights as other whites. According to historian Carlos Blanton, however, school officials justified the segregation of Mexican school children, by arguing that these students needed to learn the English language before they could join mainstream classrooms. Inadequate funding, poor facilities,

and substandard instruction plagued the so-called Mexican schools that became common throughout Texas and the Southwest. This policy is behind
the author's recollection of attending a segregated primary school along
with other migrant students in old dilapidated barracks that had housed
Japanese, Italian, and German internees during World War II.[22]

Throughout the Winter Garden area, schools implemented an unofficial
skills tracking system in which Mexicans were relegated to the lower skills
tracks. Not surprisingly, Sánchez mentions (in chapter 16) the low expectations for Mexican students held by the high school counselors in Crystal
City. The European American teachers and administrators of these schools
often believed in Mexicans' inferiority and sought to enforce a policy that
stipulated that so-called ignorant Mexicans made better laborers.[23] Many
school districts in Texas, including the one in Crystal City, continued to
segregate Mexican schoolchildren even after the landmark 1948 *Delgado v.
Bastrop Independent School District* case that prohibited the segregation of
students of "Mexican or Latin descent."[24] In a moving and revealing passage
in chapter 7, the author describes the shame and sense of self-hatred that
gripped him as a child, comparing his own experience to the psychological
trauma experienced by the plaintiffs in the *Brown v. the Board of Education*
case (1954).

In addition to enrolling in segregated schools, many migrant children
in Texas could not attend school regularly because of their family's participation in the migratory labor circuit. At various points in his memoir,
Sánchez describes the challenges of arriving at school in Texas in October
or November, long after the school year had started, and leaving school
in April, before the school year ended. He describes his first days back at
school as chaotic and disorienting. Unlike most migrant students, Sánchez
persevered in school even though he believed he had never quite caught up
with some of his fellow students. For many migrant schoolchildren, these
interruptions created insurmountable obstacles because they fell behind in
their classes and were not able to catch up. As a result, some of them would
eventually drop out of school. Even if they persevered, migrant students
faced additional challenges in the Midwest because they were expected to
contribute to their family's income. Despite the passage of the Sugar Act of
1937, which prohibited children under fourteen from working in the sugar
beet harvest, farmers routinely ignored this law. Midwestern school admin-

istrators failed to enforce the child labor provisions because they supported farmers' requests for additional labor. In addition, administrators did not want to ask teachers to spend more class time on Mexican migrant children who might need additional instruction and supervision. Some white teachers and parents claimed that allowing Mexican students in schools would lower educational standards. Not surprisingly, many migrant school children failed to attend school during their stay in the Midwest.[25]

As migrant families journeyed north, they continued to experience segregation in many aspects of their lives. Migrants learned to avoid specific towns along the way because of the antagonisms they encountered. Many restaurants refused to serve traveling Mexican laborers. At those restaurants that did serve them, Mexicans were required to sit in segregated sections or were ordered to eat outside. As Sánchez explains, drivers often avoided such segregated restaurants, and they also restricted who could get off the trucks when visiting gas stations in hostile regions.

If traveling migrants were involved in traffic accidents, medical personnel in certain towns refused to treat them. Drivers also encountered hostile law enforcement officials who staged raids to stop trucks with Texas license plates. To make matters worse, officials occasionally jailed stranded migrants on spurious charges or while they confirmed that the laborers had valid work contracts.[26] Once they reached their destinations, Mexican migrants typically lived in segregated camps, removed from local residents. As Sánchez notes in several chapters, residential segregation was intentional to keep Mexicans separated from local white residents. Labor camp housing typically consisted of makeshift and dilapidated structures, including old barns, chicken coops, and abandoned houses. Migrant families often had to haul their own water for cooking and washing because employers failed to provide running water and proper sanitation.[27]

The journey north also involved other risks. In chapters 6 and 10, Sánchez describes the dehumanizing and dangerous transportation of workers in open-stake trucks. Beginning in the 1930s, such trucks were used by labor contractors, some of whom were former migrant workers themselves, to transport laborers to the beet fields. According to Dennis Valdés, this *troquero* system (named for the crew leader who served as the troquero, or truck driver) emerged because of the wide availability of open-stake trucks and in order to transport various families in one vehicle. The labor force during the Great Depression began to include several extended families that often came from the same town. The troquero collected a registration fee from each worker and charged for transportation, a system that resulted in workers becoming indebted before they even arrived at their destination. A crew leader would establish oral contracts with the workers that specified the wages and the type of work required. Sánchez's account corroborates research showing that up to fifty workers were required to stand in the bed of a truck, and drivers often avoided stopping except when absolutely necessary for fuel or emergencies. The 1935 Motor Vehicle Act further complicated the multi-day trips from Texas. Because it stipulated that drivers register their trucks, limit their driving time to ten hours, and submit their vehicles to regular inspections, truck drivers would drive at night, choose back roads, and cover the truck beds (including passengers) with tarps to conceal workers from authorities. These strategies to avoid detection and stops made the 1,600 to 2,000-mile trips even more dangerous than they had been before the MVA and resulted in several tragic deaths from truck accidents.[28]

By creating labor shortages as Americans left civilian industrial jobs to join the military, World War II led to new opportunities that would have a long-term impact on farmworkers like the Sánchez family. In turn, the agricultural industry struggled to find laborers because rural workers migrated to cities for better-paying and more stable jobs. Moving to California for nonagricultural jobs, the Sánchezes were part of this movement, as described in chapters 4 and 5. After the war, many veterans returned to their old jobs, displacing those who had been more recently hired. It is unclear from *Rows of Memory* if Saúl Sánchez's family was among those who lost their wartime employment to returning soldiers, but the end result was that part of the family resumed their work as migrant agricultural laborers, while others remained in cities.[29]

The working conditions under which they labored after 1945 would continue to be influenced by wartime policies. The need for labor in U.S. agriculture had risen sharply in the early 1940s because agricultural production expanded as the war reduced competition from Europe and many agricultural workers moved to the cities to take nonagricultural jobs. To meet this increased need, in 1942 Mexico and the U.S. established the Bracero Program, a guest-worker program that employed Mexican male workers in agriculture and railroad maintenance on a contract basis. The program's success in supplying workers through managed migration prompted Congress to continue the program in the agricultural industry even after the war. In 1951, the U.S. and Mexico formalized a new agreement, Public Law 78, which extended the Bracero Program to meet the labor shortages caused by the Korean War. Renegotiated in 1954, Public Law 78 would be renewed continuously until it expired in 1964. Ultimately, the result of the Bracero Program was to push many Mexican Americans out of agricultural work. For those families like the Sánchezes who continued as farmworkers, the availability of guest workers through the Bracero Program meant that employers were able to keep wages low and had little motivation to improve living and working conditions.[30]

By the 1960s, Mexican Americans' limited educational opportunities and political disenfranchisement in places like Crystal City sparked their civil rights activism. Throughout the Winter Garden area, ethnic Mexican workers were socially and residentially segregated from Anglo Americans during the first half of the twentieth century. Although they were a minority of the population, Anglo Americans controlled county and municipal offices through a combination of intimidation and legal obstacles like poll taxes. In the 1950s, Mexican Americans had waged electoral campaigns for school board, but they had failed to win elected office. With the assistance of the American GI Forum (a Mexican American veterans' organization), they had also attempted to desegregate local schools, but they were unsuccessful. By 1960, Mexican Americans constituted 85 percent of Crystal City's population. However, many continued to live in poverty, which forced some 80 percent of Mexicans, like the Sánchezes, to migrate annually as agricultural workers.[31]

In addition to school segregation, students faced teachers and administrators who had limited educational expectations for Mexican Americans as Sánchez confirms in chapters 11 and 16. Despite substantial challenges, Mexican American school enrollment had increased in the 1950s when parents began changing their migration practices to lessen the number of school absences for their children. Private neighborhood preschools and schools, like the one that Sánchez mentions in chapter 5, became more popular as parents sought to prepare their children for English instruction. By 1960, the majority of Crystal City's high school students were Mexican

Americans, and they began to increase their participation in school activities, clubs, and sports. They also ran successful campaigns for student government office, and in the process learned about organizing and civic participation. In response, school administrators began reserving distinctions and honors (such as "most beautiful" and "most handsome") for European American students as Sánchez mentions in chapter 13. Certain activities and clubs (such as cheerleading) had unofficial quotas to limit participation by Mexican Americans. The administrators' attempts to manipulate awards to preserve white privilege created resentment among Mexican Americans and motivated them to organize.[32] Although too young to vote, these students played a pivotal role when the Political Association of Spanish-Speaking Organizations (PASSO) and the Teamsters Union came together to support a slate of five Mexican American candidates for city council in 1963. The students helped register voters, promoted candidates through their social networks, and held fundraisers to pay poll taxes. As Sánchez recounts in chapter 16, the 1963 electoral win of the five-candidate slate of former migrant workers led to an increased confidence among Mexican Americans in Crystal City and throughout Texas.[33]

Today, laborers in the agricultural industry continue to face similar challenges to those described in *Rows of Memory*. Agricultural work remains among the lowest paid in the nation, and it is the second most hazardous occupation after mining. In addition to exposure to pesticides, agricultural laborers are subject to heat and sun exposure, poor sanitation, and working conditions in which accidents are commonplace. Farmworkers, therefore, tend to suffer from health problems more than the general population, but they lack access to affordable healthcare.[34] The low wages and dangerous working conditions have led to an exodus of U.S. citizens from farm labor and to the industry's increasing reliance on immigrant and foreign workers. The number of agricultural laborers has declined steadily over the last century, and presently stands at approximately one million. Approximately 33 percent of these are U.S. citizens, 50 percent are unauthorized immigrants, and the remaining are permanent residents. The majority (83 percent) of farmworkers today are Latino—most are Mexicans (72 percent), but there are also some Mexican Americans (8 percent), and other Latinos (3 percent).[35] The number of migrants who follow the crops, as did the Sánchez family, has steadily declined—they make up only 5 percent of current farmworkers. About 75 percent of farmworkers today live permanently near their workplaces.[36] These trends have increasingly led the agricultural industry to turn to the guest worker program to hire foreign contract laborers, and to lobby for the inclusion of an expanded guest worker program in the current immigration reform proposals. As the United States considers expanding the agricultural guest worker program, it is important to remember that contract farmworkers have had very limited labor rights (for example, unionization is prohibited), unenforceable protections for working conditions, and severely restricted avenues for workplace complaints. In addition, critics have accused farmers using the guest worker program of racial bias for favoring malleable foreign workers over local African Americans.[37] An expansion of a guest worker program would permit agricultural employers to keep wages low and working conditions poor for domestic farmworkers, just as those described in *Rows of Memory*. Ultimately, Saúl Sánchez's memoir is valuable for its insights into the considerable obstacles that continue to confront farmworkers and for the unique story of one migrant's ability to overcome such challenges.

Notes

1. Examples of such memoirs include Ernesto Galarza, *Barrio Boy* (Notre Dame: University of Notre Dame Press, 1971); Francisco Jiménez, *Breaking Through* (Boston: Houghton Mifflin, 2001); Piri Thomas, *Down These Mean Streets* (New York: Knopf, 1967); and Esmeralda Santiago, *When I Was Puerto Rican* (New York: Vintage Books, 1994). Explorations of multiple identities, acculturation, and linguistic adaptation also occur in Sandra Cisneros, *House on Mango Street* (New York: Vintage Books, 1991) and Gloria Anzaldua, *Borderlands: The New Mestiza = La Frontera* (San Francisco: Spinsters/Aunt Lute, 1987), although these are not strictly memoirs.

2. Elsa Treviño Hart, *Barefoot Heart: Stories of a Migrant Child* (Tempe, AZ: Bilingual Review Press, 1999).

3. Richard Rodriguez, *Hunger of Memory: The Education of Richard Rodriguez, an Autobiography* (Boston: D. R. Godine, 1981).

4. Frances Esquibel Tywoniak, *Migrant Daughter: Coming of Age as a Mexican American Woman* (Berkeley: University of California Press, 2000).

5. Omar S. Valerio-Jiménez, *River of Hope: Forging Identity and Nation in the Rio Grande Borderlands* (Durham, NC: Duke University Press, 2013), 182–84.

6. David G. Gutiérrez, *Walls and Mirrors: Mexican Americans, Mexican Immigrants, and the Politics of Ethnicity* (Berkeley: University of California Press, 1995), 45; Paul Ganster and David Lorey, *The U.S.-Mexican Border into the Twenty-first Century* (Lanham, MD: Rowman and Littlefield Publishers, 2008), 66–67.

7. David Montejano, *Anglos and Mexicans in the Making of Texas, 1836–1986* (Austin: University of Texas Press, 1987), 106–10.

8. Manuel G. Gonzales, *Mexicanos: A History of Mexicans in the United States* (Bloomington: Indiana University Press, 1999), 133–38; George J. Sánchez, *Becoming Mexican American: Ethnicity, Culture and Identity in Chicano Los Angeles, 1900–1945* (New York: Oxford University Press, 1993), 188–206.

9. Omar S. Valerio-Jiménez, "The United States-Mexico Border as Material and Cultural Barrier," in *Migrants and Migration in Modern North America: Cross-Border Lives, Labor Markets, and Politics in Canada, the Caribbean, Mexico, and the United States*, ed. Dirk Hoerder and Nora Faires (Durham, NC: Duke University Press, 2011), 228–50.

10. Montejano, *Anglos and Mexicans in the Making of Texas*, 106–107.

11. Marc Rodriguez, *The Tejano Diaspora: Mexican Americanism and Ethnic Politics in Texas and Wisconsin* (Chapel Hill: University of North Carolina Press, 2011), 16–17.

12. Rodriguez, *Tejano Diaspora*, 16–17; Valdés, *Al Norte: Agricultural Workers in the Great Lakes Region, 1917–1970* (Austin: University of Texas Press, 1991), 52.

13. Valdés, *Al Norte*, 52.

14. Dennis Nodín Valdés, "Settlers, Sojourners, and Proletarians: Social Forma-tion in the Great Plains Sugar Beet Industry, 1890–1940," *Great Plains Quarterly* 10 (Spring 1990), 113; Zaragosa Vargas, *Proletarians of the North: A History of Mexican Industrial Workers in Detroit and the Midwest, 1917–1933* (Berkeley: University of California Press, 1993), 20–25.

15. Zaragosa Vargas, "Armies in the Fields: The Mexican Working Classes in the Midwest in the 1920s," *Mexican Studies/Estudios Mexicanos* 7:1 (Winter 1999), 52; Valdés, "Settlers, Sojourners, and Proletarians," 111–14.

16. Valdés, "Settlers, Sojourners, and Proletarians," 112–13; Vargas, *Proletarians of the North*, 26.

17. Juan R. García, Mexicans in the Midwest: 1900-1932 (Tucson: University of Arizona Press, 1996), 27; Vargas, *Proletarians of the North*, 21.

18. George T. Edson, "Mexicans in the North Central States," *Perspectives in Mexican American Studies* 2 (1989), 107–108; Teresa A. García, "Mexican Room: Public Schooling and the Children of Mexican Railroad Workers in Fort Madison, Iowa, 1923–1930" (PhD diss., University of Iowa, 2008), 58, 61.

19. Peter Vega interview in "Lehigh Row Remembered," *The Forum: Sunday Registrar*, April 29, 1990, in Vega Family Papers, Mujeres Latinas Project–Iowa Women's Archives; García, "Mexican Room," 63; Janet Weaver, "From Barrio to 'Boicoteo!': The Emergence of Mexican American Activism in Davenport, 1917–1970," *The Annals of Iowa* 68:3 (Summer 2009), 218.

20. The additive Americanization model tended to emphasize cultural pluralism, while the subtractive model was informed by nativist sentiments. Carlos Blanton, *The Strange Career of Bilingual Education in Texas, 1836–1981* (College Station: Texas A&M University Press, 2004), 59–62.

21. Blanton, *Strange Career of Bilingual Education*, 82–84, 90–91.

22. The United States interned some 3,000 Italians, Germans, and Japanese who were deported from twelve Latin American countries to the United States. The Crystal City camp housed 2,264 Japanese from Latin America. The official reasons given by U.S. authorities for interning these Latin Americans was to prevent sabotage in the Western Hemisphere, and to use the internees to bargain with Japan for captured American prisoners. The internment, scholars have argued, was the result of wartime hysteria, ingrained stereotypes, and widespread anti-Japanese sentiments. Alice Yang-Murray, "The Internment of Japanese Americans," in *What Did the Internment of Japanese Americans Mean?* (Boston: Bedford/St. Martin's Press, 2000), 3–5; Michi Weglyn, "Why Did U.S. Officials Intern People of Japanese Ancestry from Central and South America?" in *What Did the Internment of Japanese Americans Mean?* (Boston: Bedford/St. Martin's Press, 2000), 84–99; Emily Brosveen, "World War II Internment Camps," Handbook of Texas Online, Texas State Historical Association, http://www.tshaonline.org/handbook/online/articles/quwby. Accessed April 23, 2013.

23. Montejano, *Anglos and Mexicans in the Making of Texas*, 168–69, 191–95; Rodriguez, *Tejano Diaspora*, 43; Blanton, *Strange Career of Bilingual Education*, 88–89.

24. Rodriguez, *Tejano Diaspora*, 35–36; Blanton, *Strange Career of Bilingual Education*, 114–17; Neil Foley, *Quest for Equality: The Failed Promise of Black-Brown Solidarity* (Cambridge: Harvard University Press, 2010), 109–111.

25. Vargas, *Proletarians of the North*, 26; Valdés, *Al Norte*, 82–84.

26. Zaragosa Vargas, *Crucible of Struggle: A History of Mexican Americans from the Colonial Period to the Present Era* (New York: Oxford University Press, 2011), 194–95; Valdés, *Al Norte*, 56–57.

27. Valdés, *Al Norte*, 64–65.

28. Valdés, *Al Norte*, 54–56.

29. Vargas, *Crucible of Struggle*, 260–63; Vargas, *Proletarians of the North*, 37.

30. The Bracero Program, which ended in 1964, employed approximately 4.8 million Mexicans. Some workers agreed to multiple contracts over the course of several years. Most braceros found employment in border states (three quarters of the total worked in California and Texas), but a few obtained jobs in the Midwest and the Pacific Northwest. Garcia y Griego, "The Importation of Mexican Contract Laborers to the United States, 1942–1964," in *Between Two Worlds: Mexican Immigrants in the United States*, ed. David Gutiérrez (Wilmington, DE: Scholarly Resources, 1996), 45–85; Manuel G. Gonzales, *Mexicanos: A History of Mexicans in the United States* (Bloomington: Indiana University Press, 1995), 170–75; Omar Valerio-Jiménez, "The United States-Mexico Border as Material and Cultural Barrier," 228–50; Vargas, *Crucible of Struggle*, 263; Rodriguez, *Tejano Diaspora*, 24–36.

31. Montejano, *Anglos and Mexicans in the Making of Texas*, 143–45; Rodriguez, *Tejano Diaspora*, 16–18.

32. Rodriguez, *Tejano Diaspora*, 43–46.

33. Vargas, *Crucible of Struggle*, 294–95; Rodriguez, *Tejano Diaspora*, 46–53.

34. "Farmworkers in the United States," *Migrant Health Promotion*, http://www
.migranthealth.org/index.php?option=com_content&view=article&id=38&Itemid
=30#3. Accessed May 2, 2013.

35. National Agricultural Workers Survey, U.S. Department of Labor, http://www
.doleta.gov/agworker/report9/chapter1.cfm. Accessed May 2, 2013.

36. "Farm Labor: Background," USDA Economic Research Service, http://www
.ers.usda.gov/topics/farm-economy/farm-labor/background.aspx#Numbers. Accessed
May 2, 2013.

37. Ethan Bronner, "Workers Claim Race Bias as Farms Rely on Immigrants," *New
York Times*, May 6, 2013.

ROWS OF MEMORY

INTRODUCTION

‖‖‖

I write this memoir to leave behind some testimony of a way of life that has disappeared perhaps forever. It is a personal narrative based on experience, taken from memory, and written years after the episodes it narrates. These episodes may not sound exalted or seem like exceptional accomplishments to the reader, but they are to the author. They are exalted because the people who appear here sacrificed a great part of their lives, and in some cases all of their lives, for the benefit of their families. And they are exceptional because it is the narrative of a people who not only survive for years under shocking living conditions but also because most of those individuals who appear in these pages managed to triumph in their lives. If we also add the fact that these people spoke Spanish and not English, it is not difficult to understand why they embody those exalted and exceptional qualities that one finds in epics.

This memoir comes from collective memory. It is not a critical history such as is written by academics. The English historian David Lowenthal, in his critical study of heritage and history, says that collective memory builds community, creates identity and, in the final analysis, makes history possible.[1] My intention is to bring that heritage back to life and massage it gently in order to hear its voice echoing through time. In this case we are talking about events experienced by three different generations: my grandparents, my parents, and me, the author. Chronologically, this is a period of time that begins just after the Mexican Revolution and ends some time during the Vietnam War.

If we want to understand in depth the ancestral heritage represented by these generations, then we should know something about their language. The words used in English, "migrant" or "migrant worker" or "migrant farm worker," to identify the members of this community of migratory agricultural workers were not used by us. They were, and still are, used by English speakers to refer to us. I purposefully place emphasis on the term *English speakers*. It is another way of saying that we have a double identity, one in English and one in Spanish. For us, during those times, English speakers were the gringos.[2] A person who speaks in English about this topic brings in a different perspective: that of someone looking at us from the outside. Since we expressed ourselves in Spanish, we knew very well that saying to each other "I'm a migrant" or "I'm a migrant worker" sounded ridiculous. The truth of the matter was that we lived in our own universe. It was an organic universe full of vitality; it had its own flavors, its own images, its own color. We did not need to classify ourselves; we knew very well who we were.

We had many ways of identifying ourselves. "The people" was the most common expression used: the people from Texas, the people from The Valley,[3] the people from Monterrey. The part of the country that we returned to at the end of the working season carried strong emotional associations for us. We honestly thought that each group had its own personality, its own traditions, its own way of life which corresponded to its geographical origins. The people of Monterrey were thought of as being cheaters, for example, while those from The Valley were considered sloppy workers, and we, of course, were the good workers. They probably felt the same way about us. It was precisely for that reason that there were several categories of people, because it depended not only on the region of the country they were from but also upon the circumstances they found themselves in. During festive occasions, for instance, the people were called *la palomilla* (working class).[4] With that name, one was really adding sort of a fraternal tinge to one's countrymen because one had certain things in common with the group. The term could be heard in baseball games up north when the Mexicans played against the gringos.[5] It was heard on weekends at the dances that were held in the barracks and labor camps and especially when there was plenty of work to go around. Quite to the contrary, though, if things were going badly those same people became *la peluza* (low class) or *la chusma* (poor masses) or *los chicaspatas* (unwashed masses).[6] When there were too many people and there was not enough work, one would say, "Where did so much *peluza* come from?" When the cheaters offered to work for less, we would say, "The *chusma* is here," or "Let's get away to where there aren't so many *chicaspatas*." It was our way of debunking the competition. It was how we let it be known that things were going badly, that work was scarce, that there were too many people looking for work. There were also *braceros* (guest workers) and *mojados* (wetbacks).[7] They worked at the same things we did, but we considered them different and thus the name. We knew they had something to do with the government. The Mexican government sent them, the United States used them, and we sometimes dealt with them, sometimes not. When we referred to them we would say, "They are Mexicans," or, "They are *raza*" (of Mexican descent).[8] It was our way of saying that we had something in common, that we understood each other, that we even looked a little bit alike. But work was work even if the politics were different.

Aside from these generalizations, the people also created their own subcategories for identification purposes, and these varied according to the quality and talent of the individual. In picking cotton, or spuds, or cucumbers, or tomatoes or fruit, we were just pickers. We were known as thinners while doing sugar beets, as cutters while cutting spinach, and as packers in the packing sheds. There were the truck drivers, the weighers, the contractors. Each made a living in his own way. The truck drivers owned their vehicles, and some of them knew enough English to make deals with the growers who needed laborers. The drivers ferried workers back and forth and took that burden off the grower's back. For their services they charged very well: the workers paid them to take them back and forth, and the growers paid them for the workers. The cotton harvest in west Texas lasted roughly between August and November, and it was during that time of the year when weighers took to the fields. The most enterprising amongst them, I remember from listening to their stories, peaked between 1900 and 1950. It was during those years that Mexicans picked by hand most of the cotton in Texas, Arkansas, and California. Those old-time weighers hung their scale on a two-by-four nailed to the side of the truck, and there they weighed every single sack full of cotton brought by the pickers. It was rare to see a weigher go into the fields to pick. Most spent their time keeping an eye out or smoking their aromatic weed while they waited for pickers to come in for a weigh. If they saw that their friend looked a bit worn out late in the day, they'd offer him a draw from their smoke to lift his spirits and help him pick more. The more cotton pickers brought in, the more money they'd make.

The contractors can still be found where there is fieldwork and there are people in need. For us there were good contractors and bad contractors. The bad ones were the more interesting ones because there was always more scuttlebutt about them. They took advantage of people, they were greedy, they had a lustful demeanor. People did not trust them. That was how we knew who the bad contractors were. They always brought in new workers. The others, the good contractors, treated people with respect, and the people, in turn, followed them. Many had other good qualities: they would lend you a few dollars when you were broke, they would stop along the road on long trips to let people go relieve themselves, and they were just fair with everyone.

Then there were the loafers, the ones who always tried to avoid work or who looked for ways to get away with the least effort. *Flojo* (lazy bum) was the nicest word used to refer to them. The word was used in mixed company, amongst men and women or young and old, and no one felt seriously aggrieved. *Arrastrado* or *rastra* (lazybones) was a bit more delicate;[9] not just anyone could call you an arrastrado or a rastra to your face. To call someone *güevón* (loafer) or *güevona* (loafer) meant that things were getting really serious.[10] That refined term would be used amongst people who knew each other well or with outsiders if one wanted to insult them. There were two other categories which were considered even lower: *mantenido* (welfare bum) and *sinvergüenza* (shameless bum). These were serious fighting words. You'd better be prepared for what was coming if you used them. There was a lexicon for authority figures as well. We could always tell who the people from Monterrey were because they called the boss *amo*. People from The Valley called him *patrón*. For us, the workers from Texas but not from The Valley, he was simply *el viejo* (the old man).

Finally, there was another way we could tell who was who. This was an observation that was used to establish, in general terms, a migrant's chronological status. It told us, for example, which generational cycle a person belonged to. The elderly ones, the family members from the first generation, sprinkled their conversations with references to grubbing, to working with pick and shovel, to topping (cutting off the tops) sugar beets. They would tell us how they had lived in tents set up in the open and that they travelled in Model T's. Their migratory cycles were limited to areas around the state of Texas. They began to arrive from Mexico during and just after the Mexican Revolution. Their sons, the next migrant generation, made the transition from pick and shovel to crop pickers. At first they made their way picking cotton toward the coast around Corpus Christi; from there they extended their travels in the other direction, toward Lubbock and other points out west. Some went all the way to Arkansas. The workers from this generational cycle had their heyday between the two World Wars and lasted through the 1950s when the mechanical cotton pickers came in and displaced them.

In our family the transition from the second to the third generation, to which I belong, begins with the journeys up north. Those long journeys into the heart of sugar-beet country constitute the third migratory cycle. People soon started going up toward the Red River Valley in the states of Minnesota, Iowa, and North Dakota in search of work. There they found a well-established sugar-beet industry with factories such as Great Western Sugar Company and American Crystal Sugar Company. These companies were really the ones responsible for initiating the third cycle. It started when they began sending their recruiting agents to Texas to find workers to do the beet work.

Each of these generations distinguished itself in its own way. One of my mother's uncles started college at around sixty years of age. He received a degree in theology four years later and served in the Presbyterian Church. Two aunts on my father's side became businesswomen during World War II. They operated kitchens for braceros in California and were financially successful. At least three uncles fought in World War II and one in Korea. They left the fields, learned English, overcame obstacles, and opened the door for us. We—my generation—started in the fields and some of us ended up graduating with bachelor's, master's, and even doctoral degrees from American universities.

CHAPTER 1

〔||||||||||||||||||||||||||||||||||||||||||||||||||||||||||||||||||||||||

The Spinach Capital of the World

W hen I was young I used to hear members of my family say that our ancestors had come to the Winter Garden Valley of Texas at the beginning of the twentieth century, and that they came from the same area: the border between Mexico and the United States. What I have been able to ascertain is that they arrived during the time of the Mexican Revolution in the case of our maternal grandfather and a little after that in the case of our paternal grandparents. The best known version tells how in 1913 our maternal grandfather found his way to the ranchlands around Sabinal and Knippa, small ranching communities less than a hundred miles from the border. He was fifteen or sixteen years old and he came from Buenaventura, Coahuila. He had come alone, looking for work to support himself and to save money to send to his siblings. Of the five—four brothers and a sister—he was the eldest. He worked as a sheepherder and in time became a sharecropper. With the money he was saving, he managed to bring over first one brother, then another and another until they were all living in different ranches in the area south of San Antonio. One day while he was working around Sabinal, he met a young lady who was a native of the region, and they were soon married. He was a Mexican from the north, and she a native of the border area. They both had good genes. The aunts and uncles lived long lives. He died at the age of ninety-six or ninety-seven; his sister was 104 when she passed away. I got to know her. Our parents would take us along when they went to visit her when we were children. She lived in Knippa, next to the railroad tracks, in a tiny wooden house with a wood-burning stove inside. She was dark skinned, short and a little stooped. No sooner had she greeted us than she was stoking the fire in the stove, making tortillas the old-fashioned way. The smoke from the stove came out a long pipe sticking out the roof of her hut while we ate fresh beans from an earthen pot and freshly made corn tortillas. How can I forget the lingering aromas, the sweet laughter, the indelible memories that those gentle, humble people imprinted in my young brain?

The version that I know about how and when our paternal grandparents arrived contains some ambiguities. One version comes from collective memory; another comes from stories I used to hear my father tell. Putting both versions together, we can arrive at something closer to the real story. First, what is known without any doubt whatsoever is that our paternal grandparents had a very large family. The version that comes from collective memory says that there were sixteen kids. My father used to say that he didn't know for sure, but that he thought there were fourteen or fifteen. I've counted, with some help from my siblings, no more than thirteen. Even though my grandparents were born in the States, all of their children were born in Mexico. My grandparents met over there at the turn of the century, and that's where they married. They survived the years of the Mexican Revolution because my grandfather owned a dairy farm, and he donated cattle and mules to the combatants. They, in turn, would leave them alone. But not long after that, he was involved in a somewhat dramatic love affair. In the version I heard, he fled in the middle of the night because someone went looking for him to kill him. He literally abandoned the mules and plow to save his skin. Many years later, when we were adults, my father would remember interesting details of that unsavory incident: the midnight flight to an unknown land, a chest full of money, a half-sister no one wanted to claim. After the danger was over and grandfather returned to Mexico, my grandmother stayed behind in Texas with the younger half of the kids. My father, the youngest, was eight years old.

In 1927, the year he, his mother, and the other siblings, including two nieces and a nephew, crossed into the U.S., the economic boom that made Crystal City into the Spinach Capital of the World was just beginning.[1] To cite the 1930 census, a local newspaperman says that in the decade of the twenties, people came to Crystal City from every state in the Union.[2] The population of the area increased rapidly thanks to an advertising campaign that local investors initiated in the northern states and even in Europe. The same article gives the following figures: during the winter of 1930–1931 Crystal City exported 3,959 railroad carloads of spinach, 443 carloads of onions, 397 carloads of mixed vegetables, 214 carloads of different plants, 140 carloads of stock, and 38 carloads of wood, for a total of 5,191 railroad cars of goods exported.[3] A little further down on the same page, this quote appears: "Since spinach harvesting required an abundance of labor, immigration from Mexico increased spectacularly, aided by the turmoil of the revolution just ending."

The torrent of publicity that the developers of the Winter Garden Valley unleashed gave fruit. People came from everywhere according to a preconceived land-ownership program. The Anglo Americans arrived from the northern states to buy up the land and put it to commercial use, and the Mexicans and Mexican Americans came to work for them. It was under these circumstances that the hand of destiny brought our grandparents together in the same place at the same time. When they first worked cutting spinach, they were paid five cents a bushel. I have seen pictures of these bushels bulging with spinach. Old-time cutters said they weighed around thirty-five pounds each when full. They would cut two different kinds of spinach. One they called *tronco* (with root), the other *hoja* (leaves only). To cut hoja was a reference to the order that came down; that is, the order as received from either Chicago or New York. If the order was for spinach leaves only, that was what they would cut that day. If the order was for spinach plants with root and all, that was what the people would cut.

They would use one kind of knife blade for cutting spinach leaves and another for tronco. They squatted or knelt as they worked between the rows cutting handfuls of spinach. As they moved along they also had to remove the yellowed and withered leaves from each bunch before dropping it into the basket. The idea was to fill each bushel with thirty-five pounds of green, fresh leaves or *tronco* of spinach that was unblemished. If a cutter mistreated the plants or put withered leaves in, the overseer would overturn his bushel, and he had to start all over again. Not everybody could do that kind of work. To make a dollar during their time, they had to cut twenty bushels. If you multiply that it comes out that, to make one dollar, it took seven hundred pounds of spinach cut, cleaned, and packed. Years later, when I was cutting spinach during the fifties, they paid fifteen cents a bushel. It took 245 pounds, around seven bushels, to make a dollar.

I still remember a couple of incidents from those times that my father told me about much later. Spinach was cut in the winter. Since it was wet when they arrived early in the morning, cutters waited in their vehicles until things dried up a bit before they started to cut, or they would build small fires to warm their breakfast tacos and keep themselves warm while waiting for the order to start working. One day there was a large order; the contract called for several thousand bushels. The overseer was under pressure to complete the order. Just to let everyone know how serious he was, he parked his pickup where everybody could see it. He remained inside to keep an eye on the workers. One of my aunts, like all the female field workers at the time, was wearing a skirt over her slacks. Because of the cold, wet weather conditions, ever so often she would set her cutting knife down in the row and go warm herself up by the fire. The overseer did not approve because he needed to finish the day's order. He did not want to see cutters wasting time. One of the times my aunt got up to go warm herself and dry her wet skirt, he got there before she did. Without her knowing what was happening, she went up to the fire and was met by a loud popping. The overseer had dropped some bullets into the fire to scare her away.

The other episode dates from about the same time. One day my father and several other family members went to a field a few miles out of town with some contractor to weed cotton. When they got there they did not agree with him about the rate they were getting paid that day. There were discussions and voices were raised. They decided that they were not going to work for what they were offered. When the contractor saw they were walking out of the field, he confronted them. They exchanged words, and the result was that they had to run away as fast as they could through the *chaparral* (brush country) and then walk home.

The spinach boom didn't last more than a dozen years. The growers, in their eagerness and greed to extract the maximum profits, practiced one-crop planting and soon exhausted the land. A plague wiped out the spinach, so people began to leave the area in search of work. Another migratory cycle had begun. This time the people did not restrict their search to the Winter Garden Valley. They followed routes that took them to the cotton fields. I still recall the names of some of those places that the elders were fond of remembering, places like Sinton, Taft, Robstown (they called it "Robestán"), and Corpus Christi. And, frankly, there were legitimate reasons those memories were kept alive. Two of my aunts ended up marrying young men they had met there. We still have cousins living in the area who are the offspring of those unions. Even though it was the work that brought them together, clearly there had also been occasions where the young could socialize. People used the word *algodonales* (cotton laden) when referring to those places because the crop was so abundant, as were the pickers. In Texas these cotton-laden fields extended from the coastal areas around Corpus Christi all the way up to Levelland and Lubbock near New Mexico. I've seen a picture of one of the labor camps where they lived at the time. It was taken in the late twenties or early thirties. It shows a brother and sister of my paternal grandmother's looking into the camera from a few feet away. Behind them one sees the outhouses and tents set out in the open. Judging from the heavy clothes they are wearing, it was taken during the winter, so it was not cotton they were picking but some other crop. According to family lore, though, tents were where our migrant ancestors lived before they began going up north.

CHAPTER 2

Following the Migrant Trail North
to Iowa and Minnesota

Our grandparents went from cutting spinach and picking cotton to doing sugar-beet work. The transition from doing one type of field-work to the other occurred for the same reason that the others did: it was a question of economics. But it is also important to understand that other factors contributed to that momentous change. At this point it is worth recalling some of the oldest stories that I remember on the subject. I have no doubt that there's some substance to them because I remember hearing them from my father as well as from other family members. Some of those stories are told and retold whenever cousins young and old on my father's side get together for family reunions. What they tell is that a brother and a sister of grandmother's were the ones who started the tradition of going up north during the harvest season sometime in the 1930s. Some *compadres* (godfather/friend) of theirs had gone to work in the onion harvest in Minnesota with other families who had been recruited earlier. When they returned at the end of the season, somehow they ended up in Crystal City. Later in their conversations with my great-aunt and uncle, the *compadres* told them about their having gone up north, about all the work they had found there, about the money they had made. It seems that it was those conversations that convinced my great-aunt and uncle to go see for themselves. The end result was that a few months later, at the end of April, the heads of each of the families got together, formed a caravan and headed up north. They wanted to find out what it was like on their own, but poverty and the Depression were undeniable factors in their decision.[1]

At this point I need to rely on some less well-known details, perhaps make some assumptions, as to how they ended up in Iowa. The stories their *compadres* had told them were about harvesting onions in and around Hollandale and Albert Lea, Minnesota. But somehow they ended up in Mason City, Iowa, working in the sugar beets. No one up to now has explained to me, nor have I heard stories about, how they ended up there. But, given what I know now about sugar-beet harvests, it is easy to surmise what happened. Onion harvests up north take place around July and August; sugar beets are thinned around May and June. Sugar-beet company representatives used to come down from up north to recruit workers for the sugar-beet harvest as early as March, but most hit town in the month of April. What is most probable is that our families were recruited by the sugar-beet company representatives in Crystal City for the sugar-beet harvest in Iowa before they left. Once there, they headed north across the border into onion country around Albert Lea and Hollandale, Minnesota, a few weeks later when the onion season started (figure 1).

Sugar beets, as I mentioned, are thinned in May and June. Then there's a three- to four-week waiting period before the weeding starts. It was during that break in the sugar-beet harvest, between July and August, when they headed for the onion harvest. The timing worked out just fine. And in fact that is what took place. In late May and June they did the blocking and thinning with the short-handled hoe. Once they finished that, they took off for Minnesota to work in the onion harvest while they waited for the sugar beets to mature and the fields to grow weedy. Having finished harvesting the onion crop in that three- to four-week span of time, they returned to the Mason City area to continue with the sugar beets. There still remained the weeding, the *tapeo* (topping) of the mature beet plants to separate stalks from tubers, then the loading and hauling off to the processing plants. In their case the plant was the Crystal Sugar Company in Mason City, which had sent its recruiting representatives south the previous March to recruit our ancestors to work in the sugar-beet fields that were planted in abundance in and around the Red River Valley back in those days.

So our grandparents didn't just decide one day to abandon the cotton fields in Texas to go up north and do sugar beets. It was an incremental transition. Their method of decision making was logical for those times. People acted as members of a family rather than as individuals. As they

1

The author's great-aunt and great-uncle pictured
in Texas in the 1930s. They belong to the first
generation of sugar-beet workers who journeyed
north to hoe sugar beets in the states of Iowa and
Minnesota beginning in the early 1930s.
Courtesy of the Estate of Santiago Montemayor.

were traditional families, they were bound by powerful family ties. The decisions made by the elders, especially by the older brothers, directly influenced the lives of all the members of the extended family. Both our great-uncle and our great-aunt had been widowed, and both had remarried by this time. They each had families from two different spouses. I got to know several of those aunts and uncles. And that was what we called them, aunts and uncles, because even though they were cousins, they were even older than our parents. It was from them that I heard some of these early family stories.

They recalled in their conversations how they had worked in Texas when they were young. I remember one of those elderly uncles vividly. He would show us his hands when he talked about those times. You couldn't help noticing his crooked fingers and the disfigured joints when he gestured to explain how he dug up mesquite stumps in the field or busted a cactus stump with a pickax. By that time his body looked fragile. I would sit there and listen without saying anything, but his story affected me deeply. He would tell us that his hands looked the way they did because of the grubbing he had done with pick and shovel from sun up to sun down from the time he was a little boy. Another uncle, a brother of his, was less talkative, but they resembled each other physically. It was obvious to us that their physique was the result of hard work. They were extremely sunburnt, with slender muscular bodies and calloused, disfigured hands. Their parents, our great-aunt and uncle, had strong personalities, and they were very traditional. Both married and unmarried sons respected them and followed them wherever they went during the harvest season.

When I accompanied my father to the homes of some of his other cousins where they practiced their guitar music before serenading people on St. John's Feast or other saints' days, they would sit down and chat after practice. These cousins were the half-brothers of the uncles I refer to above. During those conversations, one could tell they had a lot of respect for each other even if they were only half-brothers. They also told their own stories, and they were likewise old-time tales of a remote past full of nostalgia: how when they were young they all headed north together in long family caravans, how they came back with brand new cars that our great-uncle or great-aunt had paid cash for. They remembered their parents' favorite models: our great-uncle preferred four-door, eight cylinder Buicks "because they had the pulling power of a train." Our great-aunt was partial to large trucks because she could carry all of her kids in them along with whatever else she wanted and she didn't have to go around asking anyone for favors. And one always detected that family pride and respect for authority in their conversations. They themselves would tell how, even after they were married, they did not dare smoke in front of their parents, how when they got paid at work they gave all their money to the father or mother. I also remember how two and three generations lived packed together in the same house and no one complained nor asked for any explanations. At least that was how it seemed to me back then. Since they lived like that year after year, one can only imagine that they must have had ways of working things out. Perhaps their accepting behavior resulted from the way they were raised. They came from large families where everything was shared, and their own parents had kept a very tight rein on them when they were growing up.

I think it was due to those old-fashioned ways and the strict personalities of our ancestors that, when the sugar-beet company reps came to town to recruit workers, our people did not find it difficult to make the transition from picking cotton to hoeing beets. The aunt and uncle decided right then and there to sign up, and thus began the long tradition of following the crop harvests up north every spring. The following year when the uncles invited my grandmother to join them, The Great Depression was at its height. Even though she also had a large family, by that time she only had three of the sons, one daughter, and three grandchildren with her. One son died of pneumonia soon after they got to Texas. By then, Grandfather had already returned to Mexico with the older sons. Grandmother refused to follow him. She chose instead to follow her brother and sister north to work in the fields. For reasons I did not learn until many years later, she no longer wanted to live with Grandfather. It was under such circumstances, and for reasons shrouded in an ancestral enigma that remained hushed up until many years later, that our family first began going on those journeys up north. My father, the youngest of the fourteen or fifteen children she had borne, was then an adolescent.

The field agents that came to town to recruit sugar-beet workers back then were representing the interests of the sugar companies. The history of sugar beets in this country is fascinating. It is one of those topics about which there should be less ignorance than there is. As I outline it here I'll limit myself to some general details. I am interested in exploring and explaining the whole question of working the sugar beets from the point of view of our ancestors. There is an excellent study of migrant sugar-beet workers by Dennis Nodín Valdés titled *Settlers, Sojourners, and Proletarians: Social Formation in the Great Plains Sugar Beet Industry, 1890–1940*.[2] It's an academic title, but his research provides valuable perspectives on the economic and cultural forces that shaped the industry and how those forces directly influenced the lives of the people recruited by the companies to harvest and process the sugar beets.

Valdés writes that by 1890 there were already sugar-beet processing plants in California and Nebraska. The American Sugar Beet Company was incorporated in 1899 with four sugar refineries. In 1900 another factory went into production in Rocky Ford, Colorado and by 1910 these plants had extended into Nebraska, Minnesota, and Iowa. Some powerful Wall Street investors in New York had discovered that sugar beets could be a real bonanza. By 1920 over one hundred such factories had come into being thanks to such investors and the government subsidies they received. One of these plants, the Crystal Sugar Company, opened its doors in Mason City, Iowa, in 1924. Our own ancestors were amongst the people they recruited to harvest their sugar beets at the time.

The first requirement that sugar-beet recruiters looked for in a labor force was that it come cheap so as to increase company profits. Likewise, it was just as important that the labor force—the sugar-beet workers—not threaten to upset the local lifestyle and at the same time be strong enough to work like brutes. These sugar-beet companies and growers associations first recruited Russian Germans from Europe. These new immigrants satisfied the demand for a while, but World War I and the type of contracts that the companies agreed to soon put an end to that source of sugar-beet workers. These people had come as families, not as single men like the Japanese workers that were recruited later. And they were Europeans. That is to say, they received loans, equipment and other provisions to help transform them from beet workers to beet growers. They received the support they needed to buy their own land to grow beets. It didn't take them long to abandon the fieldwork and farm the crop themselves. In no time at all, and thanks to their benefactors, the growers were again forced to seek other sources of sugar-beet workers, also known then as thinners.[3]

They brought in Japanese thinners from California. These people were already familiar with that kind of work. But there weren't enough Japanese workers to do the job, nor did they want to live in labor camps because they were not treated well, and the local people didn't want them around. That source of cheap labor also soon dried up. But before moving away, these Japanese workers had left behind a new way of harvesting sugar beets. The Europeans who had arrived earlier had used a long hoe to block the beets, and their kids came behind the blockers to thin the rows with short handled hoes. Since the Japanese workers had no children to do the thinning, they did the blocking and thinning at the same time. In order to do the job properly, they only used the short-handled hoe. With this pool of workers also exhausted, the sugar-beet companies and their agents then began to look south. At first they recruited workers in New Mexico, and when not enough could be found, they went to El Paso, Texas. From there it did not take them long to arrive at the Winter Garden Valley where they found our people willing and able to do the work.

The Mexicans that the sugar-beet companies recruited back then to work in the sugar-beet fields did not receive the same treatment that was given to the Russian Germans brought from Europe. The companies did not lend them money to buy land; they did not offer them any equipment, seed, or utensils to help them work the land bought with borrowed money. The new arrangement was ideal for the investors and for the local growers, even if it was not so for the new workers brought in from Texas. In place of loans, they received credit in company stores to obtain their foodstuffs while they completed the harvest. And they were not paid until they finished. At that point they were paid for all their work at once minus what was owed at the store. They did not live in town either; there were separate labor camps for them to keep them apart from the white population. The only tools the companies allowed them, which were also purchased on credit from those same well-stocked stores, were the ones perfected earlier by the Japanese: the short-handled hoe.[4]

For a person to be stooped or arched over ("stooped steep" as people would say with a touch of ironic humor) while hoeing with a hoe that has a ten- or twelve-inch handle for as long as eight, ten, or even twelve hours a day is how I would define the word *torture*. That was why Europeans would thin the sugar beets on their knees or block the rows of beets with long-handled hoes. But Mexicans adopted the short-handled hoe from the Japanese, and thus was born the myth of the genuine sugar-beet worker as I learned it: the authentic beet thinners, the original ones, used a short hoe. With the one hand using his hoe he did the blocking, and with the other hand he did the thinning, both actions simultaneously. It was a punishing way to make a living. One needed to have exceptional mental and physical fortitude. That was why the best sugar-beet thinners in the area were adolescents or men in their physical prime. For women and older men, on the other hand, to work with a short hoe like that was pure agony. Many simply

2

Three of the author's paternal uncles from Texas thinning
sugar beets in a field near Billings, Montana, in the late 1940s.
Blocking (with short hoe) and thinning (with the left hand)
are done simultaneously. Plant shoots must be left at
a distance of approximately 12 to 14 inches from each
other for mature tubers to produce quality sugar.
Courtesy of the Estate of Santiago Montemayor.

couldn't do the work. We had an expression for the good ones, though. People would say "Such and such . . . has no quit in him/her." It was my good fortune, during my years as a beet thinner, to work alongside some of the very best (figure 2).

My father was one of those. He and my mother met when they were both living in labor camps around Mason City, Iowa, either in 1937 or 1938. At that time his immediate family consisted of two brothers, one sister, my grandmother, and two or three nephews and nieces. But they didn't go up north alone. As I've said, they accompanied aunts and uncles and joined them in caravans that made the yearly trek from Crystal City. From Mason City they moved north across the state line into Albert Lea and Hollandale, Minnesota, to harvest onions with the other families.[5] They did that work in July and August after they were done thinning the beets and had to wait a few weeks for the sugar-beet plants and the weeds to grow so they could do the weeding and topping. After the onion harvest, they returned to the Mason City area to finish with the sugar beets. They returned to Texas at the end of October, sometimes in early November.

Beet thinning was paid at eight dollars an acre at the time.[6] The fast thinners, my father and some of his cousins, were able to thin close to an acre a day though not always. Rows at that time were thick with unwanted varieties of weeds and grasses. It was not so difficult to tell how much one had thinned in a day. Fields were rectangular. The rows were generally a half-mile or a quarter-mile long. These were the more common lengths of sugar-beet rows. We knew that eight rows a mile long equaled one acre, and from there one could calculate how much ground one had covered on any given day. I recall bits and pieces of stories the old timers would tell about the first time they went up north to hoe beets. They saw the effects of The Great Depression everywhere: people begging in the towns they drove through, railroad cars full of hoboes coming and going—the devastating poverty.

Yet my father's uncles and aunts came back at the end of the season driving brand new cars and still had money in their pocket. They said that they had done well because they were willing to work hard. The only work to be found was fieldwork. They also said that the gringos would rather go begging than to go hoe beets with a short hoe or go harvest onions in the fields. Be that as it may, in time what happened was that the uncles and aunts bought land in town with the money they had made working in the fields up north. They built large homes with lots of rooms in those plots of Texas land because theirs were large families. And they built them in the neighborhoods where they had lived before, amongst their own people. In the living room of one of those homes, I remember, the family placed a modern piano just like society people had. They were beet thinners, sure, but their lowly occupation did not keep them from aspiring to a more sophisticated level of culture. Those homes still exist, although they are now old and dilapidated. But even in that condition, to me they remain a quiet testimony to the willpower and determination of those aunts and uncles and the large families they had under their authority.

They bought and paid for it all with dollars earned with the sweat of their brow. The country was in the depths of the Depression, but they could have cared less. When the sugar-beet company reps came to town to recruit workers to go up north, they did not grow weak-kneed. On the contrary, they signed up right away. With a short-handled hoe and the will to work, they had transcended the limitations poverty and circumstance had imposed upon them. People back then, when referring to migrants who had done well working in the fields, said it was because they had plenty of intestinal fortitude. By whichever term one chooses to refer to their work ethic, when it came to surviving in those hard times, our forefathers chose to follow the migrant stream and worked their way up from there. The migrant tradition that I was to inherit had begun, and it has borne good fruit.[7]

CHAPTER 3

||||||||||||||||||||||||||||||||||||||||||||||||||||||||||||||||||||||||

Leaving for California

The American Crystal Sugar Company was operating several sugar-beet processing plants in various parts of the country by the beginning of the twentieth century. One of these, which started operations in 1924,[1] was the Mason City plant. In order to plant, cultivate, and harvest sugar beets profitably, an abundant and reliable supply of labor was essential back then. Identifying just such a labor pool became the job of company recruiters. As Valdés explains in his study of sugar-beet workers, sugar companies first experimented with German and Japanese workers, but for different reasons, the results did not turn out as expected.[2] Recruiters soon began seeking out workers in other parts of the U.S. As I've explained, first they recruited in New Mexico, then in El Paso, Texas, and they finally found the kind of people they were looking for in the Winter Garden Valley. From there, and in particular from Crystal City, over the years, the company recruited agricultural laborers to harvest sugar beets. In most instances these were the same people who had come to the area years before to work in the spinach harvest during the boom, and when that crop failed they turned to picking cotton. Their lives revolved around hard work. They were physically adept and held fast to their conviction that they could handle anything. And they were in dire need. All of these circumstances, at least from the point of view of the companies, made these people an ideal source of labor. Before long company agents descended on the town to recruit as many of these people as were willing to go work in the sugar-beets fields up north.

This is not a full portrayal of how our ancestors, and my parents in particular, became migrant sugar-beet workers. It is simply meant to show how they took those first steps as the heads of each family signed up to go up north to work in the fields. As was to be expected, some of those families did better than others. The stories I heard about those times, the thirties and forties, came from my father. Not all, but most of them. It should be kept in mind that the concept of collective memory includes the experiences of an entire community. During those times people lived a communal existence. They travelled together in caravans, they worked together, and they even lived together in labor camps segregated from the local people. It was part of the plan to keep them apart from the locals. That is why, even after many years, the stories that were told about life back in those times by different individuals sounded pretty much the same. Each person told them from their point of view. But that just makes the stories richer and more fascinating to our modern ears. Theirs was a collective experience. They had little choice but to stick together.

What they talked about as they grew older, then, were the hard times they went through working in the fields. I heard stories told by different uncles of that first generation of how difficult it was to thin a single acre of sugar beets back in those days. Stories too of the soil being so hard and the weeds and grass so thick that the hoe bounced right back when it hit the dirt. Stories of the men and women wrapping their faces and necks with towels and hankies or whatever they could find to keep from being tormented by the mosquitoes while they hoed. Some of the stories had a dramatic turn to them. My father remembered the beet thinners he worked with and would tell us that even though they were all family, nobody wanted to play second fiddle, that sometimes they would eat and hoe at the same time because nobody wanted to fall behind and play catch-up, that at the end of the day they came home so tired they fell asleep right where they were sitting. At one time or another they each had vomited right there on the rows from the draining toll their bodies took as they tried to keep up the brutal whack-whack-whack pace of the elite thinners who set the pace. My mother remembered that when they got married, my father had a twenty-nine inch waist. He wore the same size for many years.

But I also recall stories, as I said earlier, about how some of the uncles returned to Texas from up north with good money in their pockets and driving brand new cars. I would be captivated by the elaborate descriptions they gave of the snazzy cars they said their fathers had paid for in cash and brought back home. And of course in the telling, they didn't forget to include the minor detail of how, a mere six months earlier, they had all been packed together in the back of a truck headed north with nothing much to their names except their self-reliance. I have already mentioned the large homes they built in the barrios with some of that beet money. Some of those homes can still be found where our uncles built them. In their time they were as modern as some of the better ones owned by the gringos. It's heartbreaking to see how old and dilapidated they are now. All of this happened at a time when all over the country, people were living in desperate poverty. The Depression meant most people were unable to find work. Our people, the migrants, did but not in Texas. That was why, following their better judgment and their migratory impulses, they had headed north when the sugar-beet company reps came calling.

When my parents met in one of those labor camps run by the American Crystal Sugar Company, they were both adolescents. A year or two later, in 1939, they were married in a civil ceremony in Crystal City. The little barrio store where they held the ceremony is still standing. My father pointed it out to me many years later. They lived right next door. As was the custom back then, they all lived together in the same place: my parents, one or two brothers, a sister, my grandmother, and the grandchildren. That was their way. The home was rented. I did not understand until much later why there were such vast differences in fortune amongst the families themselves even though they all went up north and did the same kind of work. If it was true that the large families made good money working in the sugar beets and they returned to Texas driving new cars and built new homes, it was also true that my father's family did not fit the pattern. He had lots of cousins. They went north together and they came back together. They lived in the same labor camps. But his fate turned out to be different from theirs. His own father never went to the fields. After he left for Mexico with his eldest sons he never returned. Grandmother was the one who directed the family's affairs. She was the one who followed her brothers north, taking my father and the rest of the family with her. One nephew, a niece, two daughters, and two sons had remained behind. She had seven strong, healthy sons at the time, but the adult males were unwilling to follow her into the fields. As a matter of fact, my father was the only one in his immediate family who grew old doing that kind of work. Of the two remaining brothers who had stayed behind, one died in his twenties, and the other married and then left. By the time my two oldest sisters were born in Mason City, one year apart, the family consisted of six women and my father.

My mother's family was also large. But because my maternal aunts and uncles had been born in Texas, they had had some schooling. They spoke English, and they could read it and write it as well. It didn't take the older ones long to go their own way. The Second World War was beginning, and there was a big demand for working people in California. Besides, there were other kinds of jobs to choose from besides fieldwork, and the wages were better. The older ones left. Not long after, Grandfather and Grandmother followed, and thanks to my mother's influence, they themselves ended up going over there. That was in April of 1943. Instead of heading for Mason City, Iowa, to hoe sugar beets as they had been doing since the late 1930s, this time they went to California.

Surrounded by a growing family and finding himself pulled in another direction, my father relented. He and my mother packed my grandmother, her nephew and nieces plus their little ones and drove to California in a Model T. After crossing the Chihuahua Desert and parts of the Mojave, they stopped at a place where a sign read Meyer's Ranch No. 3. The ranch is still there, not far from a rural town called Chualar, and it is located in the heart of another famous valley, the Salinas Valley. Even though they did not know anybody there, and my father barely knew English, it did not take him long to find a job. Since the town was located in the middle of an agricultural area, it was surrounded by fields of all kinds of crops. But this time he did not go to work in the fields. He was hired by a meat-packing company to drive a delivery truck. He recalled years later how he delivered merchandise all over the Valley, from Salinas to Soledad and back.

My original birth certificate, which is still in my possession, provides some fascinating details about those times that help guide me in writing this. On it, my name appears as Zaul Sanchez. It is well known that English-only speakers in this country either do not care or do not know anything about written accents in language. That ignorance stands out in the document. It shows the date, June 16, 1943; the name of the ranch where I was born; and some personal information about my parents and paternal grandmother. It gives their age (he 22, she 19), where they were born (Mexico for him, Texas for her), and then, confounding their nationality and ethnicity, classifies both of them as Mexican. Their occupations are given as agricultural laborer and housewife, respectively. Where it asks for the name of the person who delivered me, there's an X. It belongs to my grandmother. She could neither read nor write. My mother signed for her. I recognize the handwriting.

Impossible to say I remember any of that. Of course not. But I do have a gem of a family story from those times that I think is worth passing on to posterity. Several people have told the story, including my father, who lived it. It happened in 1945 or 1946—I have not confirmed the year. It has to do with the famous Mexican singer and movie star Pedro Infante. He was on tour at the time all along the California coast, from Los Angeles to San Francisco. He stopped for gigs at the smaller towns along the way where there were Mexican-music aficionados. During the War, California agricultural growers from the Salinas Valley had depended heavily on Mexican labor to bring in the harvests, and Salinas and San José were fast becoming Mexican and Mexican-American population centers.

Infante, who at the time was just beginning his professional career, was not as famous then as he became later. But he was already well-known as an aspiring singer and had already appeared in several movies. The night he stopped in Salinas to do a show he was short one or two musicians. Two men came to the ranch where we lived asking for my father. How they ended up there or who told them about him I have never found out. But according to my aunts, who went to the show that night, my father was one of the *mariachis*[3] who appeared on stage that night with Pedro Infante. He told us stories later of how Infante himself had helped him put on his tie, that he had lent him a vest, that he was more or less his height "because I was looking at him face to face," and that "he was well-built." For me what was interesting about those stories was a small detail that at the time seemed rather insignificant. When later that evening Pedro Infante asked my father to consider playing with him for the duration of the tour my father said no. He never told us why. The actor even asked him to join him in Mexico as one of his regular mariachis. My younger brother, who came right after me, had just been born or was about to be born. That might have had something to do with it. But it is never easy to know why those things turned out the way they did.

That was in the mid-1940s. There are still two or three family members left who remember the episode. When they tell you about it, the gleam in their eyes and the little details make it come to life. They remember whom they went with (another sister, a brother, and his wife) and what they wore that night (store-bought outfit), who took them to the show (their older brother—my uncle), and even what color the cars were (shiny black). They are in their eighties now, but they still remember. My mother, who was pregnant, wasn't there.

CHAPTER 3

||||||||||||||||||||||||||||||||||||||||||||||||||||||||||||||||||||||||

CHAPTER 4

The Migrant Experience from Birth to Age Five

The French writer Marcel Proust, who died in 1922, wrote a very interesting book on memory. The title is *À la recherche du temps perdu* (*In Search of Lost Time*). In his book he tells of the times when, as a child, he would accompany his mother on their Sunday visits to see an aunt. His aunt had the habit of serving them tea with sweet breads during those visits. Proust describes those childhood visits in minute detail, evoking the exquisite aroma of the tea and the lingering taste of the sweet breads. Time and habit impress upon his unconscious mind the pleasures derived from that experience. Many years later, as he is writing his book, he seeks to revive that episode from the past. But he soon realizes that his attempts at recalling those childhood memories are futile because they are not accessible to his intelligence. They are hidden in the unconscious. Then, on his way back home one winter day someone offers him a cup of tea and some sweet breads. At first he refuses, but then, without knowing why, he accepts. Having been served, he dips the sweet bread in the tea and puts it in his mouth without thinking about it. He tells in his book how, at the moment his palate tastes the sweets, he grimaces involuntarily. Suddenly, he explains, he is overcome by an extraordinary sensation. An unexplainable transformation begins in him; he no longer feels mortal or mediocre. Fascinated, he later attempts to recreate the same sensation by the sheer force of will. Nothing happens. Then, after again putting in his mouth another bite of sweet bread dipped in tea, he is once again overwhelmed by the absolutely vivid images from his childhood. He has revived his past. Proust calls this experience "involuntary memory." He next explains that, as he understands it, what happens is that these intimate memories are stored intact in our subconscious mind without our even suspecting as much. On any given day some random association evoked by some material object awakens those memories lying dormant in the depths of our subconscious.

A somewhat similar experience to Proust's involuntary memory happens to me when I speak of the Salinas Valley. I am overcome by a strong feeling of elation now, sixty years later, when I realize I still have vivid recollections of some of those places. Mentioning Watsonville, for instance, brings to mind row after row of carrots buried in the mud and lots of people stooped over pulling them up by the wet, green stems. I see those same people grasping long, cone-like drums of carrots, some of which are full and some only half full, and other people in the middle of the rows emptying them into burlap sacks. The memory of that experience is accompanied by a cold sensation in my hands. Then follows a sharp pain at the tips of my fingers, between my nails, as I stick my hand into the mud to remove the buried carrots my parents are leaving behind. The pain was caused by the slivers of carrot that got pushed into the flesh as I poked deep into the cold mud to extract the carrot. They were carrots with no stem; that was why adults were leaving them behind. Adults were concerned with filling sacks full of carrots. They couldn't afford to lose time digging out buried ones. They left that to us. It is one of the earliest memories of the fields that I have.[1]

If Watsonville awakens memories of carrots, Gilroy makes me recall plums. In this recollection, we are under one of many shady plum trees. My father has just shaken the tree limbs with a long pole with a hook on it. The fruit comes tumbling down, as if it were raining plums. The ground is covered with the ripened fruit. It is of an intensely purple color. In this particular image, only the three of us appear. My mother is pushing handfuls of fruit toward me so I can fill my own basket ahead of the competition, my father. He makes funny faces and is playing around with me. He laughs, then grabs two or three handfuls of plums and quickly fills his basket ahead of me. I begin to whine because I have lost the contest to him. My mother keeps an eye on me while she joins my father as we all continue picking, but for me it's more play than work.

Another similar recollection is set in Salinas as well. I don't know how I know it, but I do. The image is rich in details. Again I am at the side of my parents. There are lots of people, but this time the setting is more orderly, not in disarray as in the scene with the carrots. On the contrary, people are dragging themselves alongside long, even rows of glowing red strawberries of all sizes. The aroma that rises up as people lift and splay the plants is so strong that, as one walks to and fro in the field, one has that incomparable taste of ripe, sweet strawberries lodged inside one's mouth all day long. The women sit and pick beside the rows, pushing little wooden boxes in front of them. Inside the wooden boxes are store-size, white cardboard containers, where they deposit the berries as they pick them. It wasn't hot or cold, but it wasn't sunny either. It was another workday, and there I was in the middle of everything at age three or four.[2] The place where this took place was called "Big Mama's Ranch," like in the story by Gabriel García Márquez.[3]

My father played baseball as well. I say this because there's another memory from that time where I find myself standing next to him. As he squats down next to me, I am standing between his knees with my back to him. We are next to the running board of some car. He's got a baseball glove in one hand, and with the other hand he is either eating or holding a drink. My mother is in front of us, and she is holding food of some kind in her hands. They are talking to each other, but I do not recall words or sounds. There are only silent gestures and smiles. I remember seeing many cars, all of them black, like the one we are standing next to.

Those recollections from infancy sometimes get jumbled up with memories of different places we migrated to in search of work. The recollections from California, probably the earliest I have, blend in with others that I have but that took place elsewhere. Most, though not all, are vague. I recall vividly, for example, an episode that took place in the state of Michigan where one of my younger siblings was born. Since I know that the year of her birth was 1946, there's no doubt how old I was. I had just turned three. And again the recollection of the event seems to be associated with a very specific place. We lived in a boxcar. Half of it was ours, half was occupied by another family. Down the middle of our railroad boxcar there hung a long bed sheet or drape of some kind. The people who lived on the other side, I found out later, turned out to be my godparents. The episode becomes clearer as I recall how my sisters and I one day ran wild over green, grassy hilltops that surrounded the boxcar. At some point during the day, we went under an electric wire fence that we had been told to stay away from. But, being kids, we paid no mind. Inside the fenced-in corral there was a large bull. That was why we had been told to stay away. As we walked up the hill, enjoying the green grass and the sun, we completely ignored the danger. Soon we were running for our lives. As we headed back to the boxcar we were running so hard we grabbed on to the live wire to slide underneath. Our eyes were on the rushing bull, not on the single strand of wire running between rickety poles. The charge was strong enough to knock us down. But somehow we all three managed to make a safe escape to the other side. The voltage could not have been very strong. Strong enough to leave that scare in my memory, though.

We had gone to Michigan to pick cucumbers. I have no recollections whatsoever from the cucumber fields because we little ones only accompanied my mother when she went to the fields to bring my father his lunch. He picked alone. There's a brief anecdote here that comes from my mother and my older sisters. I should explain first that cucumbers were paid by size when picked by hand. The smaller the size the more you got paid; the bigger the size the less. On a certain day some gringos stopped by the side of the road to watch my father pick. They were struck by how fast he worked. Finally one of them got off the car and came over to where my father was working. Somehow they talked and were able to understand each other. My father told my mother that afternoon that they wanted him to go pick for them before the processing plant closed down for the weekend. So, he did. He went and picked their cucumbers, alone. While he was picking, those same gringos, who were kindhearted and well-intentioned, kept bringing him ice-cold water so he wouldn't get dehydrated or suffer sunstroke. They wanted to make it easier for him to keep picking. In cases like that, everybody involved, picker and the growers, wanted to harvest as much of the crop as possible in as short a time as possible. The reason for that was that, over a single weekend, if cucumbers remained on the vine the large ones would spoil and the smaller ones would get bigger and be worth less.

But the combination of so much cold water, the hot sun and my father's insistence on not stopping to take any breaks during the day caused him stomach cramps and he passed out in the field. After a while he came to, got up, kept picking, and they paid him. This comes from the collection of family stories, and it belongs not to me but to the collective memory. I heard it many times in different contexts. Some of it must be true.

Our first trip to Montana belongs to this same stage of my infancy. We went to Hysham, between Billings and Miles City. Our last sister, number eight, was born there. The year was 1950. A few months later, after we had returned to Crystal City, she died. My parents' tomb rests at the feet of her tomb. Even though I have no recollection of what she looked like, I do remember some things from that time. I remember getting to the place. There was still snow on the ground. The men did not start to work until several days later. In order to kill time while waiting for the sugar beets, we went bird hunting with slingshots we made ourselves. We knocked nice, fat juicy birds off the top of fence posts,[4] and along with the fish we caught in the stream next to the house, we survived until the sugar-beet harvest started. The cold weather I remember well: I was wearing a cap with earflaps and a white jacket with black spots, and my face was snotty. When the adults were done with the harvest the farmer came over to our little house to pay us. I remember the scene well because he came in and sat at the table with my father and other family members. In his hands he was carrying a bag full of silver dollars. At the time, that was how we got paid for hoeing beets. From there we went somewhere else, thrilled at having finished and at having a bag full of shiny silver dollars.

We spent winters in Texas. There was one exception: the two years we spent in California, 1943–1945. It was not so easy to travel during the War. Gasoline, food, certain merchandise were all rationed. When we went back to Crystal City we moved into my maternal grandparents' little house. I have thought about that little shack many a time, and each time I cannot help but feel amazed. Besides my parents and their eight kids, my grandparents had adopted an orphaned nephew and niece after one of my mother's oldest sisters died. There were fourteen of us living in a little place with a kitchen and two rooms. We slept on the floor and the halls and wherever there was room. We were so tightly packed in that one time, Grandfather, who always had a couple of beers before going to bed, decided to urinate from the top of the bed where he was sleeping with Grandmother all the way down to where I was sleeping on the floor. I remember I woke up with the urine splashing all over my face and trying at the same time to spit it out and wipe it off my face. Everyone was asleep, or they pretended to be, but because we were children no one took much notice of the incident. But I never forgot it. The stuff felt warm and sticky on my face.

I didn't go to school yet. My brother and I spent the day running around the tiny house and all over the mesquites and cacti in the empty lot across the street. It is somewhat entertaining to think about those days. Our cousins were older than we were; they went to school and only rarely did they play with us. But conflict was inevitable. Grandmother would pick on the male cousin. When his sister or one of us cried, whether or not he had had anything to do with it, bam! bam! he would get it with a broom or whatever she was able to grab. I still recall the terrible facial expressions he made as she was letting him have it. It was a daily routine. Two or three years ago he started calling me from California. As he remembered those times he would cry over the telephone. He still lives there.

That neighborhood was called El Avispero (The Hornet's Nest) because people were packed in so tightly,[5] as we were, fourteen souls living in a one bedroom hut. On the other side of the lot full of mesquite and cacti where my brother and I played lived my father's nephew. He ended up having twelve kids. We played with the older ones because we were the same age. He was an alcoholic but he was also a carpenter and probably the hardest working person I have ever known. No one, absolutely no one, could best him in thinning sugar beets, picking cotton, or topping onions. We worked together for many years, and if I say it, it's because I saw it. Not even my father, who was fast and beat everybody else, could keep up with him. At the end of the day he would beat him out by a row or two when we worked in the beets. With us it was more, much more than that.

But once in the barrio he became another person. When he came home drunk, at midnight or one or two in the morning, his wife had to prepare breakfast for him and whomever he had brought along with him. And it wasn't just any breakfast. She had to fix a regular breakfast with eggs, picante, beans, tortillas, and coffee. If she messed up on anything he would let her have it. By then his kids, who had spent the day playing with us, knew exactly what to do. There was a footpath that ran diagonally from one end of the empty lot across the house to the other where they lived. One or two of them would race over that dirt footpath to the house and tell my father. He already knew what was going on. He would run over to their place, us following right behind, and drag his grown-up nephew outside all the way to the clotheslines where my aunt hung the clothes out to dry. There they wrestled until my father somehow managed to prop him up and tie him to one of the railroad ties. That night, it would double as a cross to crucify my uncle and as a support post for the laundry lines. My father would leave him there until the next morning so he could sleep it off. He untied himself when he woke up and from there went off to work. I witnessed a single episode, but I heard on the grapevine that over the years there were others.

Compared to the way of life we had up north and in California, things had a different rhythm to them in Crystal City. There was a more palpable feminine atmosphere surrounding the entire place that was accentuated, it seemed, by the dreary repetition of the women's daily house chores. As I've said, I still wasn't old enough to go to school. My brother and I spent the day playing and running around. The only times we went inside were the times we ate or slept. Life was lived outdoors. The women built fires, boiled the water, washed and hung clothes out to dry. They would go inside to cook, come back outside to do more work, and then go back inside to prepare the afternoon meal for my grandfather and my father. That was the routine. The older kids came home from school and that was the start of more commotion, more scoldings, and finally blows to the oldest boy. One could say, looking at the positive side of things, that by the way the older ones were treated, we young ones learned how to behave. We obeyed without whining even though it was tough to resist temptation and curiosity sometimes.

Behind our little shack, there was a creek covered with undergrowth. There was no water running through it so long as it didn't rain. On the other side there was a large white ranch house with a parallel carport attached on one side. There were gringos living there. My brother and I would hide next to the bushes when some noise or disturbance aroused our curiosity. But we never saw anyone outside. We couldn't see inside because there were no windows at the back of the house. Eventually we would give up trying to see anything, and we'd just wander off to play somewhere else. But we never crossed to the other side because we knew what to expect if we disobeyed. And when we went with one of the older siblings or cousins to the corner store, we'd also keep quiet. Just behind the glass counters, we could see the brand new tops with new pieces of string. I felt my mouth watering, but we were well accustomed to not asking for anything. Sometimes what we saw were little fabric bags filled with marbles, and I was so tempted to sneak some into my pocket that I left the print of my nose on the glass counter. It was no use though.

That pretty much summed up my world in Crystal City before I started going to school. I was about to turn five. I was becoming increasingly aware of the unending variety of things and people and experiences that the world had to offer and that I enjoyed day in and day out. At the same time I knew deep inside that at the center of that world was our tiny little house full of people who came and went but never disappeared. And when they left for a time it was because they were working. I had learned that very early on. I had lived in California, in Michigan, and in Montana before I had turned five years old. But I was always surrounded by my people. However, once I turned five, all of the diversity of my lived experiences as a migrant notwithstanding, a completely new world of unfathomable mysteries was about to open up before my naive child's eyes. I was about to start on a long journey to a place grown-ups called la Escuela Americana.[6]

CHAPTER 5

|||||||||||||||||||||||||||||||||||||||||||||||||||||||||||||||||||||||||||||

A Crystal City Education

P eople who lived in El Avispero had their own name for the school where we went. They called it *El Campo* (The Camp). We didn't know why it was called that. To us the name just made it sound like we were going to some mysterious place in another part of the neighborhood that remained to be discovered. But, to be truthful, of all the mysteries that we encountered that first year of school, what caused us the least curiosity was the name of the school. Our parents sent us there, and that was where we went. We were not to find out until much later where the name had come from. Neither did we know that, like everything else in town, the school was segregated. It was exclusively for *mexicanitos* (Mexican kids).[1] To us, none of that made any difference. Other things were more important. In the first place, neither I nor the cousins spoke any English. Nor were we regular students. Like everywhere else, school started in early September in Crystal City. But we were migrants, and as migrants we spent the whole harvest season—almost six months—up north. We did not return home until late October or early November. We were not around the first two or three months of the school year. Then in mid-April, before the school year was over, our parents again took us out of school because the harvest season was about to begin up north.

The result was that, for me, the first day of school was always chaotic. I don't remember ever walking to school, as children normally do, accompanied by parents on the traditional first day of school to greet their new teachers. Never happened. I have no memories of adults approaching me or supervising my first steps, leading me to class. On the contrary, what I do remember is that my experiences during those early years were very much like what happened to me upon first arriving at El Campo. And what I saw that first morning was unlike anything I had ever witnessed before. As we got closer it seemed to me rather more like I was about to enter a gigantic playground throbbing with the piercing cries of wild kids, all of them running around yelling and screaming and chasing each other all over the place. I couldn't believe what my eyes were telling me. And the kids all looked like us. That meant we could jump right in and play, too. But then, as we were getting set to join them in the frolicking, some grown-ups appeared out of nowhere. Soon all the little boys and girls quieted down, and silently they started forming lines behind the adults. We were not about to break ranks. So we followed behind, and they led us to some long, dark-brown barracks with lots of windows that had neatly painted white window frames all around.

The name of the school came from "Japanese Internment Camp." It had been one of the places where they had imprisoned hundreds of Japanese Americans along with a few Italian and German prisoners of war during World War II. Officially the name was "Alien Internment Camp." When the War started the U.S. Government did a sweep throughout California and South America and arrested any so-called aliens they found of Japanese descent. They interned them in the Crystal City camp. Once the War was over, the barracks were emptied. The city was granted ownership of the place and converted the buildings into public housing. Not long after they turned two or three of the buildings into schoolrooms for a primary school. That's where I went those first years.

Most of the other memories of that school are nebulous. What I do recall vividly are the wide open spaces in which to play and run around. They had swings and slides. And, as I mentioned earlier, nobody spoke English. We spent the entire recess period speaking Spanish in the playground. But once we entered the classroom, we became speechless. Funny how I remember the noise and laughter and yelling when we were playing outside, but inside the building there was complete silence. I can see in my mind's eye the interior of one of the barracks where I was assigned that first school year. I remember the alphabet written in large black letters, both uppercase and lowercase, on cards pasted all along the walls above the blackboards. The front wall was one complete blackboard. The desks had a compartment for our school things. The top of each desk had an indentation for the pencil and a small, round hole for the ink bottle. The legs and sides of all the desks were made of metal. Things looked like they had all come from the same place. I remember all of that well. What I do not remember is the names or faces of any of the teachers. Aside from the dark brown color of the barracks with their neat white trimming and large windows, everything else remains vague.

Gringos were not sent to that school. It was specifically for migrants. They had their own schools. One of them was Zavala Elementary. That's where I went after I left El Campo. In the small collection of short stories I published in 1976, titled *Hay Plesha Lichans Tu Di Flac*[2] (I Pledge Allegiance to the Flag) there is a story titled "The First Day of School." The people and events I describe there capture something of what I experienced that first day at Zavala Elementary. I was a little older then, perhaps eight or nine years old. In the story, I bring up the usual shoving and angry threats that a new student faces from the bullies when he invades their space, my good luck in having a brand new friend save me from a sure beating, and the small white buildings we were herded into so they could try to teach us English. I mention in the story the adults with their inscrutable faces and the shock of seeing *gringuitos* (gringo kids) and mexicanitos together but separate. That gringo world had its temptations. There was a cafeteria on the school grounds and the smell of hamburgers coming out of there was tempting and inescapable when you came anywhere near the place. The little gringuitas (feminine form of gringuito) were not like the ones from up north who played with us. They didn't even pay attention to us. There was a constant feeling of rejection. The teachers were mean. They humiliated us by spanking us in public if we spoke Spanish, or else if we didn't stand straight in line they'd also let us have it.

That was part of our education there. Then, after school was out and they finally let us go, we had to endure another two hours of agony from the Catholic nuns. They posted themselves right across the street from the school every single day, Monday through Friday, like military guards waiting to snatch us up and march us to religion classes. It's impossible to forget my introduction to that alien and unyielding world of the adults that constitutes those early years of primary school education. I can't help but cry and laugh at the same time when I remember those times.

The education I received in Crystal City during those years would not be complete if I didn't mention two additional learning experiences. Aside from the segregated gringo schools at El Campo and Zavala Elementary, and the religion classes with the Catholic nuns, I also went to the little Mexican barrio school run by *Doña* (Ms) Suze. In the barrio where we lived at the time there were two of these *escuelitas* (small schools), Doña Suze's and Doña Herlinda's. I do not recall why but we were sent to Doña Suze's. That was another unforgettable experience.

The first day my two older sisters and I arrived each with a brand new Indian writing tablet and a fat new red pencil. We paid our quarter for the week and sat down. Besides being a school the place also served as a corner store for knickknacks. There was the pungent smell of garlic and tea. Cans of Pet and Carnation milk were stacked here and there in partitions along the walls. Religious candles with huge icons stared down at us. Tops and marbles in tiny bags and other stuff hung from strings strung across the ceiling. And, in the midst of all that there were small wooden benches, worn down from constant use, for the students. We went in one by one and sat down very quietly. This lady had a reputation, and we had all heard about it: sit down and shut up, or she'll let you have it. No sooner said than done. I had just settled in, proudly holding on to my new school possessions, when all of a sudden she began screaming and waving a ruler in the air. I was not sure whom she was yelling at, but it was someone close to where I had just sat down. When she let go of the ruler, I ducked under the table and didn't see what happened. But the rest of that morning I spent reciting the prayers we had learned from the nuns at our religion classes (*Forgive me father for I have sinned*) until she opened the screen door and let us out. I didn't go back there again, nor did they make me go back.

The barrio *cantinas* (beer joints) were the other places I got an education. I got hold of a small shoeshine box. I tore up some old rags and bought me some shoe polish and wax containers of various colors. I had already seen kids from school carrying their own shoeshine boxes on weekends. They would go in and out of the cantinas, and they all seemed to know what they were doing. I did not ask anyone for permission; it was simply understood that I could go out and do it, and I did. My father's nephew, apart from everything else, was also a carpenter. My father managed to find him in a good mood one day and in no time at all he made a shoeshine box for me.

That was all I needed to know, that I had permission to go shine shoes downtown, and he threw in some change to get me started. And that was what I did. The cantinas were across the street from the packing sheds and platforms where people worked day and night. They not only represented, they were, the heart of the Mexican barrio. The movie theatre was there as were the billiards hangout, the barber shops, some small restaurants, and at one point, even a taxi stand. During the winter months, when people came back from up north, business was good. The clients had money. There was always some competition, some days more than others, but there were always enough drunks to go around. I would walk all along the side of the street carrying my shoeshine box, went across the highway and the railroad tracks next to the ice plant and ended up in the barrio. I started at the Olivares Barbershop next to their tiny gas station, heading right for the places where I had heard *cantineras* (beer-joint waitresses) served the drinks because that was where the men were. The sharp dressers were to be found there; you could make them out from their Stacy shoes, their fancy hats and dressy shirts. The only thing they were waiting for was a good shoeshine for the total elegant look. I remember some club names: *El Farolito* (The Street Lamp), *El Gato Negro* (The Black Cat), The Blue Moon, Veteran's Place, and so many others whose names now escape me. I'd get home late at night with my pant pockets bulging with coins. My mother and I would count the little mounds I deposited on the table. By then everybody was asleep. It was one of the few times that I would sit with her alone and sense her approval. Then she would talk to me in a more tender tone—which was rare for her—one I was not used to hearing from her during the day. Perhaps that's why I still hold on to those memories.

My maternal grandparents finally moved to California with my cousins, and they never came back. They left us the little shack. But instead of things getting better between my parents, they got worse. I'm referring to the back and forth changes in the direction of our migration route. In spite of opposition from my father, my mother kept insisting that we move to California. One year, around 1949 or 1950, my mother's oldest brother came to the house all the way from San José. I can still remember, as if it were today, his late model green Chevrolet Fleetline. In no time at all we loaded up all our stuff and off we went again to Hollywood. My father was not with us. As was the case with so many other things back then, for men to go up north alone was nothing unusual. I can only remember having spent one or two summers in Crystal City. And in both cases my father was not there. I can still remember that because it was not normal for us to spend summers in Texas. It was also the case that for a good while after he had come back carrying his old suitcase under his arm we would all jump up and down celebrating his return until my mother would make us settle down. Another sister had also been born around that time in Crystal City. There were a bunch of us now. None of us was of working age. The male cousins and uncles would go work in the beets in Montana then, and my father went along with them. But that year, 1949 I think, instead of waiting for him in Texas, we all met in California. My uncle dropped us off in Delano with my father's kin. He then drove off, headed for San José. That was where the other half of the clan lived. The tug of war between the families continued.

‖‖

CHAPTER 6

Joining the Workforce in Wisconsin

I n 1951 we went to Wisconsin with a contractor from Crystal City. The
man, an acquaintance of my father's, transported people to a family farm
(we called them *ranchos*) just outside Wind Lake, Wisconsin. It's a picturesque rural town that lies not far from Lake Michigan, close to Racine
and not far from Milwaukee. People called the place Dick's Ranch and
everybody knew where it was and who lived there. It was another of those
migrant camps for the people who came up during the harvest season from
April through November to harvest the crops in the region. Right next to it
and just up the road was Horner's Ranch, and further up still was Burger-
meister's. There were Crystal City families in all of them. Gringos called
the places family farms, and they all planted the same crops: onions, spuds,
beans, tomatoes, cucumbers, corn, and cabbage. I learned later that they
also called that type of farming truck farming. But whatever they called the
places and whatever crops they planted, their laborers were all the same:
Mexicans from Texas.

There were ten or so of those families, plus a few single men, who arrived
at Dick's Ranch in April of that year. I remember the journey well. We were
all packed in the back of the contractor's 1949 or 1950 green Chevrolet
truck. The bed of the truck was covered with an old, weather-beaten tarp
that had a mossy sheen to it. The wooden sides and back were the height of
an adult. The tarp hung lengthwise from a raised wooden beam running
the length of the bed. That allowed for a person to move back and forth
from one end to the other without crouching. Cramped together at the back
of the bed were the women and children and above them an improvised

3

A typical covered truck for transporting migrants from South Texas
to the labor camps up north to go work in the fields. Besides their
own families, contractors normally transported additional
paying passengers in the back of the truck.
Courtesy of Mr. Oscar Pérez.

platform running from side to side. That area was reserved for family possessions. My father's guitar could always to be found amidst the assorted belongings up there wrapped in pillow cases. Bed sheets of one kind or another were strung up as dividers to provide privacy to the women's section. That also kept the light out and the unpleasant odors in, though not always. In front three drivers took turns at the wheel. They drove straight through day and night from the time we left until we arrived. For the passengers this always presented problems. The women, and some of the elderly men, carried their own coffee cans. When somebody just had to go, someone up front would bang on the truck's back wall with a shoe. The drivers knew what that meant. Since they could not make repeated stops they would try to locate a spot, preferably in some wooded area, so that anybody who wanted to go relieve himself could do so there. Those trucks hardly went over fifty or fifty-five miles an hour. Roads were narrow and freeways were unknown at the time. At that speed it was necessary to take advantage of every minute on the road to make progress (figure 3).

No one likes being cooped up and less so if it's for a long time and in the back of a truck. When we left I picked a spot by one of the corners near the rear exit. It was where the tarp was rolled up over the crossbeam. From there I could look at the world outside as we drove on. All I could see was the pavement during the day and the stars at night. I stood during the whole journey, trying not to sneak looks toward the back. People, and especially the women and young females, were ashamed to be seen in such dehuman-izing conditions. They sat on bags and bed sheets and wore head scarves. As if on cue, we all ate at more or less the same time during the trip, I guess so as not to attract too much attention if one were to be seen eating alone. My mother would send up with one of the girls a piece of bologna or a wiener wrapped in a slice of bread. Sometimes it was only saltine crackers. The idea was to eat sparingly to avoid having to knock on the back wall of the truck and announce to everyone that you needed to go. We rarely stopped in any of the towns anyway. Back then the restaurants in Texas, Oklahoma, and Arkansas separated Blacks from Whites. When on rare occasions we did stop at some out-of-the way restaurant, the Mexicans had to place their order in the Black section of the eatery. There were some places where rac-ism was so entrenched we were not served at all even if we had stopped and asked. The drivers already knew of those places. That was what discouraged us from stopping anywhere but in isolated areas. Whenever we stopped to get gas everybody knew that only the driver or whoever was going to pay got off.

It was still cold when we arrived in April. We ended up in a long, green barrack that had four or five partitions. In each of the partitions lived a different family. The people who had been there before occupied either end of the barrack. They were generally relatives of the contractor. When each of the families had been given accommodations, we ended up in the middle of the building. It was a single room, but it was spacious. In front of the barrack, just outside the entrance to our place, there was an open area and beyond that were the fields. At the back of the building there was an algae-covered water canal. For us, all of that was new. But we were in luck. We soon made friends with the one family who lived there year round.

They were originally from Cotulla, Texas, but it had been years since they had last visited their hometown. That was the first time I met people who were like us but who spoke English like the gringos. The father and the mother became good friends with my parents. That was unusual. Generally the men would establish friendships but it was rare to see my mother become friends with another woman not of the family. They seemed unusual in some ways, perhaps because they had spent the entire winter cooped up inside the house. I supposed that was why they were so glad to see other people. But their good will was genuine. There were about as many of them as there were of us, and almost the same ages. We became friends in no time at all.

The father was a true aficionado of Mexican music, and he also played the guitar. It didn't take long for him and my father to figure out that they had that in common as well. Many years later, when they were old, and we were all living in Texas, they would visit each other, and their conversations inevitably turned to those days when they had met at Dick's Ranch in Wisconsin so many years before.

They welcomed us into their home from the very beginning. Their house was a short walking distance from the barrack. It was old but spacious, and well-insulated against the cold. I remember asking one time why the windows were so thick and they explained to me that it was because of the cold winter weather. If you knocked a baseball against one of them, I don't think it would have gone all the way through. It was there that I first saw a TV set inside a home. I had seen them in Crystal City, but at the furniture store. The store owner left them on at night, and we would stop by and watch for a short while. Our Wisconsin friends didn't have to do that. They sat on sofas to watch the whole program, and nobody bothered them. There was so much for us to learn.

But in spite of their excellent English and their cultural background, life did not deal kindly with that family. The father worked with Dick year round driving tractors and handling other farm machinery. When it was time for us to go back to Texas, they all became saddened, but he took it particularly hard because he was losing his musical companion. Winters were hard on him. The experience so deeply affected him that one year he decided to abandon the secure job he had had at Dick's place. He took his family to Montana to hoe sugar beets, but that kind of work was too hard for them and they returned to Wisconsin. In a fateful move, instead of going back to the farm he moved his family to the big city, Racine. I still remember how surprised I felt the time we visited them there. They lived on the second floor of a building in the downtown area. On the floor below there was a tavern. We climbed an old, dark stairway to get to their place. We were all still on friendly terms, but the behavior of the kids and their former openness toward us had changed. Years later I was to find out about their tragedies: two of the sons were killed in fights while they were still young, the father's diabetes had led to amputations, and another son sought refuge in the bottle. A sad ending to a good family. People were heard saying that their bad luck had begun when they left the farm for the city.

At work, people got along well with Dick, our boss. He didn't meddle in our affairs at all. But there was one occasion when he went into the fields to meet with us. I remember that day well. It was a Monday. I had just turned eight. That morning we walked over the planks of the little bridge across the canal to get to the onion field on the other side of the road. There was a thicket of tall trees, and just behind began the long rows of one of the onion fields where we were to start working that morning. The workers crowded just at the edge of the rows, and I with them following my father and two older sisters. The contractor gathered the men around him and said something to them, and then we all headed for the rows of onions. As we knelt or crouched, I remember the earth was sandy and *picosita* (it stung). I was just an eight-year-old kid, but even I found the space between the rows quite narrow. Some of the adults also crouched or crawled on all four between the rows. I know my sisters did. But that was necessary because, as we were told, we were not to mess up the onion plants. Our job was to remove the purslane, thistles, and crabgrass growing between the plants by hand. At first I was all thrilled to be there with the grown-ups. Sometime during that first morning our boss, Dick, came over to where we were working. He had come to give each of us our own Social Security number. That's why my Social Security number begins with a three, not a four, like Texas numbers do.

I have relived that particular moment of my life many times over in the past sixty years since that gringo man stood there in front of us. We were in the middle of his field of onion plants. He was the boss; we were his workers. I do not recall any words, yet a surprisingly vivid image of that scene remains clear in my mind to this day. He had a writing board with him, and he would make a stop by each head of family. At the time I had no idea what it was all about. What I do know is that, when I turned sixty-five and retired, I went to the local Social Security office to fill out the paperwork.

A young lady took down my personal info, and I watched as she casually keyed it into the computer. When she had finished, she pressed the button on the printer and it started to spit out page after page of data. The young lady's reaction was one of complete surprise. She made some comment in English, like "I can't believe this!" She wasn't so much surprised at the amount of money I had paid into Social Security since that day in 1951, but rather that the government had started deducting part of my wages that far back, when I was eight years old.

That particular episode in Dick's onion field represents my introduction into the world of the migrant worker. I have to use the term in English because that was the official classification given to us that day when we received our Social Security numbers.[1] Over the years I figured out how we made out with the pay we were getting. My sisters and I got $0.35 (thirty-five cents) an hour; my father $0.50 an hour. It wasn't long before we heard that Dick took two cents out of each hour. That was our bonus money.[2] But still we were making $11.76 daily ($12.40–$0.64) between the three of us, $64.68 a week (we worked Saturdays till noon). I cannot say that I recall my parents' reaction every Saturday when we got paid. But looking at the picture from a distance of all these years, it isn't difficult to understand why we went up north. We were making good money! It was a family enterprise, of course.

The merits and demerits of engaging the entire family to follow the migrant stream in pursuit of fieldwork have been debated for years in both our nuclear and our extended family. But the fact remains that, at the time, we had few other choices. And, the work added stability to our lives. So long as we kept working, that money would keep coming in. But even more importantly, though at the time I was unaware of it, out of those field experiences there came a small pearl of wisdom I have cherished and held fast to throughout the years. When I had gotten tired of working that day, way before the hour of noon, I wanted to quit and head home to go play with my little friends. Not so fast, I was told very sternly. "You don't work; you don't eat." I stayed and worked. Many years later, when things were at a nadir for me, and the possibility of failure seemed very real, I remembered the impact that phrase had on me at the time, and I used it though with a slightly different twist: "You don't study; you don't eat." I stayed and studied.

We were paid by the hour to do the weeding. Weeding onions and beans took us from April through sometime in June. After onions and beans had been weeded came the cucumber harvest. We picked those for two to three weeks. Then came the harvesting of the mature onions, and finally, toward the very end of the harvest season, we started working with spuds. Each kind of work had its own demands, its own work routine, required its own tools and implements. When we were doing the weeding the contractor would drive us in his truck to the fields. I learned early on that, after the first few days, the coming and going back and forth day after day working the endless rows of this crop or that, inevitably turned into pure boredom. I would make up fantasies about those things that obsessed me at the time: going to town, buying comic books, eating banana splits, and Mars candy bars.

Harvesting onions was paid by the piece rate, not by the hour. First we had to pull the now mature onion plants and lay them out in the open by the side of the row. Using gloves, for guys, was a no-no. It was just understood that the manly thing to do was to use bare hands. Once we finished doing the pulling we would return to the beginning of the row and started topping the onions. Return to the beginning means we went back to the same starting point once again. The idea was to let the onions sit out in the sun to dry for a while. In Wisconsin, as opposed to Texas, we did not chop off the roots of the onions; only the stems. The growers provided clippers to the contractors who in turn handed them out to us. There were clippers with one eye (or hole) and clippers with two eyes. We all wanted those with two eyes because they were softer and cut cleaner. But they were reserved for the adults and we got the smaller ones with a single eye. Since we had to chop off or remove, one by one, the stems off the onion plants, my father quickly hit on the idea of using a long knife instead of the clippers to do the job. He would grab a big bunch of onions by the stems and, instead of clipping each one into the hampers, he would slice off all the stems at once with a single knife thrust. At first people stared at him, and of course nobody could compete with him. My sisters and I came behind topping onions with the single-eye clippers and emptying each hamper into sacks as best we could. Two hampers equaled one sackful, and for each sackful we got fifteen cents.

Tomatoes and cucumbers were also picked by the piece rate. We made less money at that because working with those crops was less consistent. Some days there was plenty of work and other days hardly any. With cucumbers, especially, we were largely at the mercy of the weather. If the nights were cool, cucumbers ripened rather slowly; if it was hot during the day, they ripened faster and were therefore worth less. The idea was to pick them when small because they were worth more. We made good money picking tomatoes too, but only for two or three weeks. Growers hired outside help when the picking was going well. The bad thing about that was the outside help did not want to come for first pickings or the last pickings when things were slow. They would show up for a few days when the picking was at its most plentiful and took advantage of that short period. But those of us who lived there had to pick tomatoes when they were just beginning to ripen, and we were also saddled with the last pickings.

During the spud picking season we made up for the bad days we had when we picked tomatoes. Most of the fields were close to the barrack where we lived, and my mother brought us lunch where we were working. It was at the time that I was picking spuds that I learned, or was taught, who is and who is not an honest to goodness migrant worker. To this day I have in my possession two articles of clothing that the growers made available to us during potato picking season. One is a thick, wide canvas belt. It has the following words embossed on the front: E-Z Way Potato Picking Belt. Boise, Idaho. The letters "E-Z" of course stand for "easy." "Way" refers to the method of picking. The message appears to suggest that picking potatoes or spuds with that particular belt is easy. Hanging from either side of the front of the belt are two long hooks that curve upwards where we would hook the burlap sacks while we picked. That is the other article: a burlap sack such as we used then for picking spuds.

I keep these things that I have collected over the years with the idea of exhibiting them before groups of students while I give them a short talk on the subject. I have made presentations before groups of students ranging from high-school age through college age. The reaction I get at the end of each presentation is usually one of silent shock. "How is it possible that there are people in this country who make a living doing that?" is what they are thinking, or something to that effect. Most of the time the students miss the irony stamped on the front part of the potato-picking belt until I point it out: there's nothing easy about the E-Z Way Potato Picking Belt. Fewer still understand the implications of the message stamped on the belt.

Not all of my memories of Wisconsin are tied to the work in the fields.

There are pictures of the canal behind the house, probably taken by my mother, where my sisters and my brother and I are riding on a raft with my father. He would take us on mini tours, poling the makeshift raft that the Wisconsin friends had assembled from old pieces of wood. To us it was an unforgettable thrill. Nothing of the sort existed for us in Texas. We also went to the small towns in the area on weekends to spend the money they gave us when we got paid. The first thing I did when they turned us loose downtown was to go buy a banana split to make up for what I had missed back in Texas where I couldn't afford a single ice cream cone. Back at Dick's place we were allowed to go fishing at his tank, and the other guys and I would spend time there when we weren't working. On Sunday afternoons the older men would play cards outside and dice nearby. We would run around playing hide and seek. And of course we would watch a little TV at our friends' home. They were all new experiences for me. I enjoyed them and I think that was why it seemed like an eternity by the time we went back after spending the winter in Texas.

We went back to the same thing the following year but with a different contractor. They were brothers, he and the contractor who had taken us up the previous year, and since they transported passengers to the same place, we took him up on his offer. The truck this time was an old dull-red Dodge. It was loaded with people to the hilt too when we left Texas. But this time what made the trip an affair to remember was the fact that a woman rode next to the guys in the back of the truck all the way to Wisconsin. She was the contractor's wife. Now that I am old, I have retold that story to friends and relatives of the lady. Instead of sitting with the women, she chose to ride with the men, and she had us laughing the entire journey. I had never known a lady who talked as much as she did. She did not stop talking from the time we got on the truck until we got off at the barracks several days later. She was chewing gum all the time she was talking. And on top of that, she never stopped smoking. Seemingly without caring if anyone was listening to her or not she just went on smoking, jabbering and chewing gum the whole way. That was probably the reason her husband the contractor had put her there.

When in the fields, as in everything else we did, we stayed close to each other. We picked together, ate together, sweated and suffered together. When we worked by the piece rate, as when we topped onions or picked spuds, there was no limit to the hours we worked. We would start with the light of day gathering and distributing the burlap sacks all along the sides of the rows. That was the first thing we did. As opposed to the way it was done in Texas, where the contractors limited workers to a given number of bushels or sacks, in Wisconsin one could work so long as there was daylight and spuds to pick. When onions were in season it was the same thing. Men and women all picked together, and nobody wanted to fall behind. With spuds, for example, it took two hampers per sack. My father and I were paired on the same row. I had to find a way to fill my hamper at the same time he did. That way we would fill one sack each time we emptied our hampers. People were picking right next to each other and looking over their shoulder to see who was getting ahead. I knew that some of the older people picked faster than I did, but the competition made me get carried away, and I did not want to look like a loser. I still remember hearing people say, at about that time of the year, that we worked like animals. Even away from the field, in people's conversations, you'd hear it said. I suppose it was our own way of letting people know that we were invincible, even if we had to work like animals to prove it. Perhaps because I heard those words said so often, I have never forgotten.

CHAPTER 7

||||||||||||||||||||||||||||||||||||||||||||||||||||||||||||||||||||||||||||

Compromises in Delano, Wind Lake,
and Burlington

y mother and father continued to pull in opposite directions. In 1953
we did not return to Wisconsin. We went back to California. We
drove in an old Pontiac that my father had dubbed "Blood and Guts."
We left Crystal City very early one April morning and we arrived in Delano,
California, three or four days later. One of his sisters lived there. She and
my uncle ran a camp for agricultural workers. He contracted workers for
the local growers, and she ran the kitchen. Behind their house, which was
in the outskirts of town, my uncle had set up a row of small mobile homes
and rented them out to workers. We rented one from him. There were a few
other families living there as well. Next to the big house they had built a
huge kitchen. That was where the women worked who served the so-called
wetbacks hired by my uncle. It was obvious that they were doing very well,
that they were people of means, as some in the family said. We lived there
for at least one harvest season. I did not know it at the time, nor do I have
definite proof of it, but I think that the reason we ended up in Delano was
because of a compromise between my parents. We did go to California as
my mother had wanted, but we did not go to live with her family in Salinas.
We stayed with my father's relatives in the San Joaquin Valley.

The women prepared three meals a day six days a week. They fixed
breakfast so that the workers could take it with them to the fields. My
uncle drove us back and forth. At noon we would all descend on the kitchen
and sit on the benches along the long tables. They cooked everything, typical Mexican food, but in oversized pots, and they used long stoves, like in

restaurants, where they boiled and cooked meals by the dozen. I remember how my aunts, my grandmother and my mother would run back and forth serving plateful after plateful of soups, meat, beans, salsas, warm tortillas, and drinks to the men eating calmly at the long wooden tables where only adults were present.

My aunt and uncle had moved to California during the Second World War and settled in the San Joaquín Valley. When we went there in 1953 it was obvious that their efforts had paid off. Knowing no English, they had worked hard, educated their kids and invested their earnings wisely. The large home, their extended properties outside of town, the brand new cars and the excellent English their kids spoke was a testimony to that success. And they were lucky. One day as we were resting out in the patio after lunch, out of nowhere the Border Patrol swooped in unannounced. A few minutes before we had all been relaxing and dozing off as if it were the siesta hour. Suddenly we heard the commotion and saw the cloud of dust coming from the braking vans. As the agents chased the illegals around the tents and mobile homes, my father pushed one of them under the mattress we had been sitting on. They hauled off several vans with illegals on that raid. After they left, we moved the mattress aside and underneath, lying flat on his belly, about to pass out, and covered in dust, lay the only mojado to escape that day's raid. Years later he married one of my cousins and they stayed in California.

We worked in the grape harvest. Since I was only ten, I did a little bit of everything. At the beginning of the season, we had to prune the grapevines, thin out the bunches thick with grapes, and finally cut and pack the grapes. We squatted under the grapevines, and with special pruning scissors, we would first remove the bad grapes from a bunch, then cut it, and finally pack it carefully in small wooden crates. When I say that I did a little bit of every-thing, what I mean is that I worked with the older pickers. After picking a crateful of grapes I would take the crate back and stack it with the others. I couldn't reach all the way to the top, so I'd give it to someone to stack it for me, or I would wait for a stack I could reach. We couldn't just leave crates anywhere. I would then grab another one and return to my row. It sounds easy, except that in the San Joaquín Valley where Delano is located, tem-peratures in the summer top one hundred degrees Fahrenheit. Underneath the grapevines, the heat was suffocating. Picking was hard work; putting up with the unbearable heat was harder. I began to notice that many of the workers back then were Filipinos, not Mexicans. The Mexicans were out picking cotton, which was also grown there. We picked mostly grapes the year we spent there because my uncle knew the grower. I still remember his name, but phonetically, because my father called him Sonny Voviche, but it sounded more like "son-of-a-bitch" to me, which he was not. He was a good boss; I remember him well. But, judging by the name he was probably Russian or some such nationality. For us, though, he was just "the boss."

I admired my aunt and uncle and resented my parents. None of their kids worked in the fields. They were somewhat older than us. The three sons were, or had been, soldiers. The girls all dressed up nicely to go to school and spoke English well. Inside the house there was matching furniture. The sofas looked fluffy and elegant, and the glass cases looked shiny and held discreetly placed pictures of all the kids. That was where I saw the military uniforms worn by my cousins. In the pictures the girls wore their petticoats and brown and white loafers, just like they dressed to go to school. They rolled their white socks down their ankles and tied an elegant sweater around their shoulders. For me it was no mystery; their parents had something mine didn't. I didn't know what it was, but I suspected that it was the English language and all the good things that came with it. During that time I got so inspired by the constant reminder of my aunt and uncle's obvious prosperity that I began teaching English myself. In the afternoons I would stop by the tents where the wetbacks lived and right there, for a quarter, I would teach them English words and phrases. "How do you say, 'I want my check?'" they would ask me in Spanish. "I want my check" I would say. I taught them other things I don't remember anymore. But with the Border Patrol raids I kept running out of students. As for my aunt and uncle, they were neither fined nor disturbed in their persons or possessions. The agents threw the illegals they caught in the vans and took off. I never saw them talk to or bother the proprietors. I wonder what would have happened if they had discovered the illegal my father had hidden underneath the mattress that day.

I shall digress a bit here to tie some things together. Many years later I returned to California under very different circumstances. It was during the month of August 1967 when, having just gotten married, I arrived in Bakersfield in the extreme southern end of the San Joaquín Valley. I had graduated from the university that year and gotten a job teaching middle school in California. I took advantage of the nine months we lived there. We went to places where I had worked back in the fifties and searched for family members who had lived in the area. Time had completely transformed the people and places from that past I carried in my memory. My aunt and uncle had passed away, and I found only one of the cousins. The longest living family member, my maternal grandfather, was still alive, and he recognized me. My uncles on my mother's side had disappeared, others had left California, and a cousin or two had ended up in prison for drugs. I consoled myself by joining César Chávez when, along with the *Teatro Campesino* (farm workers' theatre) and one of the Kennedys, he ended one of his longest hunger strikes.[1] He had done it in support of the grape pickers and other agricultural workers. He was accompanied by musicians, comrades in arms, activists, and television cameras. The setting did not resemble the one where I had been working in those same rows of memory more than a decade before. It was at that time that I began mulling over this thought in my mind: what if we, instead of having grown up working in the fields, had gone to live in the city?

It was our family's last trip to California. After that, during three harvest seasons, from 1954 until 1957, we went back to Wisconsin. This time we did not go with contractors. Things had begun to change. Since we were no longer dependent upon a contractor for work we had to find our own employment. We ended up working two years in a row for a farmer we called El Clifa. The man's name was Clifford, but that was what we called him. He was a good man to work for. I never found out how he and my parents made contact but, when we left Texas that year, we went directly to his place. His farm was just outside Wind Lake, not too far from Dick's place. We had a whole house to ourselves. It resembled the one where the friends we had first met when we got to Wisconsin lived. The outside was rough-looking and unpainted, but inside it was comfortable and it even had a porch at the front door. That was where one left the galoshes, which were snow boots, as well as the heavy winter clothing. But the best part was that we did not have to share it with anyone else. Outside, the house was surrounded by huge trees where we saw birds and squirrels that were not seen in Texas. The people who knew about those things said that winters were brutal in Wisconsin, but judging by the summertime, that seemed like a stretch to me.

By the time we arrived, El Clifa had already planted all the crops. The fields were not far from the house. We usually walked there or drove in the 1941 Buick we had bought in California. El Clifa planted onions and spuds, but there were also fields with soybeans, corn, and cucumbers. Our family did all of the work for him: weeding, picking, and loading. I don't know why we only went there two harvest seasons, but I think it was because of something that it did not take us long to find out about. The man appeared to be an alcoholic. He lived with his wife, a sister, and a mentally challenged younger brother at a house at the end of the road we would take to get to our place. We called the brother El Kenete. His name was Kenneth, but since we renamed things to make them more familiar to us, that was what we called him.

Every afternoon, when we returned from the fields, my mother had supper ready. That was when Kenete arrived, too. And he never failed to show up. He was stubborn like Germans, my parents would say. We saw him walking down the little road from his house, his ever-present suspenders snug over a long-sleeved shirt, always clean and well-groomed from head to toe. But it was when he smiled that we could tell there was something wrong with him. Drivel would start running out of one side of his mouth, and he stared at you without blinking for a long time when he talked. But he had a heart of gold. He didn't work; the only thing he did was pick up the eggs from the chicken coops. My sisters said he was "retarded," but not when it came to eating tortillas. My mother would give him a nice, warm buttered one each time, and he devoured it. We finally had to tell him "Bye bye, Kenete"[2] because he kept getting in the way. We hardly ever saw his sister or El Clifa's wife unless it was by accident. We knew when his sister was there because she parked her miniature Nash outside the house. It looked like a toy. They don't make those cars anymore. We found out from Kenete that she worked in town, in Milwaukee. The wife never even acknowledged us even if we happened to run right into her by accident. She was the opposite of her husband.

She's pure German, my father would say, and that's why she doesn't like Mexicans. But so was her husband, and he always treated us well. It was his way of justifying an attitude or his way of being that made us feel uncomfortable. But there was more to it than that. We never saw them together; he would remain at the tavern drinking for hours on end. When he failed to pay us, my father would go look for him there. I would go with him sometimes. I remember the signs behind the bar: Hamm's—From the Land of Sky Blue Waters. We would usually find him there drinking alone. He was bald even though he could not have been more than forty years old.

Those two harvest seasons, one of my sisters and I went to a rural school there in Wind Lake. At the beginning of September they would not let us go into the fields during school hours. We walked along the narrow dirt road each morning with our Mexican lunch: tacos in brown paper bags. Everybody else had a lunchbox with bologna sandwiches and a thermos for their milk. There were other *gringuitos* waiting for the bus there. They were from the next farm down the road. I hid my lunch under my jacket as soon as they came near. Dale, one of the *gringuitos* who had a big head and blond eyelashes, became friends with us, and we would talk while we waited for the bus. That first year my teacher was a nice but strict lady. On the first day of class she put me in front of the class and introduced me as Roy because I told her that was my name. The name had been given to me by an elderly couple from the area. And when I was amongst gringos I would say that that was my name. I knew they could not pronounce my name correctly and the last thing I wanted was to call attention to myself. It really bothered me then for anyone to find out that I was a Mexican. As if it was not obvious. They were all fair-haired except for my sister and me.

But they did not reject us; on the contrary, they accepted us without hesitation and treated us nicely. During our first recess I met Nancy. Several gringuitas came up to me, but I chose to play with her and chase her around the school yard. I think she also decided to be friends with me at the same time because I didn't speak English well, but we understood each other instantly. We became inseparable friends. She and her brother lived on a farm down the road. From then on, each time we drove by her home, I would look to see if she was playing outside. It seemed I only went to school to see her. But it was just that it was the first time a gringuita had played with me. To be honest, she never invited me to her home. One day at school, we were all busy working on some assignment the teacher had given us. As was her habit, that day she was walking back and forth checking on her pupils. All of a sudden, a man walked into the room. Everything had been very quiet so the noise made us all turn around to look toward him. He was holding something to write on. Without so much as pausing he asked in a loud voice, "How many Mexicans do you have in your class?" I sank down in my desk as low as I could when I heard the word *Mexican*. "One," said the teacher, and they all turned to look at me. The man thanked the teacher and left. My blood turned to ice. At that time that was my biggest fear: for gringos to find out I was a Mexican. Growing up in Jim Crow Texas, one quickly learned that the word was loaded with derogatory connotations.

It happened to me again. One particular weekend evening we were all leaving the movie theatre—my parents, brother, and sisters—when I saw Nancy's family walking toward us. I looked for a place to hide so she wouldn't see me. That sense of shame I had of being seen with my own kind, of having the gringos find out who I was, came from deep inside me and stayed with me for many years. I've heard the expression "false consciousness" used in reference to that syndrome. At the time, I didn't know what it was called, but I knew how it felt. All I remember is that, at that moment, I was gripped by an uncontrollable fear, and that my evasiveness was an intuitive reaction. It was very real.

I think an explanation can be found in the landmark civil rights case *Brown v. Board of Education* argued before the U.S. Supreme Court in 1954. That year the blacks from Topeka, Kansas, launched a series of protests against the segregationist policies of the local school board. Backed by the NAACP and the federal government,[3] the blacks won the case and dismantled the legal statutes upon which racial segregation was then based. The testimony of the psychologist for the plaintiffs was one of the key pieces of evidence that helped decide the case in favor of the blacks. He asked that a large table with dolls be placed in front of the jury. The dolls had been made especially for the case. Some were white with white features; others were black with black features. The psychologist, who had preselected a group of school children to testify, brought in one little black girl at a time and asked them to climb up the platform where the table was. Up until then those little girls had attended segregated schools from the district. They were between eight and twelve years old. After they had walked up to the table in front of the jury the psychologist would ask each of the girls to sit down and choose the dolls she liked the best, the prettiest ones. All of the girls, without exception, did the same thing: they chose the white dolls. The members of the jury were shocked at what they were witnessing. The psychologist's conclusion was to state the obvious: the little girls associated beauty and kindness with the white dolls. Not one of them chose a black doll because they looked like them. And if they resembled them, they could not be attractive or nice at all.

The practice of separating blacks and whites in segregated schools, the psychologist told them, was the reason why the little girls had rejected the dolls that resembled them. It was a case of self-hatred, like mine. In Texas I had lived through the same experiences in school. Anything Mexican was dirty, ugly, and lacked intelligence. The first thing the school nurses would do when we arrived on the first day was to take us out into the school yard and pour white powder on our heads to get rid of lice. Since they did it in the morning, we had to go around the rest of the day with white powder on our heads, lice or no lice. And if you did not allow them to fumigate you the school principal spanked you. What could one do at that age? The fight against Jim Crow did not end officially in Texas until 1965.

When I turned thirteen, we went to work at another farm not far from Burlington, Wisconsin. That was the first time I remember having worked for a lady boss. I recall her name. We called her La Radke, just as we did with all of our bosses in order to make things easier for us. She had hired us to do more or less the kind of work we had done for El Clifa. We picked tomatoes, cucumbers, and spuds for her, and we also did the weeding. But in her case she had planted another crop that, by the end of that harvest season, had turned into a nightmare for us: cabbage.

We arrived at her place one April morning. My mother had always been the one to read the maps. She rarely failed us. Thanks to her, we almost always went directly to where we were supposed to go. La Radke was already waiting for us. She put us up in an old two-story house on a hill surrounded by fields. There were no neighbors; we were completely isolated. From the beginning, we had gotten a bad taste in our mouths about the place. We drew drinking water from a manual water pump with a long handle that sat outside. On the bottom floor of the house, she left a piano that played by itself at night when the rats ran over the keys. At first nobody wanted to sleep on the second floor. During the thunderstorms that struck during the night, the light from the lightning projected moving shadows onto the walls. Then the thunder would strike, and we all flew downstairs. But in time and overcome by the weariness we felt from working all day in the fields, we gradually got used to all the fuss. It was a question of willpower. We knew that next day we had to go work very early in the morning. On another occasion the water pump outside sank into the ground. The next day we found a huge hole on the ground where the water pump had been. Thereafter there was no way to convince my sisters that no one was buried there. For them that was proof enough that the place had been a cemetery at one time. After that it became even harder to convince them to go upstairs.

But we also had much to be grateful to La Radke for. She would come to the house every Saturday, or she would meet us in the fields just before finishing a job, and she handed my father the check. We always dealt with her. She told us which field to go to, what to pick next, where to start loading. She spent the day coming and going in her pickup, her husband always sitting by her side. We never so much as saw his face. But just like Dick and El Clifa, she left us alone when we worked. Somehow she and my father understood each other. She did not speak Spanish, and my father knew no English. She had no trouble giving us orders, though.

Every Saturday without fail our parents would drive us to Burlington in the back of the truck to buy knickknacks. The girls would go store to store checking out the merchandise, and in the afternoon they returned with the same stuff they always bought: blouses and head scarves and nail polish. That's what it looked like to me and my brother anyway. He and I got five dollars each on weekends. With all that money in our pockets and looking nice and clean, we would head straight downtown looking just as happy as my sisters. But our appetite was for junk food: hamburgers, ice cream cones, and sundaes, Butterfingers and Mars candy bars with almonds, and of course, Bugs Bunny and Donald Duck comics. No doubt we looked like some rare species of animal to the town folks. People with black hair and brown skin coming and going in a red 1947 Dodge truck with side panels, a tarp on top, and Texas plates sitting right in the middle of downtown. But in the calm and casual atmosphere that was typical of rural midwestern America at the time, nobody seemed to notice. They just left us alone like when we were in the fields.

In the end we let La Radke down. That was the first time in my life that

I saw my father decide to abandon a workplace without staying until the harvest was complete. I remember well what happened. It was already October. There was ice in the fields. All of us had worked on that last remaining cabbage field, but by then, he and I were the only ones left. The weather had been turning much too cold, and my father didn't want my sisters or my younger brother coming out to work in such damp and dreary conditions. After we had finally finished with the cutting, he and I had started loading the cabbage onto a big truck La Radke had left with us just for that purpose. The side panels were extremely high; at least, that was how they seemed to me. Using our long-handled three-pronged fork we loaded the cabbage by launching it over the sides of the truck. Working nonstop from early in the morning till late in the evening, the two of us barely managed to finish one truckload. Every day it got a little bit colder. I remember that my hands felt frozen, and the colder it got the more difficult it became for me to get the cabbages over the sides of the truck onto the bed. I just couldn't get them over; as I launched them with the fork they were not reaching all the way to the top. They kept dropping back to the ground. My father had already noticed I didn't have the strength to get the cabbages over. He worked one side and I tried to work the other. After he finished his side, he would come help me on my side then move the truck a little further down. Then he'd climb down, take his fork, and do the same thing all over again. I kept jabbing at the cabbages with my fork but no matter how hard I tried to get them to go over they kept falling back. What was happening was that they were getting damaged from falling to the ground over and over again. And the more damaged they were the lower the price they fetched.

That day my father looked so overwhelmed that we quit in the middle of the day and walked from the field back to the house. We left the truck where it was, half loaded, the forks by the side of the rows of cabbages. When we walked in, my parents said something to each other. At midnight we were already on our way in our 1947 Dodge loaded down with all the stuff the girls had been buying all summer in downtown Burlington. A few days later we were in the midst of a Texas heat wave.

CHAPTER 8

〡〭〭〭〡

From La Grammar to Elk Grove Consolidated

During those years we were going back and forth between Texas and Wisconsin to work in the fields, between 1954 and 1956, I started grammar school in Crystal City. We called it La Grammar, with a capital G to signify the importance and respect we in the barrio attached at the time to going there. It represented a new world for me. The voice of authority still spoke English, but with a drawl, and the rules of social etiquette and convention were still as strictly enforced as classroom discipline. But the door had been opened, and I crossed back and forth countless times for a span of about two years, carrying my private dreams, hopes, and fears. I don't know how I survived, but somehow I managed to make the transition from there to middle school.

I do remember the morning when my mother dropped me off very well. We had just returned from up north, the day before I believe. She lost no time getting me out of the house. Before even finishing her chores, that morning she drove me to school. But she didn't do it because she wanted to spare me the long walk. She took me in the car because she wanted me to know where the school was. After that I went back and forth on foot every day. And if I wanted to eat at noon, I would take off running the one mile distance to the house, devour whatever she put in front of me in a hurry, then run back and make it in time for class. There was a cafeteria in the school, but it took a long time before I got up the courage to go in there and eat with strangers, and money was scarce.

She dropped me off a block from the school. From there I could see bunches of kids running all over the place. Behind the playground where the gringuitos and mexicanitos were playing stood the two-story, red brick school building with a shiny fire escape attached to the side. "There's the school. Get off." Those were my mother's exact words. She seemed so serious, and at the same time her words sounded so urgent to me that I've never erased the scene from my mind. I got off the car and walked along the side of the road toward the building. I remember thinking, "There are darker Mexicans than me here playing with the gringuitos. If they can do it, so can I." Climbing up the stairs to the entrance, I remember a fleeting sensation of pride coming over me, as if I were someone important because I was going to a school in town where both gringuitos and mexicanitos were allowed to play together. I was no longer going to the all-Mexican school where they had sent me before.

At the entrance, the receptionist came up to me and asked me to follow her. We walked toward the interior of the building and went into an office where there was an open door. The principal sat on a rotating chair and turned to face us. He asked me a few questions that I answered with exaggerated enthusiasm in my voice, as if I were delivering a speech, so he could see that I knew English. He said something like "Sounds pretty good to me" or "Sounds okay to me" to the receptionist. And with that she led me to a huge room in one wing of the building. When she opened the door, I noticed there were only Mexicans inside. At the front, there was an old Anglo lady with gray hair holding a book in one hand and talking to the students. She left me there.

It turned out to be a time of triumphs and tribulations, of fears, hopes, and new friendships, some of which have lasted a lifetime. Everything started out innocently. As I walked in I noticed a smallish group of students in the front of the room and a larger one sitting toward the back. Between them, there were empty seats. I walked toward the front and sat down. I purposefully left two or three seats and four or five scattered students in front of me. The teacher greeted me with a smile and handed me a book. They were reading on such and such a page. After a short while I noticed that she would only call on the students in front to read. She completely ignored the ones at the back. A few days later I found out why. They were *Chucos* from *México Chico*.[1]

Chucos was short for *pachucos*. The word was used in reference to adolescents who imitated California zootsuiters and dandies in their style of dress. It's a word that, to this day, is loaded with stereotypic meanings, both affirmative and negative. For us at the time it was no more than a way of distinguishing between Mexicans who liked school and those who did not. But making up this group were also kids who were older than the rest and therefore terrorized the younger ones. Because they wore their shirttails on the outside instead of tucked inside their pants and unbuttoned down to their navels, we said that they had no shame. It was an accusation they would always suffer from. And they would also pick fights. If there were any differences between them and someone else, their way was to settle those differences with their fists. They fought dirty, of course, and hung out in gangs. They were the bane of the so-called good students. And I considered myself one of them.

As soon as I walked in, I became one of their targets. A few days after I joined the class the teacher asked a question about something we had all read. I noticed that only one or two in the whole class raised their hand, so I raised mine to show that I knew what was going on. She called on me and I answered in the same haughty English I'd learned up north and that I had used a few days earlier with the school principal. The teacher smiled at me approvingly. But a few minutes after I answered the question some intuition led me to turn around, and I saw the fists coming up and the threatening looks of the Chucos. For an instant I felt my blood running cold. Then I understood. I had upset them because I had answered correctly and in the process had made them look bad.

From that day on and for the next few weeks it was a matter of who ran faster. During recess I'd get close to those students I more or less felt comfortable with or who were related to me. But after school everybody had to look out for themselves, and I had to rely on my very own self. It got tough. My mother ended up taking me to a *curandera* (faith healer) to cure me of fright. At other times, I would hide behind some tall weeds instead of going to class. When everybody came out at the end of the day, I had a whole block's advantage over them.

But I noticed that the teacher liked me. Toward midyear she divided the class into two groups. One group would read out of one book and the other group out of another. In the classroom, she went back and forth from one group to the other. Those of us that she placed in the advanced group she asked to read standing up so everybody could hear us. That made things worse because it was deliberately asking for trouble. The Chucos from *México Chico* did not look well upon anybody who made them look ignorant or backward. If we knew how to read, their favorite descriptive terms for us were *queer* and *fag*. I finally went to the principal. I told him that I was not afraid of them one on one, but that if they ganged up on me, there were too many of them. At the same time, I had begun making friends. I had gotten so close to the new group that one day, they invited me to join them for lunch at the school cafeteria. I didn't have enough money, but they all pitched in for me. Since it was my very first time eating there, I walked behind one of my new girl friends. I would do as she did. Inside I found that there were benches full of students who were not in my class. Then it dawned on me. I realized at that moment that they had placed me in a class with a slower group. We were the ones who came back from up north in October or November, a mixture of pachucos and migrants. As far as these people are concerned, I thought, there is no difference.

There were gringos and Mexicans eating together at the cafeteria. We got in line with our trays and utensils. They even provided napkins. I would pick whatever my new friend would pick. I would point to what I wanted and the ladies with white aprons behind the counter placed it on my plate. As we left the serving line I was straining to see who was sitting up ahead in the direction we were headed. I marveled at the realization I could be part of a group like that, students who dressed and acted differently from those in my class. But just as I was beginning to admire the sights, I accidently stepped on food someone had dropped on the floor. I threw the tray up in the air with the food and drink and utensils and landed on the floor rear first. To my great surprise, though, the accident had not been the great spectacle that I had expected. Nor did my new friend abandon me. My girl friend placed her tray on a table and helped me pick my things off the floor. I no longer remember if I did or did not eat, but what I do remember is that someone had lent me a hand. From then on I knew that I could fall but that I'd get up again and the world was not going to end.

At La Grammar there were no more nuns to run away from nor oversized kindergartners to jump us at recess. I gradually got away from the gangs who had terrorized me the first few weeks. Slowly I got closer to a small group of friends who spoke English and knew how to read. I even made friends with some gringuitos, and because I wanted to impress one of them,

I got into trouble. His name was Jerry. He had a reputation for being a class clown, and I did what he told me so he'd let me be his friend. "Where do evergreen trees grow?" the teacher asked me in class one day. I knew the answer because we had studied it, and I had read it in the book. But instead of giving the correct answer I told the teacher "On the ground," and Jerry and I laughed at her tantrum at the same time. "Stay after class," she said. My friend and I knew what awaited us as soon as everybody had left. Said and done. Five blows with her paddle for clowning around in class. I started getting away from Jerry, and he also lost interest in me after that. Thanks to that paddling, I straightened out and went through the rest of the school year successfully. At least until the middle of the following April.

I still keep two of my report cards from the 1955–1956 school years. At my age (I'm 67 years old) I find them fascinating documents. Not only do they represent the chronological element in my education during those years, they also give a pretty good idea of some of the other issues and psychological conflicts that defined my personality back then. The first report card says on top Grammar School, Session 1955–1956 followed by my name, Roy O. Sanchez (without accent) and Fifth Grade. The word Grammar and the numbers 5 and 6 after the 195_ are written in the same handwriting as my name and grade. It's the handwriting of the same teacher who gave me the spanking. Her name is on the back of the report card.

The school year is divided into six vertical columns each representing six weeks' duration beginning with 1st Six Weeks and ending with the 6th Six Weeks. There are also two columns for midterm exams (Term Exams), two columns for the midterm averages (Term Average) and one for the final grade (Yearly Average). There are sixteen horizontal rows. They cover from Days Present to Days Absent to Deportment and Application. Next comes the list of subjects: Language, Reading, Spelling, Writing, Social Studies, Arithmetic, and Science. Spanish as a subject is crossed out and has the letters WT written over it. I don't know what they mean. We did not receive Spanish language classes then. Those started in the eighth grade. Then the list of subjects continues: Physical Ed., Health, Music, and Drawing.

There are no grades or marks in the column for the first six weeks. The column for the following six weeks shows that I had attended school a total of four days. To put it another way: of the eighteen weeks that make up the first semester I missed eleven weeks of school. That day that my mother dropped me off at La Grammar, it was already the month of November. Looking at the rows and columns for the second semester, it can be seen that I did not go to school the last six weeks either. By the middle of April, as I've said, I had to leave. Out of the thirty-six weeks that comprise the school year, I attended only eighteen weeks and a few days. I had lost half of the academic year. The grades for the last term were not too bad; on the contrary, there's one C, two B's, three A's, and three S's for Satisfactory.

When my parents took me out of school early in the spring to go up north, we headed back to Wisconsin again. That time we were not going to work for any particular grower. We ended up living in some tiny dilapidated houses, and from there we would go in search of work weeding and topping onions until the time came to pick tomatoes. Supposedly that was what we were there for. Someone had convinced my father that the tomato-picking season at that place was a long one and that pickings were really good. What they did not tell him was that a lot of other people already knew about the place and so the picking season was short-lived. We looked for work in different places and with different growers. We'd pick here and there. It was in one of those fields where I first heard Elvis Presley sing "Don't Be Cruel" for the first time. There were other families from Crystal City picking right next to us. One of them owned a red and white 1955 Chevrolet. It was a two-door hardtop, luxury model, and the young driver moved it along as we were picking and left the door open to listen to the radio. The girls also wanted to listen, and they'd get close. That was the idea.

That was the year I started driving a tractor. One of the growers we worked with pulling corn stalks was known by the people as a good guy. We went to work for him and that was where I first earned $1.00 an hour. But I had to drive the tractor and pull stalks, too. Whenever he dropped by the field where we were working and noticed I was driving and not pulling stalks, he'd tell me that he was not paying me a dollar an hour just to drive the tractor. I had to pull cornstalks, too. He told me off, and I could do nothing about it. I don't know if anybody else saw him do it because we were in the middle of a grown cornfield. I had to swallow my pride and keep working.

Since we already knew some people in Wisconsin, we would visit them in the neighboring farms. We went in search of our Cotulla friends who had taken us in when we had first arrived a few years before. They had already moved to Racine. My parents packed our whole family into the car one weekend and we drove off to the big city to look for them. That was the time we visited them in their downtown apartment. I have already described where they were living when we got there, on the second floor of a building above a tavern. I didn't understand then why I felt so sad to see them living there. They weren't ill, they seemed to lack for nothing, and they welcomed us warmly. Perhaps it was that the apartment was dark, and they seemed to be imprisoned in it, that they lacked space. Later I found out the father had even been willing to follow us when we went to work in other states just to keep playing his guitar with my father. And that was what they did. The following year they ended up in Montana hoeing sugar beets with a short hoe. But that kind of lifestyle was just too difficult for anyone not accustomed to it. They returned to Wisconsin, settled down in the city this time, and everything changed for them after that.

Not long after, when the tomato harvest was over in that part of the state, we ended up in Des Plains, Illinois. A friend of my father's had convinced him to follow him and his crew there. He was a contractor from La Pryor, Texas. That was how some of the decisions were made back then. People who knew each other would talk, and that was how they found out where to find work. Again we ended up living for a while in some barracks. By that time it was no longer surprising to us that wherever there were people living in barracks, we were sure to find people just like us. And they were there for the same reason we were: to work in the fields.

While the adults went to work in the chicory (endive) ovens in town we stayed behind picking pumpkins. The fields were right outside the barracks. My brother and I were sent to work with a couple of black men who were pulling a wagon with a tractor. We'd load the trailer to the top with pumpkins, climb on top, and they would drive to the other end of the field where a semitrailer was waiting for us. We would unload the pumpkins carefully then return to the field to pick and load another wagonful. That was how we spent the day. We got along well with the guys, and we'd share stories when we rode behind on top of the wagon or when we were picking. They would teach us new words in English, and we'd teach them Spanish. After the first week or so, it seemed natural to spend the day telling jokes and laughing with the guys while we worked. But one day a gringo came to the field and told us we couldn't work any longer; we had to go to school.

The other school report card I still have in my possession is from Elk Grove Consolidated #59, the school that the three of us who were under sixteen years of age had to attend: my sister, my brother, and I. Two other kids, one about my age and the other a bit older, accompanied us. They knew more English than I did. From the very first day, I already felt inferior. We would walk along a narrow road all the way to a bus stop where a wide, yellow school bus picked us up. My mother packed a lunch for each of us. We did not own a lunchbox for sandwiches; we had *chorizo* (sausage) and bean tacos in a brown paper bag. The grease from the tacos stained the bag, of course, and it was the first thing that the gringuitos noticed. They wanted to know what was in the paper bag.

From the time we got on the bus, my sister and the two older boys started arguing who was more intelligent and who was going to start at a higher grade. The kid my age said, "I'm in seventh grade." The other one said, "I'm in the eighth grade." My sister, who was no pushover, said, "So am I." I had not been to school since the previous April when they had taken us out to go up north. I was thirteen. I was supposed to be in eighth grade. But the truth was that I had only just gotten out of La Grammar, where I was in the fifth grade. Even though I was a migrant, nobody was going to take that into consideration. So were the others. When we finally got to the principal's office we all waited in line to register. We were all asked the same questions: "What's your father's name?" "What's your mother's name?" "What grade are you in?" I told them that my father's name was Julian, but I pronounced it in English, "jewli-ann"; that my mother's name was Nellie, and that I was in the seventh grade. None of it was true. My mother's name was Manuela, but I didn't want to say her name out of fear that the gringos would laugh when they heard me pronounce a word in Spanish in front of them. And I said that I was in the seventh grade because if I said the truth, that I was supposed to be in the sixth grade, the other kids were going to pick on me on the way back home that afternoon calling me "dummy" and "retarded." I paid dearly for that lie. The report card that I have from Elk Grove tells the story well.

Next to where my name appears, Roy Sanchez, it gives the name of the school and the grade, Seventh Grade. Where it says Attendance, it shows that I went a total of twenty-one days during the month of October. Inside the front cover it says, in capital letters, ACHIEVEMENT LEVELS, and asks for the average grades in four subjects: Reading, Arithmetic, Language, and Work Study Skills. Next to each subject it shows the grade I received: In Reading a 64; in Arithmetic a 0; in Language a 46; in Work Study Skills a 49. Written inside the loose pages of the report card are various comments from the teachers. One of the comments has two signatures, a Mr. Turner and a Mrs. Coston. It says, "Roy has not been in school long enough to give an accurate account of his grades or ability." A few empty pages follow, and then there's this jewel, handwritten and signed by a Mr. Hinnebery at the bottom of the page: "Works very hard but is not able to accomplish much."

##

CHAPTER 9

Youthful Rebellion in Billings, Montana

The whole family was in a joyful mood as we returned to Crystal City at the end of that harvest season. My parents were finally able to purchase a home. I never found out how they did it, but I know that the man who had lent us money in the past to go up north had something to do with it. It was a decent-looking barrio house with a pink slate exterior: three bedrooms, a kitchen and a small but comfortable living room area. It had no inside plumbing; there was an outhouse at the far end of the backyard as was the case with almost all barrio homes. The area was considered the outskirts of town; right across the street was a huge cotton-gin complex. We were told when cotton was in season, in August and September, there were mounds of cotton strewn all over the street. By the time we got there most of it had blown away. Little white plumes remained here and there, strung by the wind over electrical power lines or on top of trees. As the cotton gin was the area's most conspicuous landmark, the barrio got its name from there and so it was called *El Gin*. We were known as *los del gin* (the ones from El Gin).

There was room for all of us in that house, and within a few months there would be more. My oldest sister's suitor had grown so insistent on marrying her that he sent my parents a committee of what in the community are known as men of respect to ask for her hand. My father rejected the gesture. A few weeks later he sent another one. This time he ran out of excuses why she couldn't get married and so he and my mother gave in. There's a picture of bride and groom with my parents taken at the wedding.

Their deadpan facial expressions tell it all. They were not, to put it mildly, in the best of moods.

From the beginning of my sister's relationship, I had been brought in as the go-between. I would carry their secret correspondence back and forth. In return I got hamburgers, cheeseburgers, and banana splits. That was how my sister's suitor rewarded me for penetrating the home defenses and bringing my sister his letters without my parents knowing about it. Little by little I had begun to accept the role of messenger. At first I had been very protective of my family against intrusions of any kind. Besides, I had been working shining shoes after school and even landed a job in a restaurant. I was a waiter. That restaurant was across the street from the business owned by the family of my sister's suitor. I worked there a few months and learned things unknown to me until then. The owner was African-American, and he treated me well. He offered me the restaurant food, paid me a small salary, and allowed me to keep tips. One night we were chatting and he pointed to some kids who had come into the restaurant, and he told me he was having sex with the brother of one of them. I became so confused that I wasn't sure what to think. By some coincidence, it was then that my future brother-in-law offered me work, and I accepted. I would distribute movie flyers around the neighborhoods, and he paid me well. At first that was all I did, but as time went by he asked me to do more things. He was trying to gain my confidence. I did not become aware of it until later when I was a well-paid messenger.

A new chapter had begun in my life. I was thirteen years old; I began to see things differently. I stopped shining shoes in the neighborhood cantinas (beer joints). I learned that there were people who made money without going to work in the fields. I would go watch the billiards players with my sister's suitor, and I saw how the good players beat the bad ones. They beat them with their minds, not with raw strength. I noticed that girls liked guys who combed their hair nice, who smelled good, who knew how to fix themselves up, and who walked and looked a certain way. In the barrio I no longer played ball alone. I had my own team, and we would go play against teams from other barrios. We would often walk from one end of town to the other just to go at it to see who was the better team, to see who won and who lost the game. I became a good pitcher; I learned how to throw curve balls so batters couldn't hit my pitches. The adults would come watch us play because they knew we were good players. I felt my ego expanding.

But that growing feeling of independence, of having a will of my own, had no effect when it came to my father. At least not at that age. He continued working in the fields, cutting spinach and harvesting onions during the winter season. When the work in the spinach or onions was going well, he would take me out of school for two or three days. Everybody knew where I had been: with the adults working in the fields. Those times when I had to go to work instead of being allowed to go to school, I'd be in a foul mood. I worked but I didn't talk to anyone. I felt even worse when I realized there were no other kids my age working there during school hours. I'm not sure if my father ever knew what a terrible mood I was in, but he must have. It did me no good, though. If there was plenty of work cutting spinach or harvesting onions, I found myself joining the adults in the fields again, running back and forth after bushels and twine.[1] I'd go back to school after two or three days but I felt disoriented. Each time that happened I'd fall behind the other students, and of course, they would outscore me on the exams. And that was what happened. The good thing was that a few days later, I'd catch up, though not with everybody. I never was able to keep up with the intelligent ones. Then spring came around, and again there was that familiar commotion at home. The time had come to start getting things ready because the family was headed back up north once again.

That was the year I accompanied my father for the first time to the place where the company agents signed people up. It was there that I learned how people managed to go up north even though they had no money. I saw how things worked from the inside. I was able to see how far the growers' reach extended. Like everybody else who had gone to sign up that morning, we arrived at the place empty-handed. The place was called *El Teatro Nacional*[2] (National Theater). It was located in the heart of the Mexican barrio. We walked into the cavernous building. It was dark and cold inside. The seats had been piled up along the sides of the walls, and what had earlier been the movie screen was now an empty hole covered with old threadbare sheets hanging from the ceiling. All that was left was the shell. It had been years since they had shown movies there. The owners had either died or left town or lost out to the competition. It was there that the Great Western Sugar Company from Montana rented a space to recruit workers. They were looking for laborers to work in the sugar-beet fields. Each head of family received a certain amount of money in advance for the journey north. That was how the sugar companies guaranteed that the growers from Montana got people to hoe their sugar beets. Adults received $8.00 per person and minors half that amount. If you wanted to work, they would sign you up; it didn't matter how old the workers were or how much school they missed. My father accepted and that April, after my sister's wedding, the whole family left for Billings, Montana. We had one less helper.

The day we arrived I met the farmer's daughter. I don't recall her name but I do remember what she looked like because she had what they call in English a hair lip. We parked under some enormous trees. Right in front we could see the grower's family home. She was the first to come out and greet us. I could not understand her English well at first because of her lip. But because she was good-natured and she was all excited now that she had someone to play with we started chatting as if we were old friends. I figured she was about fifteen, kind of chunky and tomboyish. Right after that the mother arrived, and the two of them showed us the interior of the house where we were going to live. It had everything inside, from plates to pots and pans to window curtains. It was the workers' quarters, but it was well-kept, and it looked like it was in better condition than some of the huts we had lived in back in Texas. My mother spoke English, and the two of them lost no time in working things out. There was room for everyone. That was one of the few places where we did not have to leave our things stuffed in burlap sacks the whole time we were there. We even had room to hang our clothes. It didn't take us long to get settled in, and my brother and I were soon off to explore the place with our new friend.

That particular grower raised mostly sugar beets. In that part of the country they wanted sugar-beet workers, not pickers for the tomato or potato crop as had been the case in Wisconsin. He had planted around two hundred acres. We were one adult and four adolescents: my father, my brother, myself, and two sisters. Before starting we went out in the car to check out the fields. There were three. One was in front of the house, another about a mile away and the third one ended at a golf course. This was the setting where I was destined to begin my life as a sugar-beet worker.

When we got there, the grower had already started to cultivate the rows of beets. Cultivate in this case meant bordering the soil so as to leave a narrow raised row where the young sugar-beet shoots were coming up. They used an implement called a cultivator, and that was where we got the Spanish version of the word *calavera*.[3] Two discs were used, some three to four inches apart, leaving room in the middle for the plants. As the tractor pushed the discs through the furrows, a raised strip was left behind, and that was considered a row of sugar beets. The implement attached to the tractor, the cultivator, took up to six rows at a time. If there were lots of weeds or grass or both, as was common, the narrower the row or strip of soil where the beets grew the better for us. The thicker or more *pachón* as we called it, the worse. The reason rows were sometimes thick or bushy (*pachones*) was that the young sugar-beet shoots were bunched up together when they broke through the soil. But they did not come up alone. They were generally accompanied by a thick carpet of weeds and grass. The prevalence of these weeds and grasses varied with the season and with each particular field, but they never failed to come up.

The art of thinning the beets lay in removing that narrow strip of soil where the plants grew ("blocking" it was called) with a short hoe, then removing the weeds and grass and finally leaving a single sugar-beet plant every fourteen to sixteen inches. Why a single plant, and why fourteen to sixteen inches apart? In order for the beet tuber to produce the proper amount of sugar when it matures, it needs to grow up to a certain size, neither too large nor too small. That is to say, after years of experimenting, growers have learned what the ideal size is for a sugar-beet plant to reach in order for it to give the maximum amount, and the desired quality, of sugar. And the tuber reached that size only if it had six or seven inches around it in which to grow. That was per tuber, meaning for each individual plant. If two or three small shoots are left together, the tubers will not reach their proper size, and the grower doesn't make as much money, and he takes it out on the beet thinners. The sugar-beet worker's job, then, is to leave a single plant a certain distance from each other on every row. It is not acceptable to leave two shoots together, nor weeds or grass next to them. Nothing but a single sugar-beet shoot will do. To leave them in pairs was a mortal sin. If an inept thinner, called *chambón* (careless) in Spanish, did poor work the grower got rid of him. One also could not leave the row with too few plants. Two quick swings of the hoe (whack, whack) with the right hand, while the left hand removed unwanted shoots, weeds, and grass, with one plant left standing. Another two swings (whack, whack) with the right hand, and the left removed unwanted stuff around the plant, with a lone sugar-beet plant left standing. Not quite an onomatopoeic rendition of thinning sugar beets with a short hoe, but it gets the sense across. Short-handled hoes were essential for that reason: one had to be stooped or bent over so as to reach the ground with both hands at all times. With one hand you did the blocking and with the other the thinning. To do it right you had to be bent all the way down and moving down the row at a steady pace at the same time.

We did not get paid until we finished doing all of the work. All season long we ate food purchased on credit. The grower and the town merchants entered into an agreement so that workers got food on credit during the harvest season. When we finished, we got paid for all of the work completed minus whatever we owed at the store. But whether on credit or not, food up north was always more abundant. And, thanks to my mother, we always ate very well. By four o'clock in the morning she had already started making tortillas. We'd get up before five and we ate something light, corn or oatmeal with homemade biscuits. By five thirty we were in the field. Between nine and nine thirty she brought us the main breakfast at the field: bean, potato, and meat tacos along with sweetbread, Kool Aid, and more water. My younger sisters did not go to the fields; they stayed home and helped with the housework. At noon we'd go home for lunch (figure 4).

Sugar-beet work is done by the piece rate, not by the hour, but there was no way to convince my father to give us an extra half-hour break. At five minutes after one, we were already on our way back to the field. That was the hardest part of the day because we'd get sleepy after eating. It was hot and we were hot. Only by sheer force of will, and following the example of my parents, were we able to overcome that overwhelming desire to lie down and rest after eating. Siestas lasted no more than a few minutes. My father was not harsh; when the girls complained about something, he would let them stay home. But the males were not allowed to complain.

We started on the field nearest the house. From the beginning my father got into a rhythm with his hoeing and the rest of us adapted ourselves to it. There was a certain strategy to his method. He tied a piece of cloth to the handle of the hoe and wound it around his wrist so he wouldn't lose his grip when his hand tired. He stuck one knee on one side of a set of three

4

The Pérez family having lunch in the middle of a
field during the noon hour in the state of Minnesota.
Courtesy of Mr. Oscar Pérez.

rows, and he would hoe that row as far as his arms reached. When he had
extended his arms as far as he could, he hoed in reverse on a second row.
Then he would shift to the other knee as he hoed and thinned the third
row up to where he had reached with the first one in the middle. He was
not so much kneeling as squat-walking, as if he were walking on his knees,
while hoeing on three different rows at the same time. It was an unusual
sight to see to say the least. How he did it is best demonstrated in practice.
I remember on at least one occasion the grower brought the field agent who
had recruited us in Texas to come out to where we were working to see us
at work. They stood there staring at my father's dexterity with the hoe.

The fields were usually fifty, seventy-five, or one hundred acres each, all
in rectangular or square plots. At first they had appeared to us like they
were way too much for so few workers. But my father led the way, and then
I came, followed by my brother, and behind him my sisters. The three of us
opened more and more distance between us and the girls as the day wore
on. It somehow seemed the natural thing for my brother and me to do, to
keep up with my father all day, although he took three rows at a time while
we did one at a time. And little by little, as we finished hoeing one more
swath of rows and turned right around and cut another one, the far end of

the field seemed just a little closer. At the end of the day, after packing hoes and water jugs into the trunk, we surveyed the area covered. Satisfaction shone on our faces as we looked around. Soon, we knew we would be done hoeing that one field and then . . . It was a question of great endurance and lots of heart.

We called it "the field next to the golf course." It was where my brother and I debuted as rebels. I included a short story by that title in *Hay Plesha Lichans Tu Di Flac* (see chapter 5, note 2), the collection I published back in the mid-seventies. I'll summarize the main points of the story. We, my brother and I, had more or less perfected our hoeing skills by then. When my father first introduced us to thinning with the short hoe, we stuck behind him day after day, he doing three rows at a time, the two of us and my sisters one. But by the time we finished the first field and started on the next one, the one by the golf course, we had developed enough confidence in ourselves to strike out ahead of him, albeit still one row at a time versus his three. I led the way, then came my brother. Not long after we started going up and down the quarter-mile long rows, we began to encounter little white golf balls in the middle of the field. At first we'd stick them in our pockets. After a while there were too many, so we launched them back into the golf greens when nobody was looking. Of course we competed to see who could throw them the farthest.

One morning, just before reaching the end of the rows we had been hoeing, we noticed some old men in short white pants and big straw hats standing at the edge of the golf course, as if beckoning to us. We weren't sure what to do, so we ignored them, turned around, and began hoeing back the other way. The girls got uncomfortable, so they stopped in the middle of the field and waited for them to leave. They did after a while. We kept hoeing, and over the next few days two or three of the similarly-dressed old geezers would come up to us, smile, and say something. Our immediate gut reaction was to ignore them. Then we began to feel annoyed by their presence. We didn't know if they were just acting friendly and wanted to converse, which was probably the case, or if they were being condescending. Either way, we didn't like it.

We kept running into their little white golf balls, and we'd throw them back. When we finally finished hoeing that field next to the golf course, my brother and I and my sisters reacted with elation. Somehow we couldn't escape feeling like bona fide *machitos* (diminutive of Macho).[4] We were the real thing now, genuine *betabeleros* (beet thinners).[5] To celebrate the occasion, that afternoon as we were walking through the field checking for stuff we'd left behind, my brother and I couldn't resist the temptation to deliver our own message. As if on cue, we took our short hoes and launched them into one of the greens nearest the edge of the beet rows. It felt good doing it, not so much because it was an expression of youthful insolence but rather because it released the accumulated frustrations and resentments that had built up over time. They played golf, we hoed beets. I don't know that we thought that at the time. We simply felt the need to strike back. And that was how we did it. Of course, before walking back to the car to go home, we went to retrieve our hoes. We needed them for the next field coming up.

My father used another strategy to help us all accomplish more at work. His conversations were meant to fire our imagination. Each day he would tell us how we were going to make enough money to pay for our home, to buy a good car, to get nice clothes and shoes. As the season wore on and the sun got hotter, we oftentimes felt like quitting, like just getting rid of the damn hoe and start walking home. Hoeing row after row, dirt and sweat and the back pain growing ever more intense, meant we had to learn mental tricks to fool our brain and our bodies so we could take the strain. So he gave us pep talks. That became necessary because, looking out in front of us, all we could see were acres and acres of more sugar-beet rows as we slowly hoed our way through another huge beet field. The thrill of having finished the previous one, even after having capped it with our rebels' gesture, hadn't lasted long. It had evaporated as soon as we landed at the foot of the next one, a monstrous fifty- or seventy-five acre field.[6] Even though we were learning to refine our survival strategies, we were only twelve- and thirteen-year-old kids. Somehow we still had to learn to suffer in silence because we were all going through the same thing.

In Montana we didn't go downtown much during the thinning season. There was no money. But that changed once we were done with the thinning. We were not allowed to start weeding the fields right away. The growers made us wait for a week or two. The idea was to allow the weeds ample time to grow before we went in to do the weeding. That was when we took advantage of our idle time to make a little extra money. We didn't stay home to loaf. The three of us would go out looking for extras. What that meant was that we drove out every morning to find growers where we noticed the workers had fallen behind with the thinning. Their fields had become overgrown with weeds because some members of the crew had fallen ill or they were too slow, and the crops were in danger of failing. The three of us would go in, and within two or three days we would help the locals get caught up. That was how I began to find out that few sugar-beet workers got after it as hard and with as much drive as we did. They went along at their own slow pace all day and didn't bother to push it beyond that. We'd catch up to them and pass them but they didn't seem to mind. They just kept going at their usual steady pace, but slower than ours.

The good thing about the extras was that we got paid day by day. It was how we managed to go downtown on weekends. One weekend, two buddies from another ranch nearby picked me up, and we went riding around downtown Billings. We knew each other from Crystal City. One of them was my age, the other a bit older. Their father had lent them the family car. We took a nice bath and headed straight to the park downtown. From the scuttlebutt, we knew that it was the place the girls hung out to see and be seen. I don't remember if we ate or not, but I do remember the girls we picked up. At that notoriously fecund age, other things besides food were becoming more urgent. We found a group of them, and we picked them up. I wasn't driving; I didn't have a driver's license. I used that excuse to concentrate all of my attention on the girls. And it didn't take one of them and me very long to pair up. We drove around enjoying each other's company until it got dark. That night each of the guys went off with one of the girls. I stayed with the same one. She invited me to her house. I went and told the guys, and they dropped us off.

She lived alone in an apartment. At least that was what I had thought until we walked in. There was a child asleep in a crib in the living room. How long she had been alone or who had been taking care of her, I never found out. But we climbed on her bed and we stayed there until early the next morning. When she got up to go to the bathroom I looked outside. The guys were asleep in the car waiting for me. I said good-bye and left. I woke them up, and they made some clumsy jokes, but I was in no mood to listen. By the time they dropped me off at the ranch, the sun was coming up. I went in as quietly as I could, but I became alarmed when I saw my mother sitting on a chair in the kitchen. She was crying. She didn't get after me or say anything. My father came in a short while later, and without saying a word to me, he gestured toward the door in the direction of the fields. Just as I had been dressed when I came in, without sleeping or eating anything and with only water to quench our thirst, we worked nonstop all day, just the two of us. He was testing my mettle. I had just turned fourteen.

CHAPTER 10

Competition in Moses Lake, Washington

n 1958 we went to Moses Lake, Washington, for the first time. We travelled in the back of an uncle's truck, a red 1951 Studebaker. They don't
make those anymore, neither the trucks nor the cars, but back then they
were a common sight on the highways. I am not referring to migrant trucks
like the one we were riding in. Those carnivals on the road, as we sometimes referred to ourselves and the contraptions collectively, were unusual
sights to say the least. We avoided being seen in them except when we were
being transported up north, or when the occasion demanded it around
labor camps. Owners kept them out of the sight except when they were
being used to ferry workers back and forth to the fields. They were cum-
bersome to drive, and their freakish appearance was a constant reminder
to the locals that migrant workers were nearby. But owners profited from
them, and thus they served their purpose. Contractors would usually fit
twenty-five to thirty persons in the back and another three in the cab. I no
longer remember the going rate per person for transporting us from Texas
to Washington, but I imagine my father chose to go with relatives because
he was able to negotiate a more economical deal. We were packed in just
like we had been when we travelled to Wisconsin: the women and children
up against the back end of the cab, the men bunched up toward the rear
of the bed. A bedspread down the middle offered some privacy. All those
trucks had a tarp covering. The tarp extended from one end of the bed to
the other. A raised two-by-four was run the length of the bed to raise the
tarp. It protected us from the rain. All the belongings were stacked together
on the platform just above the heads of the women toward the back. They

therefore had little or no standing room. The men, on the other hand, rarely sat. We slept standing up. The chauffeurs drove nonstop all the way; once in a while they'd stop in some out of the way place to let us out to relieve ourselves. There was no stopping in any town except to fill up with gas.

As usual, it was April when we left. Moses Lake, Washington, lay some two thousand miles from Crystal City. It took four or five days to get there. It was not just that we travelled at a low rate of speed. There were times that all the men got off the truck to help push it up steep grades. Close to Pecos, Texas, there was a particular canyon that had become famous amongst migrants. It was called *El voladero del diablo* or Devil's Canyon. The old trucks couldn't make it all the way up on their own power. The loads they carried were excessive. The drivers were usually experienced, and they already knew what to expect. Going downhill they would let the old jalopy pick up all the speed it could. If it didn't make it all the way to the other side, just before it came to a complete stop we'd jump off. The driver put the transmission in low and kept going, but if the truck stalled we pushed to help it reach the top of the *voladero* (canyon). That was how we managed to get to the other side that time. I don't remember exactly how long it took us to get to the other side of the canyon, but it was a matter of hours. No one said anything or complained about the delay; it was an expected part of what everyone considered to be just another journey.

The people who headed for Washington to work in the sugar-beet fields did not have any kind of contract, nor were they given any assurances of work. The area we were going to was known as the Columbia Basin. Thousands of acres of sugar beets were grown there along with other crops like asparagus, spuds, and beans. Like everybody else on that particular trip, we were going there to hoe beets. One of the attractions of hoeing sugar beets in that state was that work was arranged following the open market economic model: everybody had to fend for themselves. There was an element of risk involved in traveling all the way over there without knowing where we were going to work. As was customary, we based our decision on our own faith and in other people's stories. We had joined other family members on the trip, so we were not totally at the mercy of blind faith.

When we got there, in the early morning hours, our legs were stiff from standing up for days on end. People started getting off the truck slowly, the men helping their wives and other family members come down the ramp.

My mother and sisters were, understandably, in a foul mood from breathing the exhaust fumes the entire trip. Yet in spite of their suffering, such hazards were hardly even commented upon. One simply endured, whatever the price to one's lungs or sanity. Still, it didn't take us long to take up residency in one of the barracks. Inside we found that there were already some metal bunk beds. We brought in the bags with our belongings and each one picked a corner to go and rest. Everybody was a genius at improvising. We made tables from discarded cans and boards; my mother had her small kerosene stove, the kneading board, and rolling pin which she carried everywhere.

With the light of day, early next morning we went out to explore. Outside we found that ours was one of three or four long barracks set a few yards apart from each other with ample space in between. They all looked the same with their green slate siding. They resembled military quarters, and most probably had been dragged there from the local military base when the government condemned them. Even the common soldiers found them unacceptable. Perfect for sugar-beet workers. Just like in Wisconsin, we had ended up in a large central partition of one of the barracks. Both of the end partitions were already taken up. At one end lived the family of one of the drivers; at the other end it was the family of another one. Those people had been going to that same place for several years in a row. The place, another labor camp in the outskirts of town, would be our home for the next four or so months. But the people who had put up the camp had thought of providing its dwellers with extra amenities. The place had showers and water toilets! They were communal, not private, but it didn't take us long to find out how things operated. The best time to use them was not early in the morning or in the afternoon. The best time was late in the evening. Everybody was already asleep by then, except the young lovers who would sneak out to exchange pleasantries with each other for a few minutes at the restrooms and showers before being found out.

My father had made arrangements with a family member to take us to a place where we could find us an old used car. He took us the very next day after we got there to visit an old friend of his who owned a junkyard. The gringo turned out to be a nice guy. He did well selling to the Mexicans from the camps. He'd buy the used cars off the soldiers from the military base and resell them to us. He made money at both ends. The soldiers sold their cars at a loss when they found out they were being deployed outside the States. Once they received orders from the government, they had no choice but to get rid of their vehicles. He paid junkyard prices for them. The sugar-beet workers from the area picked them up in no time because he gave them good prices with credit. With interest, by the time we finished paying off a car, it turned out not to be such a great deal. But that was how one learned to survive. We got hold of an old four-door Studebaker that lasted the entire harvest season. The front of the car looked like a torpedo, and that's what we named it. We paid it off well before the end of the harvest season.

To this day we laugh and tell stories about some of the experiences the family lived through during those years we went to Washington. We went six or seven times to the same place. I had a girlfriend there; I met sugar-beet workers from San Antonio, from The Valley, from Monterrey. I went to dances, I saw fistfights, I had some close calls as a consequence of running around with the wrong crowd, and I learned how to manufacture my own fantasy world to escape in my imagination from the depressing conditions under which we lived. This did not happen to me all at once. I was fourteen years old when we made that trip. I was almost twenty when I hoed sugar beets there for the last time. By then I was not only an experienced beet thinner but had other more transcendental accomplishments to my credit. But I don't want to get ahead of myself; let's let things just fall into place.

There were bedbugs in the barracks. It was our first encounter with them. And oh how they made one's life miserable! They only came out at night when we were dead tired and all we wanted was to fall asleep. But they made us lose precious sleep night after night until we left the place. They came out of the straw we used to fill the burlap sacks we used for mattresses. I remember so very well those nights and how one suffered just to get something as simple and necessary as a good night's sleep. First there were the bedbugs. We went to bed early even though it didn't get dark until late. Washington lies way up north; in the summer, darkness does not set in until after nine. But by then we were exhausted. As soon as darkness fell they came out for blood. They were the size of a tomato seed but punishing like a mosquito. They would come out to bite, we turned on the lights, and they scurried away between the pillows and mattresses. We'd squash as many as we could get to. We'd turn off the lights and fall asleep again. Half an hour later we would be scratching ourselves again. We turned on the lights and the same thing all over again. It was a never-ending story.

Then there was the noise from the hallway traffic. Working people spent the whole day in the fields and we'd get home tired. We all wanted to sleep and rest like everybody else. But not the children and kids. Once it got dark outside, mothers kept them inside and they ran up and down the halls. They ran back and forth, dragged toys and threw stuff against the walls. Those walls were not made of the best materials and one could hear everything. Between the bedbugs and the noise outside, it was difficult to sleep. It was during one such occasion that I swore, I remember, that someday I would sleep a whole month nonstop just to make up for all the sleep I'd lost. It wasn't that I was exaggerating. Things were not that easy. We went to sleep late because of the bedbugs and the noise. And just as it got dark late because we were so far north, in the summer the sun also came up early. And you can add to that a third factor that also contributed to those sleepless nights: competition.

The way of life for sugar-beet workers in Washington was totally different from that of sugar-beet workers elsewhere. It wasn't the work; that was the same everywhere. In Montana and Iowa, people had already agreed to a contract from the time they left Texas. The company agents assigned each family a particular grower to work for depending on the number of workers ("hands" they called them) in the family. People didn't just take off blindly. A certain obligation was entered into as soon as the workers accepted the money advanced to them by the company. In Washington you went to compete against all the other sugar-beet workers from the area. In a manner of speaking that was the philosophy behind a capitalist economic system, but instead of capital, we invested sweat, misery, and brute strength. That was all we had. Well, almost. It was also necessary to have lots of willpower, and we had it.

In the beginning, without much competition from the people from Monterrey, we did pretty well. That first year we found work thinning beets beginning in the first weeks of May. There were four of us who were quite good: my father, a nephew, my brother and myself. My sisters struggled at first but eventually they resigned themselves to doing the work. With six of us each time we hit the field, we'd grab a nice-sized swath of rows. After we had done a few acres in different fields scattered here and there, we got lucky. This man, who turned out to be the first Mexican American in the whole state of Washington to grow his own sugar beets, hired us to hoe a field of approximately one hundred acres. We'd come and go every day for two weeks from the barracks to his fields until we finally finished. By then one of his sons, who wanted to get close to the girls, had found out that my father played the guitar. They invited him to the ranch to play for them one weekend. The old man fell in love with my father. He played and sang some of the old classical Mexican songs: "Dos arbolitos" ("Lovers' Trees"), "Usted" ("You"), and "Canción huasteca" (a regional Mexican song).[1] They celebrated all night.

But work was another thing. Even though we had done all of the thinning for the old man, we didn't do so well when we went to do the weeding. The man, who must have been around seventy years old at the time, had not become a grower like the gringos because he was incompetent. He loved the way my father played the guitar, but he did not allow messy work in his fields. He got into a foul mood when he found *cuatas* (doubles) we left behind or when we knocked down one too many plants.[2] When plants have reached that stage of maturity, they must not be chopped or knocked down. Once in a while we'd chop one down instead of removing it by hand, and that made him think we were destroying his mature plants. He walked back and forth between the rows until one day he fired us all. My father knew who was making a mess of things, but he would not allow only one of us to be fired and the rest remain behind working. If you fire one of us, he told him, you fire all of us. He fired everybody.

I was fifteen. Like any normal adolescent, I had my own tastes and idiosyncrasies. I loved cars. I knew how to drive, but since I had no driver's license, all I could do was daydream. Back in those times, I started reading *Hot Rod Magazine*. They published articles and pictures of California hot rods. Within a very short time it became an obsession with me not just to read but to devour that and other hot rod magazines. I still remember the names: besides *Hot Rod Magazine*, there were others, like *Car Kraft* and *Car and Driver Magazine*. I read them religiously. Every month I'd buy the latest issue. For years I kept a big cardboard box filled with these mags under my bed. I would lie there and read each one from cover to cover. It was from those magazines that I learned about engines, horsepower, and automotive engineering and design, not to mention the names of materials and of the technical terminology used in automotive manufacturing. I remember I would spend hours reading about how to take apart a V8 engine, how expert mechanics prepared a special engine called the Chrysler Hemi for racing, how to do stripping and striping, how the young people from California had developed a car culture unrivaled in the world. I knew the names of the hot rodders who won prizes and the names of the fastest racers along with the latest speeds they posted. I was fascinated by the popularity and glamour that surrounded that fantasy world centered around souped-up cars that captivated the young people of California.

It is possible that my salvation as a young migrant in those years lay in that obsession. In time those hot rod magazines became my refuge. When work became so unbearably hard that I was overcome with anger and repugnance, or if we were suffering from too much heat and dirt and hunger, I got lost in my car fantasies. As I hoed along, whacking the earth with my short-handled hoe, chewing dirt up and down the rows of sugar beets hour after hour and day after day, in my imagination I would be customizing my 1949 V8 Oldsmobile Coupe to my heart's content. I would pull out the old engine, have it rebuilt to my specs by experts, install it myself; then, I'd pull out the seats, sand down the body, exchange the old transmission for a brand new Dynaflow trans, add the requisite differential, put in new brakes, and then add the finishing touches. I contacted expert painters to have the Olds painted my favorite color: solid white with gold flames shooting out from the front all the way to the back. Of course, once I had finished working on it, I would drive it downtown for a spin so everybody could see me. But I never did finish working on it; there was always something missing. So I just let it alone for the time being. Until the next crisis hit. Then I would take it out again from where I had stored it in a specially built shop so nobody would look at it or touch it because they might leave a scratch here or there.

That mental habit of fantasizing my way out of hardship reached its peak somewhere in those vast sand-blown sugar-beet fields of central Washington. I couldn't say for sure where or how it first came to alleviate my efforts at beet thinning, but the tendency to indulge in fantasy most probably appeared as a defense mechanism, as some instinctive mental trick to help see me through the harsh surroundings we found ourselves in. The daily grind, as I've said, became unbearable: the constant heat and back pain, the sweat and sand and rash up every orifice, the unfailing certainty that the end of every row was always the beginning of another. Relief seemed nowhere in sight. To survive without coming apart required exceptional mental toughness, an almost superhuman resistance to pain. And yet somehow that first year in Moses Lake, we did not do so badly thanks to my parents' persistence, to the goodwill of the people from the barracks where we found other excellent sugar-beet thinners, and a little bit to our own blind faith and good luck.

When the beet thinning was over and we started just hoeing (not thinning) or weeding, we earned less because we usually got paid by the hour, $1.25 an hour at the time. They would let people work up to twelve hours a day if they wanted. We went in at 5:00 in the morning, we took half an hour for lunch, and we quit at 5:30 in the evening. The problem with that schedule was that there were times the growers did not believe we had worked that many hours. One of those growers, after we had finished weeding his fields close to Pasco, refused to pay us the honest number of hours we had worked for him. I know because I went to pick up the check. Every day I wrote down the names of everybody in our bunch, the time we started in the morning and the time we quit each day. When we finished hoeing his field, and I went to his house to let him know, he refused to pay. He gave me a check for half of what he owed us. When I got back to the car with the check everybody got pissed off at me but nobody did anything. We went home with half the money he owed us. So much honest, hard work for nothing (figure 5).

One Sunday my father decided we would go finish thinning what was left of a small field so we could be ready to start a new one the following Monday. There were no more than eight or nine acres left to hoe. Five of us went that morning: three adults, my brother and me. One of the adults was a friend from the barracks. He was one of those good-natured fellows who got along with everybody. He was related to us by marriage. My father had asked him to give us a hand because we wanted to finish early. We started very early in the morning, and we worked steadily for about two hours. By eight thirty or nine our friend suddenly stood up and flung his hoe out into the unfinished rows. "You all work like animals," he said and went off to sleep in the car. We kept working, all of us going full speed. It was getting unbearably hot; we were surrounded by desert sands turned

5

A Texas migrant worker, cousin of the author, thinning sugar beets
with a long hoe. After the mid-1960s growers in the Red River
Valley began planting a special variety of sugar-beet seeds that
did not require thinning by hand. The upright stance allowed
workers to thin several acres of sugar beets per day.
Courtesy of Mr. Alejandro "Elías" Guerrero.

luscious green thanks to the waters of the Grand Coulee Dam. But right
where we were hoeing the only things audible were the rhythmic thumping
and the scratching of our short hoes on the sand. Around three in the afternoon, without having stopped except for water so as not to lose any time,
my hoe fell out of my hand, and my knees buckled. I fell face down on the
sand, probably from sunstroke. My brother had already fallen behind. I had
wanted to keep up with the two adults. They picked me up, and we went
home without having finished. To this day I don't know if I let go of the hoe
on purpose because I couldn't keep up with the men or because I just ran
out of strength. The incident made an unforgettable impression on me.

At about that time another defining episode occurred in my life as a

6

Three migrant workers from Crystal City, Texas, weeding sugar beets
with a long hoe. All weeding (as opposed to thinning) was done with
a long hoe and was paid either by hourly rates or by the piece rate.
Courtesy of Mr. Alejandro "Elías" Guerrero.

sugar-beet worker. Our two families, ours and my father's nephew, whom
he called brother, had come together to work in the same sugar-beet field.
They called each other brother because my paternal grandmother had
raised them as if they were, and because they were about the same age. For
us back then he was always Uncle and his kids cousins. But even though he
was slightly younger than my father, he had a larger family. The oldest (a
girl) was my age, and then there followed ten or eleven more brothers and
sisters one right after the other. One day we all came together to thin the
same sugar-beet field. It turned out to be one genuine hoe-to-hoe battle but
without anybody openly acknowledging or admitting it. We started very
early in the morning like all good sugar-beet workers were wont to. My
uncle came first, then my father, then myself, and right next to me, my
oldest cousin, followed by the other younger kids according to age (figure 6).

The real competition was amongst my uncle and father, my cousin and
me. That was what I thought when we started. But it took less than an

hour for us to realize that our uncle and cousin were leaving the rest of us behind. When we stopped at the end of a row to get a drink, he just turned right around on the next row and kept on hoeing without stopping. My father had stayed right up with him, but eventually he too began to fall a bit behind. As for me, I can still hear my cousin's hoeing in my left ear as she followed right behind me. A woman, yes, but invincible. Try as I might to withstand the pain in my back there came a moment when I just had to stand up for a little bit and rest. She would do the same, but as soon as I stooped again to keep hoeing, she would bend down herself and start hoeing and kept up with me all the way. The experience had so enthused us that around noon, instead of stopping for lunch, we simply took a taco on our left hand and kept on hoeing with the right. We were hoeing while eating, or eating while hoeing.

That field was not a particularly large one; perhaps fifty or sixty acres total. It didn't take us but about two-and-a-half days to finish. But the lessons learned there have lasted a lifetime. I'd come out at the end of the day with my sore legs feeling all cramped up and my back burning with pain. My right hand felt numb. In order to stand up straight at the end of the day we would unstoop a little bit at a time; it was too painful to straighten up all of a sudden as one normally does. We had a drink at about the middle of the rows and again at the end if the rows were long. I couldn't leave my cousin behind at all, and frankly she had come very close to giving me the *coup de grâce*. Two or three times as we were both hoeing next to each other in the middle of some row late in the day, I thought I had made a mistake. Instead of my having taken up the third spot, perhaps she should have. As for my uncle it was just impossible to keep up with him. Not even my father could. And that was saying a lot. I had never seen anyone leave him behind no matter what the job was: not in picking spuds, harvesting onions, cutting spinach, or picking tomatoes. To see him ahead of everyone else, regardless of what kind of work we were doing, was for me like a law of nature. No one ever left him behind. But now his own nephew, the son of his oldest sister, had managed to do so those couple of days and in front of everybody. The beautiful thing about this story is that they are both (the nephew and his daughter) still alive. For me the experience was a hard-nosed catharsis.

Over the years I've tried to figure out how our uncle was able to withstand so much physical pain because what I saw him do in the fields was almost superhuman. The only thing I have managed to find out, though, is what I already knew: as soon as we hit the field, before starting to work, he would take two or three raw eggs out of one of his pockets. He tapped a small hole on top of each with a spoon and added some salt. He then downed them raw just as they were one right after the other. The other thing he did was cheat. But not against us so far as I know. I saw him in action when that grower came to pay us after we finished thinning his field. Back then the workers and the grower himself measured each field as soon as the hoeing was done. That was the way they came up with a figure to pay the workers. It was at that point that our uncle took out his own measuring tape. It was one hundred feet long and made of cloth. They would measure one hundred feet, the person walking in front drew a line on the sand with his foot, walked another hundred feet and drew another line. That was how they determined the length and width of the field. But Uncle already knew how to use some psychology to get more acres out of a field than there actually were. He asked me to accompany him and the grower to measure the field that time. He told me to tell him that he didn't know how to read or write. I knew it was true, but I didn't understand why he had asked me to tell him. When we started to measure the length of the field, the grower took off with one end of the measuring tape in his hand and we followed behind. After the first hundred feet I noticed that Uncle had bunched up some of the measuring tape in his hand. I stared at him and he just smiled. By the time we were halfway down the field he had a large lump of the measuring tape in his hand. Before we reached the other end of the field he had gradually released the bunched up ball of tape in his hand so it again measured one hundred feet. Using that trick he added another four or five acres to a field. As far as I know they never caught him at it. And I didn't know until many years later, while reading Alex Haley's *The Autobiography of Malcolm X*, why he had asked me to tell the grower before starting to measure the field that he didn't know how to read or write. He did it so as not to arouse any suspicions. He was both astute and an invincible worker with the short-handled hoe.

My sisters, who picked up scuttlebutt from other sources, insist to this day that Uncle outlasted the competition the way he did because he smoked marijuana. "That was why he didn't feel any pain," one of them will blurt out when we're together and the subject comes up. "How do you know?"

7

*Texas sugar-beet workers topping mature sugar-beet plants in the field.
The man standing holds a special machete in his right hand and a mature
sugar-beet tuber in his left. This was the last step of the sugar-beet
harvest. Beets were loaded on trucks and hauled to the local
processing plant after the tops had been removed by hand.
Courtesy of Mr. Oscar Pérez.*

another chimes in. "That's what *tía* (aunt) Constancia would say . . . and she practically raised him." "Maybe that's why they didn't speak to each other at Grandmother's funeral," a third sister adds. And thus it is that those memories, imprinted in each one of our brains and on our backs by the short-handled hoe so long ago, remain alive to this day and continue to bind us ever so intimately to that unsavory past (figure 7).

CHAPTER 11

Crystal City High

The year after our first trip to Washington, I entered high school in Crystal City. I had turned sixteen up there that summer. Because my birthdays are in June, we were usually somewhere up north every time I turned a year older. Some were memorable; others were not. The previous year, my mother had prepared a cake for us, and we celebrated my fifteenth birthday outside one of the barracks. But not this time around. When I turned sixteen, we were in the thick of a sugar-beet field hoeing away, and no one was in any mood to celebrate anything. By the time we arrived back at the barracks, everyone forgot about it. We just wanted to bathe, eat, and sleep. So, in a negative sort of way, it was memorable, too. As we got older and stronger, our endurance proved to be up to the task at hand, and we could compete with any adult when it came to hoeing sugar beets with the short hoe. That, in turn, meant more acreage hoed, and therefore, more money for the family. That was always important. It meant everybody had stayed healthy, and no one had suffered breakdowns. The crew had worked in sync throughout the critical period when we worked by the piece rate. Then, once the thinning and weeding portion of the beet harvest ended, we headed for Iowa. We spent another three months or so there picking, loading, and hauling tomatoes. By the time we got back to Texas, it was around the middle of October. We had been gone nearly seven months.

To me, getting back to Texas meant so many different things. The most important one, though, was that I'd be going back to school. That's understandable; I was young and full of life. But returning to school also signaled an uncomfortable reality: it meant another late start to the school year for me. One of the saddest things about our lifestyle was that the migrant cycle and the academic cycle ran at cross purposes to each other. I ended up missing between three and four months of school each year. In high school that could lead to disaster. For most migrants, it did. But in our family, we all depended on one another. I couldn't just quit. At the time, that was not an option for me or anybody else in the family.

I was not the only student who missed so much school. All the teachers knew and, with rare exceptions,[1] did not complain when we started the school year one or two months late. They were well aware of the kinds of lives we led. They knew why we missed so much school. And it was a topic they did not wish to discuss openly, if at all. As a matter of fact, talking about migrants was taboo in school back then if I remember correctly. And since all our teachers were gringos, with one or two exceptions, it seemed to me that it did not even occur to them that migrants who attended school might be at a disadvantage. They just stuck faithfully to their curriculum plans. At the beginning of the school year, they introduced the material for the semester, and from then on, either you learned it, or you got kicked out. It was that simple. We were the ones who had to adapt, not the other way around. That was the logical thing to do, of course. The gringos and the few Mexicans who went to school year-round were not going to be left without instruction because we were not there. But if some of us learned to adapt to an inflexible system which was the product of a racist society,[2] many other migrants who did not simply abandoned school. And they easily represented the majority of migrant students. It was not so easy after all to arrive fresh off the fields, walk into a classroom, and try to act as if you knew what was going on in chemistry, in mathematics, in physics, in English, in history, or in typing. The other students were already halfway into the text, and you were just arriving. How can I forget those first few days in school when we had just arrived from up north, fingertips still stained dull green from the months spent in the fields picking tomatoes? The stuff was hard to rub off. Like it or not, until it came off, everybody knew who we were and where we had been. It wasn't from any experiments in chemistry class, either. As I said, it was an unpleasant topic for discussion at school.

Now that all these years have gone by, I can't help turning over and over in my head that awkward, ungainly stage performance that was my academic experience in Crystal City during those years. I feel that I still need to understand not only how I did it—how we did it—but also where the willpower came from, if that's what it took to survive, the work ethic, the persistence necessary to return again and again (as the popular Mexican song "Volver, Volver" says, "Return, Return") to fight against those invisible phantoms that assailed us from everywhere. Because it did seem to me that learning proper English was like fighting against unearthly forces. The gringos laughed at us because of our accented speech. But once we left school, nobody spoke English to us. At home it was absolutely forbidden. Everybody spoke Spanish in the barrio; to speak English, or to try to speak it correctly, was cause for taunts and jeers. Then, once we were back in the school environment, even the teachers said that they knew we were Mexicans because of the way we spoke the language.[3] But what they did not do was to explain to us how and why we should correct the accented English. What they did do was to send us to the front of the class to recite Lincoln's Gettysburg Address or Hamlet's soliloquy, "To be or not to be." The result, of course, was to accentuate how correct their language usage was and how incorrect we were.

That same attitude prevailed in the other classes. In mathematics I remember sitting at my desk with mouth agape listening to the teacher, for the very first time in my life, explaining what was meant by an isosceles triangle. And it was no different from what happened to me with the slide rule in physics and with the Periodic Table in chemistry. My English, I was constantly reminded, was subpar. What to do? The only answer I came up with was to do just as I did when we were working in the fields: take whatever they dished out no matter what the price. And I began to find out, little by little, that that was something very few others could beat me at. It was evident I was not one of the most intelligent pupils. But I gradually began losing the fear of failure, especially after adjusting for the time lapse of the first few weeks I had already missed. I caught up with the slow ones and got even with the second-tier students. Perhaps if I had had a little more time, say seven or eight months instead of five, I might have raised my academic competence to the level of the top students everybody looked up to.

Crystal City High was not recognized as the kind of school with exceptionally high academic standards. It was a rural school in South Texas like so many others in small communities where the working-class population was in the majority. As often happened in such cases, the firmly entrenched bilingual and bicultural traditions of the local population created confusion for those of us who went to school and lived in the barrio. Acquiring conversational proficiency was next to impossible: whom could one practice with at home? Addressing Spanish-speaking individuals in English sounded hollow to us, so we addressed each other in Spanish. That led to a lack of proficiency which, in turn, led to emotional insecurity: whom to trust? At school our accented speech made us sound childish. That conundrum, in turn, fed our—or at least my—perennial defensive mentality. The effects of such cultural dichotomies on a people have been dissected and debated in academia for years and are well known.[4] For us, competing academically with the native-English speakers in their own tongue was like starting a race from behind the starting line. But we compensated for that disadvantage, or at least I did, by having more endurance than the regular students who attended school the full nine months. If I had to stay up all night memorizing passages from Shakespeare or writing an essay in English on Keats or Tennyson, I would do it. Then I'd go to school the next day. If in history class we were studying the War of 1812 or Woodrow Wilson's 14 Points, I would read the entire chapter in the book rather than wait for the teacher to assign it. That was because that strategy of overcoming those who were faster or better than I and beating them to the end was one I had already learned in the tomato fields. One of the loaders who worked with us was always faster than anybody else at counting the number of baskets that were stacked on top of the trailer. It had to be done rapidly, because when we were loading the tractor wouldn't stop. I couldn't beat him at it, so what I did was to count not basket-by-basket but stack-by-stack. That was how I learned to count the tomato baskets faster than him, and he never found out how I did it.

But not everything at school was a question of endurance or outlasting the others. I faced psychological traumas that left me beaten down. Perhaps I should say, to be honest, that these were traumas that were due more to the conditions of poverty we lived under than by anything else. And ignorance was part of it, too. In my case it meant that the lack of money to get professional treatment for a persistent acne problem meant that I had to suffer in silence the humiliation and stares from others that one suffers at a young age by looking different. Though I have always enjoyed excellent health, the pustules and zits that constantly marked my face and parts of my neck gave the impression that I was unhealthy and carried around loads of bacteria. The lack of hygiene at home made things worse. In the fields, we were always covered in dirt and sweat; at home we did not have the water or the facilities to bathe consistently. And in the barrio everyone had outdoor toilets, not bathrooms with running water inside the house. I did not see a dentist until I was fifteen or sixteen years old. By then I had started to get cavities.

At school these became psychological issues that sometimes led to panic attacks. I tried to avoid calling attention to myself. When the teacher sent me to the front of the room, I wanted to die. I answered or recited or spoke as rapidly as I could so they would send me back to my desk as soon as possible and not remain alone in front of the others. It happened to me more than once. On one occasion we were competing in a spelling bee at the front of the class. Each word missed meant one student less left standing. At the very end of the competition there were only three of us left, two gringas and myself. They were very good; they belonged to the top group. The teacher asked me to spell *rheumatism*. I spelled it out correctly, but I said the letters so rapidly that she asked me to spell the word again. Since we were the only ones left, everyone was staring at me. Classical them against us scenario. So that she would sit me down right away and end my torture I said, "R-h-e-u-m-i-t-i-s-m." I knew it was wrong, but it worked. "Sit down," she said. That was what I wanted. I had bested everyone in the class except those two girls. But the stares from the other students and my own timidity were too much for my enthusiasm and beet-worker's endurance to overcome. I was becoming my own worst enemy.

On another occasion, our biology teacher went around the entire class with the same question: "Where is the human brain found?" The answers given by the students ranged from the sarcastic "in the head" to the serious or esoteric "in our consciousness." And each time the teacher, an elderly man with a good heart and years of experience, would say the same thing to them: "Wrong!" and he would proceed to call out the name of the next student on his list. After about fifteen or so students (he was going by alphabetical order) he called my name and I said "In the cranial cavity." What came next was a somber lecture directed at all the lazy, good-for-nothing and ill-prepared students in our class who were within hearing range. Then he praised me to the heavens, and for a moment, I felt that I had lost my anonymity. The other students turned to look at me with disgust. But nothing changed even after his scolding. They just didn't read, or they read the material superficially, and so they could not retain it. In the fields, we took authority, especially from elders, seriously. But this was school . . . their school. After that I wouldn't answer.

I sought refuge in my history books, in English grammar, in hot rods. I started reading Hitler's *Mein Kampf* because I needed to find out if it was true that only 144,000 people in the world were going to be saved when the world came to an end, and if that were true, then no one else would go to Heaven because according to the Bible, that was the number of people who would be saved on Judgment Day. From there I found out about the concentration camps at Auschwitz, Belsen, and Dachau. Grammar had been my academic specialty since the eighth grade. That year our language teacher was the first Mexican American like ourselves that we had ever had for a classroom instructor. He was one of us—he had been a migrant worker—and he had just graduated from the university. He filled our heads with ideas taken from other Mexican thinkers who were totally unknown to me and about whom most of us had never even heard. "You can do it," he would say to us, "and I'm going to show you how." And he did. He started by teaching us, not how to speak correct Spanish like the gringos wanted to teach us, but rather by teaching us the structure of the language beginning with the conjugation of a single verb from the simple present tense to the pluperfect subjunctive. And we learned from him. He opened another window for us from which to view the world. "There are writers who write books in Spanish," he told us once. I remember clearly that I could not believe what he had just said. That was the first time that someone had told us at school that the language we used at home on a daily basis was good enough to be used for writing books. To me it was a revelation.

I started to work as an auto mechanic. I had learned from my books how to tune up engines, fix brakes, remove and replace transmissions, drive shafts, shock absorbers, and differentials. My school buddies would ask for my help with their old jalopies, with hot rods, or to adjust some old carburetor. I had gone to work at the shop of probably the best old-time mechanic in town and I learned more from him. That knowledge has helped me all my life. And I took refuge in sports. Even though we left in April for the harvest season, I played baseball with the school teams from January until we left. I became a pitcher and made varsity. But when I went to pick up my uniform on my last year of high school the coach gave everybody except me a uniform. I asked him in front of the others in a not-so-nice tone of voice, "And why aren't you letting me have a uniform this year? What's different from last year?" "Nuthin" was his answer. I went home cussing him under my breath. He was also our history teacher. On the next test he gave us after that incident, I got a 100. I even got the French expression *Laissez faire* right.[5] As he was returning the exams in class he stood for a second in front of me and said, before handing the test back, "Perfect!" I already knew it. Whether it was my beet-worker's tenacity or just plain audacity I don't know, but, as far as I was concerned I had returned in a just-so-subtle manner his own monosyllabic insult for not letting me have a baseball uniform that year.

If truth be told, the criteria or level of academic instruction, though it could not be said to have been very high, was good enough to create some distinctions between individual students. As far back as grammar school, even though I was one of those who arrived late every year, I had felt a profound desire—a psychological drive of some kind—to not be considered one of the dumb kids, to be counted amongst those students who could read books, to be part of those who answered questions and expressed themselves in English, to be one of those who came out ahead in science, in English, in math and history. It simply did not enter my head to be considered an inferior student. That distinction that I was after in my academic life was to me no different from not allowing anyone to beat me when it came to hoeing sugar beets when we were working in the fields. If someone did beat me, it was because they had some advantage over me, not because they were better. Out in the fields, my father or uncle could get the better of me; their level of tolerance for pain was higher than mine. But if I came up against someone my age, I had to come out ahead. The time one of my friends from Wisconsin got the better of me picking spuds, I started to cry. After that I wouldn't speak to him even though he wanted to play when we weren't working. But then I'd beat him at a game of marbles or outsmart him when we played a game of hide-and-seek. That was how I got even when somebody beat me. But I couldn't do that at school. What I would do then was, if they did better than I on some exam or written essay,

8

*Sugar beets being loaded onto trucks to be hauled to the
local sugar-beet processing plant. Loading the sugar beets
in the field became mechanized over time. Earlier
generations accomplished the task with a pitchfork.
Courtesy of Mr. Oscar Pérez.*

to convince myself that it was because they were gringos, or if they were migrants like me and did go up north, their parents did not let them work once school started. Then I figured they had gotten a higher grade because they went to school nine months, and I had only gone four or five. That was how I conferred upon myself the distinction of being one of those who were the very best in everything. If that way of thinking worked in the fields, it had to apply in school. At least that was what I made myself believe (figure 8).

|||||||||||||||||||||||||||||||||||||||||||||||||||||||||||||||||||||||||||||

CHAPTER 12

New Beginnings in Iowa

The trips to Washington had helped me mature. We were learning to survive in a setting which was quite unlike those of Wisconsin or Montana. If we wanted to work, we had to compete for sugar-beet fields against an assortment of traveling thinners. Even though we were surrounded by family, everyone had to go out and find his own field to work in, reach agreements with the growers, and guard against cheats. As the oldest male in our family, I was given the task of serving as my father's interpreter. That was how I learned the way things were done. I had started to work out deals from the very first time we went there: I negotiated piece rates, collected payments, helped to measure the fields we had just finished working on, and kept the books. I did that especially during the thinning season. When we finished with that, we'd go work by the hour doing mostly weeding. My father knew some contractors who lived right there in the barracks. Some were family, others acquaintances from our hometown in Texas. They usually worked things out themselves, and my skills as an interpreter were held in reserve for when they were needed. At about the time the beet-harvesting season was about to end, we used some of the money we had made to buy us a better car. We needed something that would get us all the way to Iowa. The Studebaker we had bought that first year ended up back in the junkyard where we had gotten it when we had arrived from Texas.

When July came around, we headed for Iowa to look for our oldest sister who had gotten married the year before. By then my father and mother had become grandparents. In their conversations, they talked of little else besides the granddaughter. At home those conversations turned emotional when they discussed driving over sixteen hundred miles to go find them. They just had to meet her. So we took off early one morning and crossed the states of Washington, Montana, parts of North and South Dakota, and drove through a small corner of Minnesota to get to Iowa. We were guiding ourselves by one of the letters my sister wrote to my mother every week. It had an address somewhere in Route 2. After almost four days on the road we came to the small town near where they lived. The place was called Kalona,[1] I believe.

By one of those fortunate coincidences that change a person's entire life, while looking for the infamous Route 2, we ended up in the outskirts of the small community of Muscatine, just a stone's throw from the Mississippi River. As we drove into town on a scenic stretch of some rural blacktop we saw a man coming toward us in a Ford tractor. My father pulled over on the opposite side of the road to wait for him. When he got close enough to us he said, "Go ask him where Route 2 is." He pronounced Route 2 in a Spanish accent, "rrautoo." As I was the official interpreter I knew he was referring to me. I got off and went across the road waving my arms for him to stop. "Hello," I said. He turned out to be a nice man. "Hello," he answered. He was a local grower, and I asked him for directions to Route 2. He told me more or less how to get there. "Thank you very much," I said. I was about to go back to the car when he asked me, "Do you have a place to pick?" "Dad," I yelled across the road in Spanish, "He wants to know if we have a place to pick." "Tell him no." "No, sir." "Would you like to pick for me?" "Dad, he wants to know if we want to pick for him." "Ask him how many acres of tomatoes he's got." "Sir, how much tomatoes do you have?" "A hundred acres." "Dad, he says he's got a hundred acres." That man turned out to be the grower for whom we would pick tomatoes the rest of our migrant lives. But we were not aware of that at the moment. We just wanted to know how to get to Route 2 and find the new granddaughter we were all so anxious to meet.

We found my sister's family that same afternoon. We went directly to the ranch where they were working thanks to her letter and the directions we had gotten from the man in the Ford tractor. We entered the labor camp, and my father parked near to where there were cars we thought looked familiar. Even though our limbs were stiff from the long drive, we were also emotional and anxious to see the new baby and my sister. But once we all settled down, we realized there were too many people at that labor camp. It was during the week and the time of day when people were supposed to be out in the fields working. Somehow things looked out of kilter to us. There were too many people at home. Perhaps because of what we had learned while working in Washington State, or because of some instinctive feeling on his part, my father decided not to stick around the place. It was best to avoid workplaces where there were too many idle folk hanging around. After spending a few hours there, we said our goodbyes and went looking for the man in the little Ford tractor. When we found him, he and my father spoke, and I translated. From that day on, I noticed that they had no trouble understanding each other. My father would say that we wanted to work, and he would answer that he needed pickers. At first he put us up in small one-room company shacks provided by the H. J. Heinz 57 Varieties Tomato Ketchup company. They were simple little rooms fifteen feet wide by twenty feet long. They were called "Migrant Housing" by company people. They aligned eight or ten of them, one right next to the other, on a grower's property. That was where the tomato pickers lived. But we only stayed there the first few nights. The grower offered us a more spacious place where we were to live the rest of that harvest season and every harvest season thereafter for as long as we picked for him. It was a pigsty.

I need to explain that because it sounds ugly. It is true that the small house he offered us was a pigsty, but it would not be true to say that it was uninhabitable or downright decrepit just because it was a pigsty. Proof of that was the fact that it was no more than a few hundred feet from the big house where the grower and his family lived. It looked like a warehouse, with a concrete floor and plenty of windows and a corrugated metal roof. It was used exclusively for sows with piglets. While they were in that delicate stage, the grower separated them from the older hogs because they required special care. And since those piglets were for export to foreign markets, they were treated as part of the family. That was what people said. The fact is that when we arrived they took the sows with their piglets out of there and we went to live in that very same abode.

My mother had the place washed down with bleach and plenty of water. Then she threw the windows wide open and let the place air itself out for a whole day. In the afternoon, we took our stuff in, and we each found our own place at a bunk bed and an empty burlap sack for a mattress. Year after year when we first arrived we repeated the same ritual. Many years later, while on vacation, I went to stand in front of what was left of the pigsty. The concrete slab was all there was. Before, when we were still migrants, that had been our home from the time we arrived in July until the cold weather chased us back to Texas. That usually occurred in the month of October when, after just one or two hard freezes, nothing was left for us to pick. It was then that the grower would return a new crop of sows to the pigsty we had just moved out of. After a few weeks they gave birth to new piglets. For him to leave the place unoccupied was to lose money.

We arrived in July, settled in, and soon after, we were ready to go to work. Tomatoes in Iowa are not harvested until late August, all of September, and into October. The weeding is done in July. Our arrival had been well timed without our knowing it. We started working the following Monday. Our family took up a whole *melga* (a section of fourteen rows) and worked on it several days. The grower gave us instructions in the morning and didn't show up again sometimes for days. A few melgas down from where we started working, there was another family doing the same thing, weeding tomatoes. We noticed they avoided talking to us. We could tell from afar that there were more women than men in their bunch. From what we had seen when we arrived, they did not live in the Heinz company shacks where we had spent the first night or two. It didn't take us long to find out that they lived in some old workers' quarters next to a warehouse where the grower kept his tractors and implements. We also found out they had been coming to work there for years. A few years later, one of the young men we had seen in the melgas that day would marry one of my sisters. But at the time we suspected nothing of course. We did notice they worked at a rather slow pace; they didn't push themselves like workers in Washington did. But they were steady. They started early each morning at exactly the same time with an uncanny consistency and kept up their forward progress the entire day, like yoked mules my father said. The whole family hoed and moved in unison, keeping the same steady pace all day long. They never failed to show up, either. Every day they arrived at the fields just as the sun was coming up, they ate their noon meals right there in the middle of a melga, and they left at the same time late every afternoon. In time we grew to admire their method of working slowly but with an unrelenting persistence few could match. They befriended no one. Later we would find out why, much later.

A few days after arriving, we went downtown on a Saturday afternoon. It was around the middle of July, and the watermelon crop was just beginning to ripen. The growers from all over the region were so glad to see that the Mexicans had arrived to pick their tomato crop that they decided to celebrate the occasion with a watermelon party. Generous and smiling faces called out from the loaded trailers and trucks as we walked by, offering us huge slices of sweet melon, and we would accept them with an innocent smile and a "Thank you very much." They just handed it out to people, all the watermelon we wanted to eat, free, just for the future tomato pickers. They were celebrating the earth's abundance; we reveled in all the attention they seemed eager to shower upon us. And it went without saying that we were all awaiting the arrival of the tomato-picking season. After all, our own family had managed to end up, after a 1,500 mile trip, at the small Mississippi River town of Muscatine, Iowa, where the world-renowned H. J. Heinz Tomato Company had one of its largest processing plants. Many of the town's people worked there. That was the reason they had received us with open arms and wagonloads of free watermelon. The plant processed hundreds of truckloads and wagonloads of freshly picked tomatoes and converted them into millions of bottles of ketchup that were shipped all over the country. These were tomatoes picked by the people from Texas who came there just for that. At least that is how it was at the beginning. It was a mutually beneficial arrangement. The people from the community benefitted economically, and the pickers from Texas had work for a few more months. With the free watermelon and the smiles that came with them, we were led to believe on that occasion that our presence there was appreciated. But, sad to say, the good will did not last long.[2]

The tomato crop began to ripen by August. The first picking took only a few days. People called that first round of picking "the warm-up," or the *pepena* in Spanish.[3] There wasn't much to pick. We stuck the basket under one arm and walked all over the rows looking for ripe tomatoes to collect. But that once-through helped us get an idea of the lay of the land. As we walked over the rows looking for ripe tomatoes, we could tell which melgas were the thickest and most promising. When the time came to start picking we already knew where to pick first.

We didn't have to wait long for the good picking to start. Already accustomed to going all out when we worked in the sugar beets, we hit the tomato fields working full speed. Pay was eleven cents a basket. One basket held roughly thirty-five to forty pounds of tomatoes, rarely more than that. We were always careful not to step on the plants. The idea was to keep them healthy so that the next time around there would be even more tomatoes. We grabbed the plant with both hands, picked up the vines and grabbed handfuls of ripe tomatoes from underneath. Two plants gave up one full basket. We walked each one out to the side of the melga and placed the basket snugly between the plants, sometimes one on top of another (arranged strategically of course so as to avoid crushing the tomatoes). There were fourteen rows to a melga. The males would pick in the middle rows so the women could pick in the rows closer to one or another of the sides where the full baskets didn't have to be carried far. Between each melga there was a narrow road for tractors. Those were the roads that the grower and his helpers used when they delivered the empty baskets to the pickers and loaded the full ones.

When the harvest was at its most abundant, the second and third pickings, the pickers had to leave double rows of full baskets by the side of the melgas. The men picked between 180 and 200 baskets a day, sometimes more sometimes less, depending on the weather, the availability of (empty) baskets, and if we had picked a good melga. The women picked somewhat fewer but rarely less than a hundred baskets per day. We formed a circle in the middle of an area we had already picked and that was where we ate when the best of the picking was going on. My mother brought us breakfast, lunch, and snacks to the field.

The fields were large enough so that each family got its own melga. The one hundred acres of tomatoes were dispersed over the rolling hills and valleys of the land belonging to our grower. That land lay less than a half a mile from the city limits of Muscatine. There were thickets of trees at the end of the rows, and those trees served as natural drapes. The people who drove up and down the highway right next to where we were picking had no idea we were there. And we would eventually get used to not getting distracted. But bit by bit things started to change. The war in Vietnam had entered a more serious phase. The need for fresh tomatoes brought more pickers to the ranch, and as a consequence, my father came up with the idea of proposing to the grower a change in field strategy. These changes began two or three years after we first arrived. For the time being, though, we had successfully managed our first year working for the man in the little Ford tractor we had accidently run into when we had first arrived in eastern Iowa looking for my sister. We stayed with him until we finished with the last pickings. As soon as the first frost hit the crops, he paid us the bonus money he had withheld during the picking season. That bonus money came from the penny per basket he had held back from each check during the whole of the picking season. It came just in time. Those were our savings to see us through the winter back in Texas.

CHAPTER 13

|||||||||||||||||||||||||||||||||||||||||||||||||||||||||||||||||||||||||||||||

Graduating from Crystal City

I graduated from Crystal City High School in May, 1963. I was nineteen. I was a year or more older than most of my school companions. But I was not the only one who was graduating at that age. The other two or three students in that group who were graduating at about the same age were also migrants. It was not such a rare occurrence at school. Those three or four months that we missed school each year accumulated over time, so we learned English later than the other students. By the time we graduated, we were a bit older, but if that meant we were at a disadvantage somehow, we were not aware of it just then.

What was important was something else: to continue the forward progress in our education just as if we had been regular students. To my surprise, people in the community celebrated our achievement. We were recognized for that achievement in a special mass at the local Catholic church. Families threw parties and celebrated all over town. At school we had a prom for juniors and seniors. At the local Mexican dance hall there was a dance, and speeches were given. The athletes, the outstanding students, those who won awards were recognized. I was not in any of the groups. But I did not feel excluded; on the contrary, I felt that I fit in just fine because I was amongst my own. I felt and shared in the euphoria just like everyone else. That surely amounted to a way of moving forward.

But there were distinctions. The same month we graduated, the same night I went to the prom with my friends, I stood in a corner practically all night until we were called on stage to go play. I was part of a band—two guitars, a base, drums, a singer—and we were introduced in front of the whole group that had gathered that night. We played three songs, gringo style, and that was it. The kids liked the music, but the dinosaurs would not let us continue playing. They thanked us, smiled, and that was the end of it. The rest of the night we had to listen to the perennial geriatric prom-night band: a group of senior citizens who played funeral music. The gringo students faked they were dancing; the Mexicans didn't even step onto the dance floor. We just stood at the margins and stared at all the gringos. They seemed to be in good spirits, enjoying themselves in their own environment. We, the raza,[1] just stood around politely. We were visibly uncomfortable, but there was no way out of the boredom. After my friends and I did our number I spent the rest of the night staring at a gringa whom I had liked for a long time, but I never even got close to her. There was an explanation for my timidity. The year before, the gringos had ganged up on a Mexican who had dared approach a gringa for a date. And there had been other cases where more daring Mexicans than I had tried to date a young lady of the wrong ethnic persuasion. The results were always the same: violence for violating the taboo. The idea was to remain separate but equal.

The truth of the matter was that, outside of school, gringos and Mexicans did not mix. We played baseball, some participated in the school band, a single token Mexican would be selected as cheerleader out of the five in the school squad. But once school let out, everybody went their separate ways. Racism was inescapable. The dilemma for the gringos was that when it came to choosing or electing someone based on voting, they lost. Since we held the numerical majority both in the community and at school, from time to time a Mexican would be selected for class president, to represent some club, or even as the most popular. But that was the extent of it. There were certain activities, like selecting Most Handsome, Most Beautiful, or Head Cheerleader, which were not put to a vote. The Administration saw to it that their candidate won.

And that same frame of mind that was the standard practice in school activities whereby they voted for their candidates and we voted for ours was a reflection of what was going on in the community. We were divided. Yet things had begun to change. During the 1963 municipal elections, five Mexicans were elected to office for the first time in the town's history.[2] The political and social agitation brought about by the Vietnam War, by the violence against the Freedom Riders, and by Dr. Martin Luther King

Jr.'s protest marches had raised people's consciousness across the country, and the Mexicans were no exception. Several political parties, like PASSO and MAPA,[3] were organized in town. Activists and organizers with different backgrounds came into the community and brought new methods and ideas for organizing the citizenry. Little by little they began to give some sort of ideological orientation to the voters: now they had a cause and a new leadership that received ample moral support from various quarters. When committees began to appear in support of these candidates, the organizers used propaganda tactics that I was already familiar with from when I worked in the movie theater. They hired kids from the barrios to distribute flyers in those parts of town where gringos never set foot. They announced the names of the candidates on loudspeakers mounted on top of pickups, and they played popular music to arouse the people's interest. Even I helped in the beginning.

The night when the winners of the municipal elections were announced, people gathered around the pharmacy in the gringo part of town to await the results. A designated poll watcher would write the numbers of votes next to the names of each candidate on mobile blackboards facing the street. When it became clear that the Mexicans had won, horns blared and people whooped and hollered. What happened that night is now a well known story: in Crystal City, a small rural town where gringos represented a quarter of the population and Mexicans three quarters, the Mexicans were ousting the gringos from the city council for the first time in the history of the town. Two distinct societies had been developing side by side for years. Even though they were in the minority, the gringos had always controlled the political process. They ruled, and the Mexicans obeyed. As they were in the minority, they resorted to all sorts of subterfuges in order to maintain their authority over the majority. They used intimidation in various guises. Contractors decided who worked and who didn't. The Texas Rangers parked their units in front of the Mexican polling places. They used segregation. The Mexican barrios were separated from the Anglo communities. And they undermined the Mexican vote by other means, such as the poll tax and arbitrary testing.[4]

At that time everybody knew in advance who was going to win the election: the same crowd of gringo old-timers. If someone dared to vote against them, they would lose their job, or some bank loan would suddenly come due. For years Mexicans were not allowed where gringos went. Movie theaters, barber shops, restaurants, and even the local cemeteries were segregated: one for the Mexicans and one for the gringos. It was another form of maintaining control, of imposing the will of the strong. So they voted, but Mexicans didn't. But once the new breed of agitators came to town to stir things up and arouse the Mexicans, the first thing they did was to organize fundraisers to pay the poll tax for those who wanted to vote. And one result of that campaign was the victory of five Mexicans in that year's municipal elections.

That was in April. I remember that the next day, when we arrived at school in the morning, the tension in the air was palpable. Here and there small groups of students were having heated discussions. One of the girls in my class, whom we all considered to be a sympathetic gringa, started to cry as she was walking up the stairs into the school building. From the top of the stairs she called out, in a voice loud enough so that everybody could hear, that she didn't want to go to school anymore, and that she was leaving town. She belonged to the enlightened bourgeoisie and she did not approve of a government under which she had to respect the authority of Mexicans. What she did not know—nor did we—was that the results of those elections were only the beginning of a new era.

I saw no reason for them to worry. We were obedient students. For us to progress meant just that: to faithfully do our homework and attend to whatever schoolwork our teachers assigned. If we were at a disadvantage because we were not native-English speakers, too bad. So what? If we were poor and had to sacrifice our schooling to go to work, too bad. So what? If we had neither voting rights nor political representation at the local, state, or national level, too bad. So what? What we were faced with was no less than the ugly truth of being the descendants of a defeated people: to survive we had to obey. It was only with the passing of time, little by little, that we managed to find wiggle room here and there. For instance, not all of us obeyed all of the rules all of the time. When we studied hard day and night to do well on the exams, we were being disobedient. Why? Because instead of attending school every day like everybody else, we went to work in the fields, and we still managed to keep up with the regular students. When we returned in November from up north, and the first day the teacher would tell us to go home and instead we stayed put, we were being disobedient. Why?

Because they thought we were too dumb, that we would never catch up with the rest, and they didn't want to bother with us. And when the school counselor helped the gringos get ready for college and ignored us completely even though we still managed to matriculate successfully,[5] we were being disobedient. Why? Because they thought that providing college orientation for us was a waste of time for them and for us because we were going to fail anyway. But not only did we not fail, things actually turned out the other way around. Nevertheless, there was a price to be paid at the time for not heeding the master's voice.

And so it was that we began pecking at the shell. Not only were we going to graduate from school, but we were going to make our own decisions. Should we volunteer for Vietnam? Should we continue in school, learn a profession, leave the fields? Should we follow our natural instincts, find a woman, and get married? Should we continue along the same path as our ancestors and remain in the migrant stream? When they passed out the diplomas the night we graduated, I ranked thirteenth in a class of sixty-three students.[6] Other migrants who, like myself, were the offspring of families who followed the crops up north, were ranked even higher.

Our decision was now officially confirmed. That diploma was a formal declaration of the choice we had made: it was our way of saying that we knew how to reconcile those two inimical and contradictory worlds that had already caused us to jump through so many hoops in order to survive the first twelve years of school. But it was not to be. That youthful naiveté was about to be exposed for the moral contradiction it was.

The fact of the matter was that the Vietnam War feasted on the young, and we knew it. For us, as migrants, it had become necessary to learn how to go back and forth from one way of life to the other without losing our souls: work in the fields; survive in school. Those were our enemies; that was the opposition: racism and hunger. But now, precisely because we had gone to school and were about to graduate, Uncle Sam wanted us to go fight a foreign enemy we knew nothing about. So, to find our way out of the dilemma, we turned to what we knew best. That was why on graduation night we had no plans to go on vacation at the beach or to summer camp like the other kids who were well off. Instead what we did the night of our graduation, that small group of migrants who had just received our diplomas, was to go home and pack our bags so we would be ready to leave for

Moses Lake, Washington, the next morning to go work in the sugar-beet fields.

It had not even occurred to us that we could go to the beach or summer camp on vacation. Summer meant going to work, not going on vacation. Vacation from what? Frankly, we thought it ridiculous to say that going to school was work, that one got tired from it, that it was necessary to go on vacation to recuperate. That thought was unnameable for us then. Or at least it was for me. The one thing I knew for sure was that my non-migrant classmates were not going to hoe sugar beets, either because they lacked the physical endurance or because they had no need to. We, on the other hand, did possess the requisite physical capacity and knowledge of the real world. Did that mean, then, that they would be less desirable material for a fighting force than us? Would they be spared from the military draft as well whereas we would not? I had thought all along that learning a more sophisticated English, developing my mind through reading and studying, would lead me out of poverty and away from the fields. Those had been my goals as I matured and learned to survive in the non-migrant universe. However, the members of the local Draft Board, which was composed of local ranchers and businessmen and had not a single migrant worker on it, had other plans. Our migrant lives were nothing if not a genuine paradox.

We left in our uncle's 1957 Ford pickup with thirteen passengers and three drivers. We were quite familiar with that road by now, but it still took three days and nights to get there driving nonstop. Way before we reached Albuquerque, New Mexico the guys and I started to laugh. The year before, at a Dairy Queen not far from the edge of town, we had spent a couple of days trying to fix our aunt's 1954 Dodge. She had been part of our caravan. I think I was driving her car at the time. It was a V8, but it was nonetheless unable to make it over a steep hill leading into town. We coasted and stopped at the first spacious lot we saw. It was the Dairy Queen. The rest of the caravan kept on going. They didn't find out until later that we were stranded. My cousin and I, not seeing any other alternative, decided right then and there to take the engine apart and repair it. We got our tools out and started working. First we removed the exhaust manifolds; then we removed both heads, the valves, and I don't remember what else. The next day, as the two grease monkeys worked away under the car, and my aunt and the girls fought off the boredom, one of those famous Albuquerque dust storms that lasts for hours chased us out from under the car. We had to give up and call on some professional mechanics to come help. They came out, towed the car to their enclosed garage, and the next day, we were on our way to Moses Lake, Washington.

That incident had occurred the previous year, in 1962. But this time there was no caravan; only us, the recent high school graduates with our truckload of passengers in the back. The three of us—my cousin, another buddy, and I—had driven as far as Utah when it was my turn again to take the wheel. The passengers had not asked for a stopover, so we just exchanged drivers, and kept going. Those thirteen people traveling with us had waited until school was over to leave town. They had worked things out with my uncle; they had paid him in advance to save themselves a place in the pickup truck. My uncle had always been a generous man and he helped us students out as well. We would help his son with the driving in exchange for the ride to Washington. Adolescents though we were, the families in the back trusted us and knew we were responsible enough to get them safely all the way to Moses Lake. After all, two of us were recent high school graduates, and we knew how to act responsibly. They trusted us to reach our destination safely. Well, we almost didn't. Our inexperience and overconfidence brought us within a hair's breadth of disaster.

There are places in Utah where there is nothing to see except the highway and empty spaces. That's in the daytime. At night, and especially in the wee hours, there's nothing but the darkness and the stars above. Soon enough, as I've said, it was my turn to take the wheel. No sooner had we exchanged drivers than my copilots were snoring in my ear. Their breathing and intermittent snoring were the only audible sounds besides the streaming air through the window and the steady whine of the engine. As is so common in late-night situations like that, after a while I began to struggle to keep my eyes opened. I adjusted my posture a bit and kept on going. I wasn't about to stop. Where? And for what? Everybody was asleep. So I just kept on going. But it didn't take too long to realize that I had made a stupid decision. Before I knew it, I had dozed off for I don't know how long with my eyes wide open. I was barreling down the road in the dead of night with a full cargo of people, and I was asleep! Just before disaster struck, though, I woke up. And it was literally just in the nick of time. We had not been destined to perish that night. I distinctly remember that when I came to, still half-dazed, my eyes were peering straight at the speedometer needle on the dashboard: it was pointing to seven zero. Going seventy miles-per-hour down the middle of the highway asleep at the wheel! What woke me up just then I don't remember. I do recall seeing two bright lights a short distance in front of us and closing in fast. As we crossed paths at that hour of the night just a few inches from each other going in opposite directions I saw the eighteen wheeler, horns blaring as it zoomed by us. My companions in the truck had slept through the whole thing. I don't remember if I ever told them about it later. I did tell my father, but only many years later, in his old age. He just stared at me and shook his head in disbelief. As far as I know the passengers never suspected anything. At least no one mentioned anything to me. What people did talk about, for years after it happened, was that other horrible accident: a group of migrants from our hometown had all gotten killed along that same stretch of highway not long after. It was also late at night, and the driver had fallen asleep. They had not been so lucky.

Given my new status as a recent high-school graduate, I found a girl-friend not long after we arrived at the barracks. I was already familiar with the migrant way of doing things, but now I had moved up another notch: I started dating girls who were not migrants. V. and I met at a dance and started dating soon after I arrived. Her parents liked me; they allowed us to see each other at their home. When we went dancing, my vanity got the best of me. Yes, I was a sugar-beet worker, but at the labor camp and even in town, it was already well know that I would be going to college. And so it was true I was coming out of my egg shell. With all the confidence in the world, I would tell V. that as soon as the sugar-beet harvest was over and we finished picking tomatoes in Iowa, I was going to study psychology in college. She was my age, but she had graduated from high school the year before, and she did not plan on going beyond that point. Back then higher education was not the goal, and especially for women—finishing high school and getting married or finding a job was considered having a successful career. Frankly, that was also true for males if you were a migrant. That was why, as she reminded me when we were together, and I believed her, I was the exception. As far as sugar-beet workers like me were concerned, it was true. She gave herself to me.

Yet, even though the physical attraction between us was strong, I was already beginning to believe I was different from other migrants and sugar-beet workers, that neither poverty nor V. nor anything or anyone would keep me from going to college. My father's family, several of whom followed us wherever we went, asked me foolish questions. "What good is it to work so hard?" an aunt asked me one afternoon as I arrived from working in the fields. "I'm saving up to go to college," I answered. She laughed out loud at my answer and said something stupid about how I was just wasting my time by going to school. I didn't say anything back. I knew I had been listening to an ignoramus. By then I already knew I was different.

It turned out to be a good year. By that time, there were three of us in the family who were tops at thinning sugar beets with the short hoe. Between my father, my brother, my sisters, my cousin, and me, we covered lots of territory. We'd start a fifty- or sixty-acre field, and three days later, we were putting on the finishing touches. We thinned an eighty-acre field in one week. The Columbia Basin's sandy soil was ideal for thinning extra fast. Unfortunately toward the end of that harvest season we encountered a new phenomenon that was an unexpected by-product of those good sugar-beet harvests. The migrant stream itself was attracting workers from non-traditional backgrounds. And they brought their unusual ways with them. People from Monterrey, Mexico, started to arrive at fields while we were working and offered to do the same job for less.[7] On more than one occasion, we lost out on fields where we were already working to cheaper workers from Monterrey.

As happened every one of the years we went to Washington, once we were done with the thinning and weeding of the sugar beets in July, we'd head for Iowa. That year I met V., we had gone out alone to several places with her parents' permission. The night before we left for Iowa, we spent hours alone at a local park. We decided to take along some drinks and sandwiches to celebrate picnic style. We confessed our true love to each other almost to tears. We swore we would never love another, we argued, and she cried. Since she was willing to do anything for me, why wasn't I? Why was I leaving? Why not stay, get a job in town, get married? But I wasn't listening. I was a different person now. There was no future for me in some plain job. I wasn't interested in staying around to be like everyone else, beholden to whomever was paying me. I wanted to be educated like our Spanish teacher was, like the politicians who had won elections in Crystal

City, like the grower's son in Iowa who attended university. By then I was ambitious and knew deep inside what I wanted to be. But I still needed to learn how to read the world around me to advance further. Toward what? Toward the kinds of people who were not to be found in the barracks. The next day we left for Iowa. We rode in a long caravan made up of four vehicles with brothers, sisters, aunts, uncles, and cousins, and amongst all of those migrants, one newly minted high-school graduate.

CHAPTER 14

Hauling Tomatoes to the Heinz Plant

My father was in the habit of playing his guitar in the afternoons after we got home from work. Following our usual routine, we would wash, eat, and then go outside to rest and relax our tired bodies. And also as usual, sitting underneath an enormous oak tree outside the pigsty where we lived, he would play and sing softly to himself. The songs he played were the same ones he and his cousins played and sang back home: "Dos Arbolitos" ("Two Trees in Love"), "La Calandria" ("The Lark"), La Llorona ("Hollering Woman"), and other, mostly sad, songs we had all heard many times before.[1] We sat a short distance away and listened to him, weary from the day's work, stretching out on the fresh green grass or resting against another nearby tree. We could hear his voice as it floated lazily over the guitar notes even from afar because all was quiet at the ranch. It was both comforting and soothing. I think he knew it, and perhaps that was why to the end of his days that instrument accompanied him wherever he went.

It was during one such afternoon that he came up with an idea he wanted to share with the grower: if he let us take charge of loading the tomatoes in the field and hauling them to the processing plant in town, he, my father, would purchase a couple of old trucks to do the job. He shared his idea with the small group of us relaxing there that afternoon. I immediately perked up when I heard him mention our hauling tomatoes. It meant getting out of picking all day long; it meant, even more incredibly, that we would be driving a tractor and loading tomatoes in the field like we had seen the gringos doing. We all liked the idea, and together we worked out a plan. My parents talked it over, and a few days later when the opportunity presented itself I mentioned my father's plan to the grower. Not only did he like it, he said, but he would even make things easier for us. Why go out and buy old trucks? he asked. You can use three of my trailers and the two John Deere tractors to do the hauling. Two of those trailers carried up to 237 baskets each, he said, and the third as many as 249. I think that's enough to keep up with the pickers. He didn't tell us twice. While I translated, he and my father worked things out. He would pay us eight dollars per ton for loading, hauling, and unloading the tomatoes at the processing plant. We would be in charge of the whole operation, including distributing the empty baskets to the pickers as well as keeping count in the field. At the end of the week, we were to tally the numbers and report back to him. All he had to do was hand out the checks to each head of family every Saturday morning. He did . . . religiously.

Once we took over the loading and hauling ourselves, we had entered another stage of the migrant experience. There would be no more of the day in, day out, back-breaking picking for us. On the other hand, we had agreed to take on a much bigger responsibility for a successful harvest. We started with a crew of four: my father, a brother-in-law, myself, and one of my sisters, who drove the tractor on the field. It didn't take us long to earn the grower's trust. He let us use his medium-size automatic Ford tractor to pull the wagons in and out of the melgas to load the tomato baskets. As soon as we spotted a long trail of full baskets being left by a family next to their melga, we headed over and started loading. We stacked the baskets, back to front, one on top of the other, pyramid style until we had a full load. That meant either 237 or 249 baskets per wagon. From that point on, it was a slow, leisurely drive through the various roads between the melgas to the far end of the field where we parked the load. There we would hook up another empty trailer that the haulers had left for us with the bundles of empty baskets tied to the support wall at the back. We turned right around, drove onto the field, and started to distribute the empties to the pickers. While the pickers were busy picking away, and we were loading their baskets nonstop, the haulers were hurrying back and forth to the H. J. Heinz plant downtown delivering their cargo. For that line of work the grower let us use two old John Deere tractors, an A and a G. They were old 1940s models, the one-cylinder kind that had a single enormous piston that made the unmistakable rat-tat-tat sound as they went chugging down the road pulling another four tons of tomatoes to the factory. When it rained and we got stuck in the mud, the grower let us borrow his new AC (Allis Chalmers) tractor. That monster was so powerful that it dragged everything out from wherever it got stuck no matter how deep the mud. So when I say that we earned the grower's trust, I mean not just because of the good job we were doing for him, but also because he had entrusted such expensive machinery to our care. Each of those pieces of equipment was worth many thousands of dollars. We drove them all over the place. It was a routine that lasted from early July until the middle of October. Work was abundant during the tomato harvest season. To my knowledge, there were never any idle bodies at that labor camp.

Each of the haulers made five or six trips to the processing plant each day, depending upon how heavy the picking had been and upon the availability of empty baskets. When I was hauling, I'd be the first to take off. By six in the morning, I was already on my way. The night before, I had filled the tractor up with fuel before going to bed. I had to be on my way early in the morning to be back in time with a load of empty baskets to distribute to the pickers in the field. I ate a little something, fired up one of the John Deeres, hooked up the loaded trailer the crew had left ready the previous evening, and took off. All of the fields were close to the edge of town. It took just under an hour to get from there to the plant.

Over time the method of unloading the tomatoes at the factory changed. At first everyone got in line, tractors and trucks loaded with baskets full of tomatoes, waiting for our turn with the swings where we placed the baskets one at a time. The swings were metal plates attached to hanging rods that were pulled via an overhead sprocket conveyor that circled around the plant. We placed the baskets one by one on the plates, and the workers inside dumped the tomatoes into large vats filled with water. There they stacked the empty baskets in bundles, and somebody else wheeled them to the end of the line. It was a tedious process, and we all had to wait our turn. As we moved over to the end of the line, we were given back the rolls of baskets which we had delivered full of tomatoes via the swings at the beginning of the line. We secured them with ropes to the back of the wagon and returned to the fields. If no other loads were available for hauling, we'd join the loading crew to redistribute the empties we had just brought back from the plant.

That was basically how the process worked, and our part did not vary much over the years. But for us young boys, whenever we managed to get out in the field to help pass out the empty baskets, things got a little more exciting. It was a real treat for us just to be riding in the back of the empty wagon checking on the folks picking in the field. It was our chance to do some scouting for new girls. And we did take advantage of the opportunity every chance we had, just as if it were a brand new adventure even though we did the same thing every day. When the tomato harvest season was at its peak, the grower hired outside help to come and help the regular pickers. That was the best time to check on the new arrivals. The view from the top of the wagon could not have been more advantageous: looking down at the pickers as we passed by their melgas, we'd look for a signal or small gesture from one of the girls. It was how we found out whom to invite to the movies the following Saturday. I was able to arrange several dates that way. I still remember that when I saw those same girls dressed up and transformed from tomato pickers into sophisticated-looking young ladies, I could hardly believe my eyes. To describe just such an experience, the elders used an expression back then: "Appearances can be deceiving." They were indeed.

But all was not fun and youthful adventure at the ranch. From time to time we also had to deal with cheaters or greedy and untrustworthy pickers. It seemed as if there was always someone trying to take advantage of the situation. One trick that was common was to not fill the tomato baskets to the top, but rather to only make it appear as if they were full to fool the loading crew. Once we loaded a basket onto the wagon it was credited to that particular family. The tractor kept up a slow but steady pace, so a loader could not stop to inspect each basket before placing it on top of the wagon. The person driving the tractor did that. One particular man we all knew, head of a family, would instruct his younger kids to gather only large tomatoes in a basket. The older pickers who were in front would leave their baskets almost but not quite full, then move on to another one and another one doing the same thing. The younger kids, carrying their baskets with the large tomatoes, came up behind them and placed a single large tomato on top of the incomplete baskets to make it seem as if they were full so we would count them as such. My father used to throw fits when he came upon those baskets because for us, it meant losing precious time. We had to stop the tractor and empty some of the incomplete baskets into the half full ones before counting them and stacking them alongside the others. We were continually undoing the silly little trick the man had his younger kids perform just to see if he could get away with it. But it didn't do him any good. We saw to it that he came up with less rather than more baskets. We were the ones who had to take the time to rearrange his numbers, though. I believe they picked for us only one harvest season. It was because of the half-full baskets and also because of another incident.

One typically quiet and peaceful night that same summer, around two in the morning, loud noises woke us up. At the time, all the guys slept in the same men's shack. There was a sudden knock on the door. It was my father coming to wake up my uncle so he could go help him with two men who were squabbling over empty baskets. They were fighting on top of one of the empty trailers parked under the oak tree. The men were both regular pickers from our ranch, and each wanted to beat the other to the empty baskets tied to the back of the wagon. But distributing those empty baskets to the pickers was our job. From the beginning it had been our responsibility to see to it that each family got a few baskets early in the morning to start picking. As the haulers came back from the plant with more empties, we'd see to it that everybody got enough to keep them busy. We had followed the same routine for years without problems, and until that night, no one had complained or protested. We tried to be fair, to give everybody baskets as soon as we got them back from the haulers. But during the peak picking season we couldn't always keep up with the demand; we'd run short of empties and pickers would have to sit around and wait from time to time. That was the reason the two men were fighting at that ungodly hour of the night. They both wanted to get a head start on the other by taking not some but all of the empty baskets.

My uncle pulled his pants on as fast as he could and ran after my father. Neither had on a shirt or socks. We came up right behind them. On top of the trailer, their arms wrapped around a single bundle of baskets ready to drop them onto the beds of their pickups, were the two men hurling insults at each other. My uncle jumped on top of the wagon. He pushed both of them aside. I still remember his words. "You don't fuck around with me."

He forced both men to leave the baskets where they were and get off the trailer. One of them was a relative of ours. After that incident, the families involved never spoke to each other again. A few days later, as the picking was beginning to slow down somewhat, one of the two men involved in the incident decided to leave the ranch with his family. But there was one problem: if he left before all of the picking was over, he'd lose his bonus money. He invented a ruse: he asked someone in his family from Texas to send him a telegram at the ranch saying that a sister was gravely ill and wanted to see him. It was a bald lie, and everybody at the camp knew it. I explained to the grower what had happened and why he wanted to leave. "Let him go," he said. The incident had caused the family to lose all of their bonus money.

There was no shortage of drama at that place. On another occasion we were all asleep when the wailing cries of a woman woke us up in the middle of the night. The screams were coming from one of the shacks at the back of the yard next to the creek. We jumped out of bed and ran outside to see what was happening. All we could make out in the dim light were the dark silhouettes of a man and a woman running through the weeds toward the highway. She didn't have all her clothes on. It was one of the couples who had just arrived to help with the picking. I never knew how they'd gotten there. They weren't friendly with anyone. In the afternoons when they got back from picking, they'd shut themselves up in their shack and not come out until early the next morning. We never saw them on weekends. But they weren't there long. My sisters said he would beat her up and drag her across the floor of the hut by the hair. How they found that out I never knew. It didn't seem like anybody missed them, though. We did not know they had left until someone pointed out that their car—not them—was missing.

I experienced my own bit of drama when a load of tomatoes I was pulling to the plant came unhooked from the tractor. I was chugging along as fast as the old John Deere could go on Mulberry Street, which ran right through the middle of one of the oldest and most affluent sections of town. The whole length of the street was paved with weathered red brick. Tractors and trailers swayed going over it because it was uneven in some spots. From afar one could see the undulations splayed here and there across parts of the street. But as time went by we got used to the rocking motion of the tractor as we pulled our loads along. We put the tractor in fifth gear and didn't do more than twenty miles per hour. Since on that occasion it was early in the morning, there was no traffic coming or going. So I was driving down the middle of the road on the big John Deere G pulling the usual four tons of tomatoes. I preferred driving standing up because the seats on those tractors were made of hard metal. They were hot in the summer and cold in the winter. Even though I could feel the cold in my face, I was driving with the casual confidence and distracted demeanor of a seventeen- or eighteen-year-old. As the tractor swayed over one of the undulations on the road, I heard a loud clunk against the bricks. At the same time, I felt a slight forward jerk as the loaded trailer came unhooked from the tractor. Looking back to see what the commotion was about, I saw that the trailer tongue was dragging along the surface of the road and sparks were shooting up from the bricks. A single thought flashed through my mind at that instant: block the trailer to keep it from ramming into one of those elegant homes and making a gigantic mess. I had no time to sit down, and that was what saved my life. I pulled the clutch lever all the way back. I remember my thoughts: if I can get the front part of the trailer to crash against the John Deere's tires it'll bounce back. That way I can slow the whole thing down and keep it from leaving the road.

The laws of physics don't work that way. The tractor tires lifted the load off the road and pulled the whole thing up against the seat *over which I was standing*! The gyrating force of the tires and the tractor's own power were more than enough to lift the loaded trailer that I had been pulling just a short moment ago. As the load headed up and over the rear tires of the tractor toward me, I heard a quick, loud "wonk!" followed by a thud in rapid succession just underneath where I was standing. The trailer bounced back, struck the tires again, and the whole load went crashing down splashing tons of ripe tomatoes all over the bricks.

During the entire episode, which seemed at the time as if it were happening in slow motion, I had been driving standing over the main axle. On either side of the axle there was a special metal plate for the driver to stand on so he could drive comfortably while standing up. When the load fell over I braked quickly, but I pressed the brake pedal on one side harder than on the other, and the pedal's sudden kick bent my foot back awkwardly. That was it. I brought the tractor to a complete stop ten or fifteen yards from the trailer and got off. For a few minutes I didn't know what to do, whether to start picking up the overturned baskets and put the tomatoes back, or just leave everything there and go back to look for my father and the grower. I sat there quietly for a moment. By some miracle, someone living in one of these elegant houses saw what happened and thought of calling the ranch. A few minutes later my father and the grower arrived in his pickup. Behind them in a car were the rest of the crew. As soon as I saw them I started to tremble uncontrollably.

I had never seen our grower so nervous. He looked at me from head to toe and kept asking me the same question, "Are you all right, Roy?" "Are you all right?" Other cars were beginning to pull over. Everybody came to where I was, standing next to the tractor and unable to move. When I finally got over the fright from the accident, I found out something I have been eternally gratefully for. The John Deere's solid steel seat, and the large steering wheel made of the same unbending material, had kept the fully-loaded trailer from crushing me to death that morning. What had happened was that, driving standing up over the axle, I was positioned so that the bottom of the steering wheel was between my legs. The seat itself, beneath and slightly behind me, was not fixed, but rather it had some upward and downward motion. It bounced gently up and down when one was seated, and it was attached to an iron beam, thick as a two-by-four, that went under the steering wheel. That beam angled down under the steering wheel and extended all the way to mid-frame, where a special bracket allowed it some play. The trailer, hurled forward by the massive rear wheels of the John Deere, struck the seat from below, pushed it against the steering wheel where the beam bent it slightly at the point of impact. But it didn't give. Blocked at the point of impact, the whole trailer swayed and became unbalanced.

Nothing had happened to me, save for a slight sprain where my right foot was bent backward by the brake pedal. I did not realize the seriousness of the accident I had been involved in until much later. The G weighed five tons, the loaded trailer weighed four, and I, at the time, about 155 pounds. Trapped as I was between the two behemoths as they crashed into each other, nothing, by some miracle, had happened to me. Had I been caught between the two I would have been crushed like a ripe tomato. Death had spared me a second time. Or was it a third? I don't remember anymore. What I do remember is that they sent me home after the accident, and my mother fed me some sugar cubes to cure me of fright. She also said a prayer of thanks to the Virgin, but not in front of me. That same afternoon, I went back to the fields and started working again as if nothing had happened.

CHAPTER 15

Experiments in the Iowa Fields

Not everything that happened to us in those northern climes back then revolved around hard work or took place in the fields. Even though we lived on a farm, from time to time the outside world and its attendant cares found their way into our settled migrant ways. One morning I was leaving the ranch early as usual. I had hooked up one of the loaded trailers and was headed to the processing plant in town. It was the same old trek as always; I knew it by heart and could manage it with my eyes closed. It was already October, and the weather had already started turning cold. My mother had wrapped a towel around my head to keep me warm. I pulled out of the ranch with the load and a little ways down I turned left to take the road that passed in front of the cemetery. Not a sound could be heard. The cold ground was damp. I turned right on Mulberry Street, which was paved with the infamous red bricks, slowed the John Deere to shift gears and headed toward the Heinz plant. As usual, I drove standing over the tractor's gear box. I picked up speed and shifted into high gear, doing not more than twenty miles an hour, driving along at my usual pace with the load of tomatoes. Up the road I noticed an odd-looking little car coming toward me at a slower than usual rate of speed. It was not just the unusual model and slow speed that attracted my attention. Someone inside was waving at me, not in the usual nonchalant way, but rather enthusiastically. It was a young, very nice looking gringa. I didn't know who she was. I stared at her and waved back. She turned the car around, pulled up ahead, and came to a stop on the side of the road a little ways ahead of me. She signaled for me to stop. I had taken the towel off my head without even thinking about it. By then I had become quite skilled at driving the tractor with or without a load. I came right up behind her car and stopped.

Her name was L., and she was the daughter of a local physician. They lived on one of the streets we drove through day in and day out on our way to and from the factory. When we had first arrived in Iowa in 1958, I had accompanied my mother to see a doctor downtown. By sheer coincidence the doctor who had treated my mother was her father. Over the years, whenever we needed medical attention, he was the one we went to because of his down-to-earth character and friendly personality. That morning she had recognized me on top of the tractor. She helped her father at the office. She already knew who I was, where I worked, and where we lived. I tried to keep my nerves in check at first by acting serious, but she soon disarmed me with her kindness and sweet, innocent smile. She told me she would visit me at the ranch, that she knew the grower's family, and that she would ask him for permission to come looking for me so we could talk. She was a student at the University of Iowa, and she had been headed that way when we ran into each other that morning. She said so many things to me. From that day on, I was not the same person. She went to the ranch the next weekend. We spread a blanket on the grass under the trees and spent the whole afternoon there. I had chosen the spot. From there neither the pigsty where we lived nor the shacks where we slept were visible.

She began arriving at the ranch every weekend when we were not in the fields. She would tell me she was studying Spanish at the University, that she wanted to be a nurse, and she invited me to visit the campus. I just stared at her in disbelief. I would tell her that when I graduated I planned to go to college, that I wanted to study psychology, and that they called me Roy, but that it was not my name except that I used it because gringos couldn't pronounce mine. I kept smiling so much that I forgot she was a gringa, and I was a Mexican. Until one day she invited me to the local drive-in.

We met there one night. The first thing she did was to get away from a friend who was with her, and we went to her car. It was not the same old odd-looking jalopy she was driving that morning when we first met. I never asked her whose car it was, but this one was elegant and spacious. She had probably borrowed it from her parents. I opened the door for her and she got into the driver's side. I went around the other side. We sat and stared at each other. She looked serene yet lively while I took her in with my eyes. Up until then, when we met at the ranch, all we did was talk and exchange innocent looks. There was no doubt that the attraction was mutual and that it was strong. We were getting comfortable, trying to ignore the movie and calm our nerves, when suddenly she sat up and said, "That's my boyfriend. He's looking for me." But she said it so calmly that at first I wasn't sure how to react. Was she asking me to get off, to leave, to hide? I didn't know what to do. Finally she said, "I better go."

The year I returned to Texas in the middle of September to go to college, I asked her to join me. She told me she would go. We had been talking about it those times we met under the trees at the ranch. When we couldn't talk, we'd write to each other. When the day finally arrived for me to leave, I got a letter from her. I remember it well because it was so neatly folded and because of her beautiful penmanship. In the letter she told me she had changed her mind about the promises we had made to each other, that she would not go with me to Texas after all, that she wanted to go back to her old boyfriend. I flung the letter aside after reading it and swore never to talk to her again. After that I lost track of her for many years, and then when both of us were much older, she briefly reappeared in my life.

The meadows where the grower planted his tomato crop year after year extended out into gentle rolling hills and green picturesque valleys. He and his brother had inherited those lands from their parents years before. They were just outside the city limits. When we first went to that ranch in the summer of 1958, it was there, in the midst of those hills and valleys, where he had planted the one hundred acres of tomatoes that kept us busy that harvest season and many others. He also planted lots of corn and alfalfa for fodder. On top of a little hill, just up the road from where we lived, he had a dairy farm. Between him, an older son, and some regular hired hands, they took care of the milking, did the baling, fed the animals, and harvested the corn. With the animal waste, they fertilized all of the fields, and then the Mexicans who arrived early planted the tomatoes. Years earlier, before we got there, he had contracted braceros from Mexico to help with the picking. Work was abundant at that ranch.

It was in that soil fertilized with animal waste material where truly delicious tomatoes were grown. Those tomatoes tasted so rich it was a pleasure to eat them. We ate them right off the vine; my sisters used to carry their own salt shakers to the field to treat themselves to those sweet, juicy tomatoes every time they felt like it. They were everywhere. We all loved the taste and thought they were the best-tasting tomatoes in the world. We also thought, what with our ignorance of the world, that all tomatoes were the same, rich in taste and with a firm but soft and delicate texture. One year, though, we found out that things were not what they seemed. At the beginning of one harvest season we noticed that somebody was putting in stakes at the head of some of the melgas. A small white flag or ribbon was attached to the top of each stake. At first we didn't pay much attention to them. We just knew we weren't supposed to pick there. We'd go on to the next melga and continue picking there.

Along with those stakes we also began to see, coming and going to and from the fields, some men in white lab coats. We called them "the scientists" and, without our knowing it, that was what they were. They were from Iowa State University in Ames, and they were the persons sticking those stakes with the little white flags on the ground at the heads of selected melgas. They were conducting experiments with the tomato plants. Then suddenly one harvest season we saw with our own eyes the results from those experiments. The tomatoes in those melgas that the scientists had been setting aside with stakes and white flags were not picked until the very end that season, and only once. People called them "roma tomatoes" or just "roma." They were not like the others, sweet with a delicate texture and a deep, rich red color. Nobody wanted them, neither to eat nor to pick. They were smaller than the regular tomatoes. What struck us was not only the hardness and thickness of the skin but also their lack of taste. They were all the same size, and that also surprised us when we picked them for the first time. They all looked the same, like chicken eggs, but they were red like real tomatoes. To us they tasted like boiled paper (figure 9).

They were genetically modified tomatoes. The scientists, in their white lab coats, all looked the same to us, too. When they stepped into the field, they picked a few tomatoes from each of their melgas and left. They didn't fill up their baskets like we did. But that was not what they were there for; they had come to take the tomatoes to their laboratories. And, as it turned out and as we found out later, they were scientists who were experimenting with tomato seeds to modify them. But as we were only migrants, objects and not subjects of our own destiny, no one told us anything. "They are

9

A member of the Gozález family from Corpus Christi,
Texas, picking tomatoes in a field in the state
of Iowa during the decade of the sixties.
Courtesy of Mrs. Gloria S. Casas.

grafting them," people would say about the new tomatoes. "That's why they taste different." In fact, they were the result of a hybridization program we were totally ignorant about, but with a single bite, we could tell that even if they resembled tomatoes, they were not real tomatoes. Or at least not to us with our highly developed sense of taste. We picked normal tomatoes every day; we had done it for years. It would not be so easy for the scientists to trick or deceive our taste buds without our knowing it.

Things got even worse. If we were unable to understand the tomato experiments being conducted by the scientists from Iowa State University, much less would we have been able to know what their intentions were. Nor were we able to know, ignorant as we were, that the push for those genetic changes was coming not from the growers but from large companies. Nowadays they are called corporations. Their intentions, as I understand them now, were pragmatic ones. The idea was to increase the crop yield and increase economic returns. Perfecting tomatoes resistant to rot and to plagues of all kinds, that ripened all at the same time and still retained their market appeal, would bring enormous benefits to growers, and of course, to the owners of the patented seeds. Scientific experimentation and economic gain went hand in hand. If such tomatoes could be engineered or invented without degenerating in texture and appearance, it would also be possible to pick them with a machine and eliminate human pickers. What was more, a single picking with tractors and machines did away with another public nuisance: the need to build and maintain labor camps to house migrant workers. In other words, the idea was to remove the picker from the equation. But for that to happen tomatoes, formerly nutritious and rich in taste, would henceforth be no more than a simulacrum of the original nutritious fruit. A triumphant capitalism had eliminated from our diets another tasteful delicacy of the national heritage.

That's the way things turned out after a few years. By the decade of the 1970s, almost no one hired people to pick tomatoes. Growers simply brought in a piece of machinery and dug them out of the ground. The machine had heavy metal prongs that tore through the soil underneath the plants and in one fell swoop pulled out roots, vines, and tomatoes. The crop was brought up by conveyor belts to the top of the machine where, next to a steady stream of plants heavy with ripe tomatoes, there stood four or five women pulling and shaking the vines off and tossing them to the ground. The hybrid tomatoes dropped onto another broad conveyor belt, turning over and over as they moved along, until they fell into specially built vats mounted on trucks. It was how tomatoes were picked now. Out of the fields came truck after truck loaded with tomatoes even though there were no pickers. They drove directly from there to the Heinz plant in town and dropped their loads. The truck beds were hydraulically operated; the driver need not get off the vehicle. From his seat he maneuvered the load until he emptied all the tomatoes into water vats where they got soaked. Even at the factory there were fewer people now. Yet millions of bottles of tomato ketchup made with so-called fresh grown tomatoes kept coming out of there. They were plastic bottles, of course. If people only knew!

But as times change, so do our diets, both our physiological and our psychological diets. And with the change in our diet, the digestive system adapts so as to better digest and eliminate what the new diet brings. The girl from the university was one of those changes in my psychological diet. She helped raise my self-esteem and awakened in me whatever self-confidence I had. At the same time, her words brought me disillusionment, and I came to feel that I had deceived myself for having believed her. As with my psychological diet then, so with the pickers and the tradition surrounding the tomato harvest. The analogy of the genetically modified tomatoes with the changes in my—and our—migrant lifestyle is crude but intentionally so. Just as that young girl had acted out of a sincere interest in my welfare, so too had those scientists with their experiments. They were no monsters; they meant well. They came from the same university where the grower's son went. He himself became an agronomist. It's a real possibility he had something to do with the tomato experiments conducted in his own father's farm. But one of the sad consequences of their work, which I doubt very many people are aware of today, has been the elimination of normal tomatoes from their diets. In their place, the public now consumes roma and other kinds of genetically modified tomatoes. That such modifications have led in our day to drastic changes in the taste and texture of the fruit is no secret: tomatoes are no longer the natural crop we used to pick. They have lost their original sweetness and rich flavor. The taste of those tomatoes we migrants knew and cherished when we handpicked the crop in the fields was nothing if not an exquisite treat. Today both the original fruit and the pickers themselves have mostly disappeared from our consciousness. The one was engineered out of existence by the men in white lab coats, the other by modern do-it-all technological implements. Today, it appears, both the modern digestive system and the migrants of old have themselves been modified to make them more suitable for their consumer, and market-friendly, roles. I know; I was there. How I've adapted is another story.

The political diet—our social institutions—was changing as well. Whereas before no one had any idea where Vietnam was, suddenly even the older people knew that it was some country on the other side of the world. To pickers and the children of migrants, the War in that heretofore unknown part of the world added another dimension to our lives: an escape route. Picking tomatoes was no picnic for anyone. I remember that, as far back as the fifties, young men left the fields on the slightest pretext. Going back even earlier, my own uncles on my mother's side did it. They went to wars and fought in Europe and the Pacific rather than suffer the indignities of toiling in the fields. Now I was seeing the same phenomenon in my own generation. Two of the young men who worked at the ranch had no sooner turned eighteen than they volunteered for military service. The Government made it easy.

All males received, upon turning eighteen, a letter from the Selective Service System. That agency was in charge of recruiting men for a war that, officially, did not exist. One summer I had also received my letter. We were hoeing sugar beets in Washington, and I had to go to Spokane to take some tests. I have already mentioned elsewhere what happened then. Anyway, one conse- quence of that new draft policy was that, around the time the scientists began experimenting with tomato seeds at the farm, the majority of pickers were either women or older men. I remember counting nine men and twenty-three women picking tomatoes in the field at about that time. Most of those men were elders, heads of family. The younger ones who wanted out were signing up. Some made it back, but many didn't. My sister's husband did, alive and in one piece, but that too is another story.

There's a picture I've kept where my mother, a cousin, a young niece, and I are standing by the Mississippi River. Sticking out of my shirt pocket is a long white envelope. Inside was my train ticket. I was on my way to Texas to start classes at Uvalde Jr. College. That morning, before my mother took me to the train station, I had quit working early. At about 9:30 or 10:00 in the morning I walked over to where my father was picking. He knew what I was there for. In his wallet he was carrying eight one hundred dollar bills. They were for me. He said nothing; he just took his wallet out and started counting . . . one hundred, two hundred, three hundred . . . eight hundred. I have never been able to erase from my mind that image of how, as he counted each bill, his hands trembled before he handed it to me. "I'm leaving," I said when he finished counting. "Good luck," he answered, and that was it. There were no hugs or formal partings. He and my brother and sisters kept on picking as I took the road back to Texas. I felt a knot in my throat; there was tightness in my chest. I was leaving, and they were staying behind. There was still plenty of work in the fields, but I was going away to college.

After the picture taking was over, my mother gave me her blessing. I got my bags from the station wagon. I was anxious to get on the train. Aside from the eight hundred dollars and my personal belongings I had a letter from L. inside those bags. She had mailed it to me at the farm. Before the incident at the drive-in we had spoken about college, about our studies, about the future. When I told her where I was starting college, in Uvalde about fifty miles from Crystal City, she had told me they had relatives in

Dallas, and if I wanted to, she would attend a Methodist University there, and she would be close by so we could see each other regularly. I explained to her that Dallas was really very far from Uvalde and that private universities were very expensive. I wasn't sure how serious she was, but I knew it wouldn't work. When the train finally took off, and I opened the letter and read that she was sorry, but that she would not be going to school in Dallas after all. She also said she had a boyfriend, and that he would not let her move that far away. I could not understand that kind of thinking, but I knew what she was trying to say: that she did not feel strongly enough about me to leave everything and follow me. I don't think I did either, but at the time I wasn't sure.

I had my own compartment in the train. That first night, sitting there alone and lost in my own thoughts as the train rumbled along, an attractive young gringa passed by and smiled at me. I looked toward where she sat and saw she was alone, too. She invited me to go sit with her. She was on her way to Texarkana. I don't recall her name. She told me she wanted me to spend a few days with her at her place. We chatted and laughed for a while, but sometime during the night I went back to my seat. The next morning, when the train made a stop at her hometown, I kept looking at her while she got her bags together. She smiled before getting off, but I was unsure about how to interpret her smile. I felt inept at reading non-Mexican faces. And I was still afraid of getting too close to someone I didn't know. I was carrying with me enough money to pay for a whole year of college, buy books, clothes, provisions and everything else I would need. My whole future was right there in my pocket. I felt her attraction but was held back by the heavy sense of responsibility that hung over me. And I just didn't know how to get close to her. I still couldn't read the world I was getting ready to study about.

When I finally reached Crystal City my sister went to pick me up and drove me home. It was the small pink house across the gin, off of Highway 83, the road over which a bus would transport us to and from college for the next two years. I slept I don't know how many hours straight through. The next day the guys and I drove to San Antonio to buy dress slacks and shirts for college. I spent almost a hundred dollars. But I bought everything I needed, from underwear to a heavy winter coat even though the weather was warm. I had no experience either with women, with ideas, or with handling money. I thought that $800 was a lot of money, that it would never run out. It didn't turn out that way, but when I recall my father's image in the field that morning—when I go over that episode and what it brought forth—I now understand that what my father was doing was not only encouraging me to go to college but also saving my life. Had I not gone to college, what would I have done? I had just turned twenty years old, the country was being convulsed by war, and Uncle Sam had his eye on me. For the time being, though, the local Draft Board had approved my request for student status so I could go to school. It was an enormous relief both for me and my family. I just couldn't see myself being engineered into the Vietnam War like a roma tomato.

Again I had been saved by my backwardness and migrant's intuition. When L. would come visit at the ranch, more than once we had talked about eloping, about running away and just going off somewhere by ourselves. I was able to keep my hormones in check at those times, though I don't know how. Then, when that nice gringa sat next to me on the train, and I again felt that same physical attraction, those eight hundred dollars I had in my pocket and the fear of losing them again saw me through the ordeal, though I still don't understand how. Had I gone along and followed my personal inclinations, it would have been like losing my own identity, everything I thought I was. I simply couldn't wrap my mind around the idea of failing. That migrant simplemindedness that was so much a part of me at the time had saved me one more time. Either I lacked something or didn't have enough of it. Perhaps in college I would find out which one it was.

𝟙𝟙𝟙

School and Work from Texas to East L.A.

When I left the fields to start college, I had some tools with me. At the time, I did not realize how inadequate they were, though. In fact, my whole academic preparation was laughable as I was to find out later. For the time being, though, I had learned English and Spanish grammar, some basic mathematics, and the fundamentals of sciences, such as chemistry and physics. "So I'm prepared," I thought to myself. And I was also fascinated by history and literature. No longer was I limiting my readings to *Hot Rod Magazine*, *Car Kraft*, and *Motor Trend*. Thanks to my English teachers I had read *Othello*, *Hamlet*, and *Macbeth* by William Shakespeare; I knew Lincoln's Gettysburg Address and some poems by Keats and Shelley and had even read some of Edgar Allan Poe's short stories. I didn't understand any of it, but I had read them. I had memorized "To be or not to be" and "Tomorrow, and tomorrow, and tomorrow," Hamlet's and Macbeth's soliloquies. I had learned the difference between noun clauses, adjective clauses, and adverbial clauses thanks to one of our high school English teachers who taught us that and other intricacies of the English language. In seventh and eighth grades I had even learned sentence diagramming. And, thanks to the great *profesor* Rivera, by the time I started my English language studies, I had learned language concepts that opened the door to an understanding of advanced forms of verb conjugations. He taught us, better than anyone else up to that time, the conjugation of Spanish verbs from the simple present tense all the way to the pluperfect subjunctive. It was that paradigm which made it easier for me to comprehend English concepts such as tense and mood (indicative, subjunctive, conditional, and imperative). That started around the eighth or ninth grade. What I learned there, I simply transferred over to English. Spanish grammar had thus served as a bridge to help me better understand English grammatical concepts, although my conversational skills remained substandard. But my optimism was boundless. So, with that background, and thanks to my typing skills and knowledge of academic nomenclature, I knew in my heart I was prepared for college.

At least that's what I thought. My initial experience in the academic world, however, turned out to be more of an exercise in frustration—an academic psychodrama—than anything else. Misunderstandings plagued me from the start. That first day, as soon as we got off the bus, we all headed for the gymnasium eager to set the academic process in motion. The college administrators crowded the freshmen from all the area schools into a gigantic auditorium. We were handed programs at the door. According to the program we were given, we were scheduled to begin with a two-hour orientation session. Once we had all settled down they talked to us about credit hours, class schedules, required courses, transfer courses, and all of that. Then the librarian, a matronly lady with gray hair, confounded us even more by talking about the card catalog, research papers, footnotes, study habits, and such. I say confounded us because I already knew all of that. They had already taught us those concepts in high school. But we were in college now. It was not possible that in both high school and college we would be learning the same thing. But that was precisely what I was thinking when they finally let us out of there to go matriculate. "If that's how it is," I said to myself, "then I'll whip this out in a year."

That was my first mistake that day. I left the gym with a bunch of papers in my hand and walked directly to the building where they had told us to go. The advisors were waiting for us there, ready to help. At Crystal City High School, our school counselor had never so much as paid attention to Mexicans much less spoken to us about attending college. And, as far as I knew, no one had ever complained; it seemed so thoroughly normal to us to be excluded from his academic orientations that it did not even occur to us to ask for help, in spite of the fact that he was the school's academic counselor, and that was what he was paid for. That was one reason, I'm convinced, that I was blindsided just as I was about to register. "How many hours are you taking?" the lady asked me as I sat down and carefully placed my papers in front of her. "Thirty-six," I answered. She stared at me for a bit, as if she wasn't sure about something. "You're crazy!" she finally told me. "Nobody takes thirty-six hours in one semester!" I didn't feel offended or humiliated; I was thoroughly confused. I had figured I could take six classes on Monday-Wednesday-Friday, five on Tuesday-Thursday, and an additional Advanced Placement course. The bus arrived at eight o'clock and returned to Crystal City at four. I had enough time to take four classes between eight and noon. I'd take an hour for lunch. Then from one to three, I'd take two more. With that schedule I still had an hour left, from three until four, to do all my homework before getting on the bus to go back home. For Tuesdays and Thursdays, one-hour-and-twenty-minute-long classes, I had written down five classes on my schedule.

I walked out of there with twenty hours: English—3 credit hours, History —3 credit hours, College Algebra—3 credit hours, Biology—4 credit hours, Speech—3 credit hours, Physical Education—1 credit hour, Advanced Placement (in Spanish)—3 credit hours. My migrant-worker logic had told me that I should come out ahead of everybody else, or that I should at least try to be among the first ones to reach the other end (graduation). I had thought of everything in terms of rows, like when we worked in the sugar beets. Since I had not seen a single person whom I thought could best me at working in the fields, I had come out of orientation brimming with confidence. If I could beat them in the fields, I could surely do as much in the classroom. Or, at least, I would be able to keep up with the best of them. As a testimony of my then new-found faith, one of the items I had purchased with the $800 was a pocket English dictionary which I carried everywhere. As soon as I read or heard someone pronounce an unfamiliar word, I'd whip it out and search for the word until I found it. That way I continuously armed myself with new terms so nobody knew more words than I did. So constant was my obsession to get ahead of everyone that in the bus, the other students made dismissive jokes every time I pulled out my humble little dictionary.

My first difficult test was neither in English nor in math. I was just beginning to adjust to my college routine when my family returned from up north. I had been alone the first few weeks, surrounded by my books, and with a good sum of the $800 still left over. Now, instead of one, there were seven of us in the small house. My own privacy, my space, hygiene, it all grew more complicated. It was a problem just to take a bath. My mother and I eventually fixed up a small area for my own use where I spent my time studying, reading, and writing. But something had begun to change in me. In spite of my efforts, I had been unable to buy a typewriter. They were too expensive for my budget. My friends and I relied on a single portable typewriter for all our work. The three of us who hung out together used it for research papers, writing footnotes, bibliographies, and citing primary sources. Thanks to our high school teachers, we had a beginner's knowledge of such things. But with the new teacher, that was not enough. No longer could we plagiarize with abandon nor hide behind pompous-sounding words. Not only was he demanding, he knew a lot, too. I received a C on my first important essay. With such a grade, it was not difficult to imagine that others had done better than I. And the same thing had happened to me in Math: C's and D's.

By November of that year, I already knew something was wrong. I had not dropped out of a single class, but neither was I doing as well as I thought I would do at the beginning of the semester. Thanksgiving came around, and our meager resources at home became even scarcer. To make things worse, late one night, as I headed home in my old blue Dodge from a friend's house where we had been studying, I smashed into a 1957 Ford. It happened downtown. He didn't see me, and I couldn't evade him in time because I was speeding. He struck my car on the passenger side and sent me spinning all the way to the gas station across the street. I ended up a few inches away from the gas pumps facing in the opposite direction from where I was coming. At that hour everything was closed so no one was around. For a few minutes I sat inside the car, disoriented, then I heard the driver of the Ford call out, "Don't call the police! I'll fix it for you. Don't call the police!" I knew I had been speeding. It was past midnight; I had been studying, and they were coming from a dance. I got off and walked around the car. I noticed that the rear panel where he had hit me was stuck to the tire. I pulled it back out with my bare hands until it cleared the tire. "You're going to pay for this!" was all I told him. "Sure . . . I'll pay for it . . ." But he had no insurance, and neither did I, and we both knew it.

At about that time, I'm not sure if before or after, I had a nervous breakdown. It was the first time in my life I had come apart psychologically. After my mother and I fixed up the little corner for me to study, I'd spend hours there alone. But studying was not the only thing I did there. I would lie awake in bed for hours on end, silently suffering from a worsening acne condition. I had started having acne early on, when I was thirteen or fourteen years old. It came and went; sometimes I would break out in unsightly pustules and blackheads. But until then I had not had an episode serious enough to land me in the hospital. One night I ended up there. I had spent three straight days and nights in bed, the covers pulled over my head, so no one could see me. My poor mother, as always, was the one who first attempted to alleviate my nightmare. The pores on my face had become clogged and infected. Reddish pimples full of pus and blackheads covered my entire face. My desperation finally reached a breaking point. I jumped out of bed in a rage and started throwing furniture around, kicking anything that got in my way, smashing chairs and tables. Good thing it was late at night; everybody was asleep. I was raving like a mad man inside that house. It woke people up. As my mother desperately pleaded with me with tears in her eyes, my father ran outside to get the car. They threw a towel over my head to hide my face when they saw the terrible infection. They knew very well what I was going through. I had not been out of that room for three days and nights, and when I did come out, I hid my face from everyone. I allowed myself to be guided into the car. I did not want to attack anyone in my family, least of all my own parents. The fury that had erupted inside of me had been brought on by a constant itching and burning, not to mention all the unsightly bumps, on my face. They were a reflection of the ones I was carrying around in my soul.

It was midnight when we arrived at the emergency room. A Mexican doctor checked me over. He looked at my face and his expression told me everything. He drew some blood from my forearm and re-injected it in one of my buttocks. He explained something to the effect that my own natural antibiotics would help curb the infection. In the meantime another doctor, a gringo, gave me the name and address of some specialist, a dermatologist friend of his from San Antonio. I felt better almost instantly: a strange tingling sensation came over my face that seemed to be concentrating around the affected areas. The next day my parents lent me the car, and I drove myself to San Antonio to look for the dermatologist. I found his office downtown, in a three-story building, and walked right in. No one had to tell me his specialty was treating acne. There was another adolescent sitting in a corner, about my age and accompanied by an adult, with his head down and trying not to attract attention. It was the classic posture of victims of that unsightly affliction. I understood very well the evasive look typical of those suffering from acne. It was bothersome for others to look at you; you were conscious at all times of being an object of curiosity.

The doctor who saw me had the perfect personality for patients suffering from my skin ailment. He was well aware that it had both a physiological and a psychological cause. I told him of my woes, and he listened attentively. He knew that ridding oneself of a low self-esteem was part of the therapy. And so it was. He treated me right there in his office; he explained how to do the treatments on my own at home. And he gave me an expensive prescription: $12 each. Alas! There was a cure for my suffering!

I went back to school feeling renewed. I could face my friends and the other students again and not feel abnormal. But the problem did not entirely go away. A few weeks later the infection reappeared, though in a milder form. The pustules began to erupt around some areas of my face even though I continued to apply the treatments. I studied as much if not more than before; I avoided my friends and hardly went out. That was about the time I had the accident downtown. The semester was almost over; we hardly had any money at home. When, around the end of November, I had no more money to buy the prescriptions and other materials for the treatments, I began to feel defeated. School itself was not the problem. Even though I did not have an outstanding grade average, I was passing everything. At the end of the semester, my very first one in college, I would have twenty-two credits (five instead of three in Spanish). But it was the complications caused by my skin condition that I had no solution for. Each time I stood in front of a class, each time I had to look at someone directly, I became more demoralized and more emotionally drained. I couldn't help comparing myself with others, especially with gringos and gringas with their perfect skin, their smooth, clear faces without any blemishes or sunspots. My desperation knew no bounds. It tormented me to know that much of my crude, uncouth physical appearance was due to my being a field worker who spent day in and day out in the sun hoeing and picking and working in the dirt. As that first semester came to an end, I was distraught, introverted and penniless. When we finally walked out of final exams that December afternoon, I had already made up my mind: I was leaving for California. I wanted to get away from myself.

When I announced the news to my parents, I could tell they were saddened by it, but they didn't object. It was reassuring to know that an aunt and uncle on my father's side lived in Los Angeles. They had a home downtown. He was a tailor; she stayed at home. I had written to them asking permission to live there while I got a job. They couldn't turn me down. In January, with what little money I had saved from skimping on my medication and skin treatments, I changed the oil in my old Dodge, cleaned the spark plugs, and fixed the spare tire. I threw my stuff along with some books and papers in the car, and very early one Monday morning, I took off to L.A. by myself. It was cold. There was no one in the car to talk to, so I meditated the whole way, driving nonstop from Texas to California as if it were just a long Sunday drive. It was part of my migrant's endurance.

At that time I was still not aware that I wanted to solve my dilemma by running away instead of confronting it. It was not really an issue of school work; I had not done badly. What had happened was that I stuck my nose in my books and paid less and less attention to my friends. Sure, I needed to study, but it was more a matter of hiding from the world and feeling embarrassed when people looked at me. When they went to dances, I stayed at home. When I did go out, I hid to avoid being seen. I would look at girls askance. I was terrified of being rejected, of arousing pity or compassion instead of normal feelings. I had gotten to the point where, instead of looking to see how my presence impressed other people, I avoided even being noticed at all.

My aunt and uncle lived in the middle of East L.A., by Whittier Boulevard and Arizona Street. Their home was a smallish, two-bedroom, one-and-a-half bath affair that my aunt kept spotlessly clean. It was just the two of them living there, and she spent the day at home by herself. They welcomed me warmly; we chatted about the family and had supper. They were not academic types; they were pragmatic. He was a tailor; she was a housewife. They were not fieldworkers like us. They had spent a couple of harvest seasons when we went to pick grapes and cotton in Delano, but my aunt had worked in the kitchen with the other women. And he had simply not been cut out for fieldwork.

They were city people who lived an orderly life. As my aunt led me to my room, I noticed how neatly arranged everything was: the night table and lamp with a soft light on, extra-thick fluffy pillows, matching carpet. She pointed to a private bathroom in the hallway. It was worlds apart from what I had left behind. My father had told me about his sister. "She gets into arguments with the TV screen," he'd warned me jokingly. "Don't cross her." The all-night traffic and ambulance sirens screaming up and down the boulevard were something new to me. I had a hard time falling asleep the first few nights. In the mornings, after breakfast, my aunt would give me her blessing, and I went out to look for work. The last thing I wanted was to return home empty-handed. My aunt did her house chores, watched her soap operas, and fixed my uncle's meals. I could see in those simple, commonplace activities the very essence and rhythm of their lives. As for me, desperation soon began to set in.

On one of those unproductive days, I got in the car, shut the doors, and closed the windows. The sun gets hot in L.A. in the winter, and it was even hotter than usual that day. With no work and no money for my treatments, my skin condition had worsened. As I had nothing else better to do, I lay sideways on the front seat, facing the sun. I shut my eyes and decided I would stay inside the car until it got so hot that my skin would be forced into a sweat. I reasoned that it was a way for me to heal myself, that as the sweat streamed down my face it would cleanse the pores. I did it for several days, determined to shut myself inside the car for as long as it took to see results. I paid dearly for that indiscretion years later.

I kept searching. Finally one day I got a job at a car wash. They gave me towels and rags and sent me to one end of the line to dry the cars as they were coming out of the wash port. At least it was something. When I got paid, I offered my aunt part of my salary, but she refused it. It was a beginning, and I could buy my antibiotics. I abandoned my improvised sun treatments, which had been a grossly stupid idea. Even after many years had passed, a dermatologist had to remove damaged and cancerous basal cells brought about, as she put it, by "an unusual positioning of the face." I never told her what that unusual positioning was or how it had come about. I only confessed to her that I had been a migrant worker for many years, but nothing about my L.A. experiment when I had shut myself up in the Dodge to try to sweat my woes away.

I had read in the paper about some openings in a state- or federally-funded training program right there in L.A. It was for manual jobs, and to qualify, one had to take some kind of dexterity tests. I went and registered. Inside the warehouse, there were rows of people standing on either side of long tables. They were poor people from the barrio, mostly winos and drug addicts with tattoos and reddish noses. Not all of them, but some. The guy next to me was one of them. The first test consisted of inserting little sharp sticks on perforated boards, then to loop rings on the sticks, and stuff like that. They were typically government-issued exercises to help classify the masses of unemployed people into groups from the most to the least employable. When the administrator arrived, he instructed us to stand in front of our utensils, and he pulled out a stopwatch. He gave the signal and we started inserting and looping. Since I was a baseball player, knew how to type, and had ample dexterity on both hands from hoeing sugar beets, I finished the test in no time. The *cholo* (California zootsuiter) standing next to me didn't like that I had beaten him.[1] When the whistle sounded for everybody to stop he continued inserting the little sticks and looping the hooks on the board. The girl on the other side and I stared at him, aware he was cheating, but it did not seem to bother him. Only when the test monitor approached to check our work did the cheating *cholo* stop poking at the board.

I did so well that the director called me into his office the following week. He asked me some questions; I told him who I was and where I came from. I had shown him some of my grades from the first semester at the junior college, and he asked if I were interested in attending UCLA. "Of course!" was my answer. "I can help you get in," he said. But I left too soon and nothing came of it.

My luck was beginning to change. The following week or so, I received a call to show up at the Square D Company employment office. At the time they were one of the premiere manufacturing companies in all of Los Angeles. They manufactured electric transformers for home and industry. I could start as soon as I was ready. I went the next day. My aunt and uncle congratulated me, and I noticed a sigh of relief when I told them. They had not been indifferent to my plight; on the contrary, they had been very supportive. My uncle, a patient man like all good Mexicans, chatted with me and took me to his shop. He offered, in jest, to make me a fancy double-breasted suit when I got married, and I promised I'd wear it. That dream never came true.

With my first check, I took off in my Dodge to visit family. My maternal grandfather lived with an aunt north of L.A. Another uncle lived in the San Fernando Valley. I found him sweeping a drive-in parking lot. He held two jobs, both sweeping theaters. As always, he was very helpful and attentive, but I sensed something was wrong. He stayed at work while I went looking for my aunt. It was then I realized that they were barely making ends meet. As she came out to greet me, my aunt was crying. She expressed her regrets; she had nothing to offer me. I said hello, and we chatted for a while. I asked her permission to go to the store, and I shopped for groceries: rice, beans, tortillas, fruit, and whatever else I thought necessary for her family. I even got them some ice cream, I remember.

At the Square D warehouse where I ended up working, rows of industrial-size screwdrivers hung from the ceiling, one per workstation. They were pressure driven and very powerful. In seconds they screwed or unscrewed the panels, and they never ran out of juice. As the panels passed in front of us, we picked up one at a time from the assembly line, aligned them in a pre-determined pattern, and screwed them together as fast as we could. I had been placed next to a nice guy who gave me tips on how to improve my skill at assembling and screwing the panels together. He befriended me from day one. He gave me pointers every day, but even with his help, I kept falling behind. The panels slipped out of my hands; the noise was unbearable. By the time I filled up a delivery truck with assembled transformers, the others had already started work on their next batch. I'd go, deliver my load, bring the truck back, and start on the next load. By then my companions were delivering their next load. I arrived early every day, with my lunch, and assembled transformers from eight to twelve. I took an hour for lunch, then continued doing the same thing again for another four hours, from one to five. They paid me a good salary, but even though I knew I was on a trial basis, I couldn't put my heart into the job I was doing. I was getting better, and my confidence grew. But there was no life for me in that world. I did not know anyone; my only outings were visits to family members. When I was called into the director's office one afternoon after my shift was over, it was already March. I had worked there for a little over five weeks; I had already received one check: $300 for one month. Before I got my second one, they fired me.

In my family visits, I had made it a point to come see my aunt where my maternal grandfather was staying on a more regular basis. Her brother, my maternal uncle who worked at the drive-ins, lived not far away. After losing my job I went to visit him again. He offered me one of his two jobs. "Thank you, uncle T. I think I'm leaving for Washington." From there I went to visit my aunt and grandfather. By then I had already given some thought to the idea of going up to Moses Lake to work in the sugar beets. My parents had arrived at the barracks at the beginning of April. Everything pointed in the direction of my leaving. When I arrived at my aunt's house, her husband was also there. I had not seen him in previous visits. He drove a rig delivering celery and lettuce all over Southern California. I hadn't seen him in years. After greeting each other warmly, we stepped outside to chat. We remembered the days when his younger brother, the one with the long blond braids, and I played and ran around together at the McCullum labor camp outside Salinas. We talked about his parents, the siblings, and the days gone by. Then he told me something that caught me off guard: they didn't have any transportation. He drove large company rigs, but they didn't own a car. Right then and there I told him I would be leaving soon for Washington, and that he could keep the Dodge. His face lit up with a smile that made me remember all the way back to when he had just married my aunt, when his kid brother and I were the best of friends. Now, wearing that depressed look, he seemed like a different person standing there in front of me. I had admired him so much back then, and now he was telling me they were barely making ends meet like my other uncle. Things were not what I had imagined them to be; the images I had in front of me did not match those I had carried around so long in my head. A few days later, having bought my train ticket to Washington, I went and left him the car we had bought at the gringo's junkyard the year before. It didn't make it back to Moses Lake. I left it in California with a banged up rear fender I had straightened out myself with a crowbar and a hammer.

CHAPTER 17

Working the Rows between Classes

From Big Bend Community College back to Uvalde

V.'s letters arrived at my aunt and uncle's address, on Whittier and Arizona, in Los Angeles. When I was at work or had gone out for some reason, my aunt left them on my night table next to the lamp. In her letters she told me she missed me a lot, that the weather was freezing, that she was bored. Her little sister, like her, was starting high school, and she was thrilled about it, just as she had been when she had started high school. Now she had been looking for work. Her folks supported her, and for now she had to depend on them. She also wanted to know, when was I going back to Moses Lake? At night I poured my heart out to her in my letters, writing until the wee hours of the morning alone in my room, accompanied only by the sirens and unending traffic of East L.A. My uncle had given me a set of earmuffs one afternoon when I told him I couldn't sleep at night because of the noise. But the truth was that I couldn't sleep because, after writing V. big fat letters, I lay in bed thinking about my draft classification. It worried me and kept me awake. It would take the college a couple of months to report to the government I'd dropped out. By then it would already be March, April maybe. I had told her all those things in my last letter from there. She wrote back that there was a college in Moses Lake, called Big Bend Community College, where I could take summer classes.

By then things were going badly for me at Square D. I knew I wouldn't last. It was at about that time that I received a letter from my mother. It came from Moses Lake. They had been at the barracks for a couple of weeks. There were only the two of them and my three unmarried sisters.

My younger brother was in Texas playing baseball. She told me in the letter that my father had given permission for him to stay behind only because the school would pay his way back when classes were over, that they would soon be playing for the Regional Championship, that they missed me.

What she did not say in the letter but that I sensed was that they were not doing so well in Washington. It was too early in the season. The work in the fields hadn't started yet. My father had managed to find a part-time job driving Cats and tractors, but they missed my brother, and they needed me. So far as I was concerned though, my immediate preoccupation was finding a way to keep from getting drafted. Going to war made no sense to me. I felt cornered; there were few choices left. I had been fired from Square D. I was not going back to washing cars for a pittance. The Selective Service was after me. What to do?

I cashed my last check and returned home to spend the night. I knew I had to decide. Next morning, having already decided what I was going to do, I thanked my aunt and uncle and offered them money. It was not much but they turned it down anyway. It was the last time I saw my aunt. My uncle came back to Texas for a visit or two some years later. He had sold the little house in East L.A. after the death of my aunt and moved back to Texas. By then he wasn't the same person who said goodbye to me that day. Without my aunt by his side, he seemed lost. From there I drove straight to my other uncle's place and gave him the keys and the title to the old Dodge. I don't recall who drove me to the Amtrak station but it was probably him, the husband of my mother's youngest sister who had become my grandfather's caretaker.

V. and her parents went to pick me up at the Amtrak station in Ellensburg, Washington. I was happy to see them, and especially her of course. She smiled at me with tears in her eyes and her beautiful shiny teeth as we hugged. She looked radiant: coiffed, tight skirt, elegant shoes. We couldn't talk about what we wanted to in the car. So we talked about family. I spoke about the trip, about the spectacular sites, and the panoramas I had been admiring on the trip, about the snow-capped mountains in Oregon and California. In her letters V. had already mentioned to me how proud she and her parents were that I was going to college. During all the time that we hadn't seen each other I had called her long distance a couple of times. She would tell me about her friends, the parties she'd been to, that she missed

me. Here she was now, sitting next to me, serene, and with that unforgettable smile she always had, as anxious as I was to get to Moses Lake. They
dropped me off right at the entrance to the barracks.

What I found inside was very depressing. As always, my mother had
divided the place into several partitions using bed sheets to separate males
from females and them from us. My sisters spent the whole day cooped up
in theirs, waiting for my father to get home from work. There wasn't much
to eat. Sugar beets were still weeks away. My father had finally been able to
find work plowing fields. When he got home in the afternoons he was covered in sand and grit from head to toe. He wore goggles to protect his eyes,
and when he removed them there remained a flesh-colored strip across his
face. The thick shabby clothing he wore to insulate himself from the cold
and blowing dust somehow magnified the already depressive atmosphere
inside the cramped space they occupied in *la barraca* (the barrack). That
evening I could tell just by the way he greeted me that things were not
going well. My mother spoke little. After greeting me, my sisters had returned to their partition. It was the beginning of April; there weren't many
people at the barracks. There was no money, either.

One of those afternoons not long after I got there, my father had gotten
home in a bad mood. He went outside to the showers to clean up, and
when he returned, he sat at the table to await his dinner. We had to wait
for him to finish eating because the table was too small. It would have been
uncomfortable to sit so close. We wanted to give him ample space. When
my mother put the plate of food in front of him something upset him and
he flung it against the wall. He tore into her right in front of us. We froze
and said not a word. Then my mother, in tears, removed her apron, placed
it over a chair and put her sweater on. She removed her house slippers
and put on some shoes. We saw her walk out, expressionless, and leave the
building. From my bunk bed, I could see her through the window walking
along the narrow road leading out of the barracks in the direction of town.
She looked straight ahead and walked at a good clip.

My father was still at the table. The girls started picking up the food
from the floor. Whispering amongst themselves they kept saying that my
mother would take the bus to California, that she would end up going to
where grandfather and her sister lived. When I lost sight of her I jumped
off the bunk bed, put on my jacket and ran after her until I caught up. Tears

were streaming down her face. I talked to her about my brother, that he'd soon arrive from Texas, and that I would be going to college right there at Big Bend Community College, and about whatever else I could think of. We walked along the road for a good while. Before reaching town my father caught up with us and told us to get in the car. At first she resisted him, but he blocked her path. She finally climbed in without looking one way or the other and we returned to the barracks. I got off and left them alone. That night they slept together.

It was two weeks of pure agony. There was no work. I had no books and no money to take V. out except on short dates. We were short of everything. One day my father gave me the keys to the car, an almost new Chevrolet four door they had brought with them from Texas. He told me to wash it and to take it to the Chevy dealer in town and leave it there along with the paperwork. That's what I did. I drove the car there myself. When I got to the dealership I talked to the first salesman I ran into. "My father can't pay for the car," I said to him and handed him the keys. I must have walked back to the barracks. I did not so much feel humiliated as desperate and angry. I can't even remember how I made it home. There was a letter waiting for me when I got there. It was from my best friend who had stayed on in college when I dropped out. He was doing well in school, he told me, but he had gotten married. I unconsciously put the letter down, and for a minute I just stared at the wall, my mind a complete blank. Then a sense of incredulity began creeping over me. "Double-crosser, coward, quitter!" My interior monologue went on and on like that. It was an anguished explosion of expletives blasting the contents of the letter. Disillusion and finally just a sense of total confusion set in. My closest friend, work companion, drinking buddy, and college acquaintance had gotten married. To me he had always personified inflexible willpower; he was the most intelligent of our group. Who did he think he was getting married and breaking off that special bond we had shared for so long? The dream of attending a large university together had helped see us through hard times more than once. He was to study mathematics, and I would become a teacher. Now he was abandoning me and we weren't even halfway there. I sat down that night and wrote him a letter I never mailed. I still have it somewhere.

My brother finally arrived from Texas. We had just started hoeing sugar beets, and we were beginning to make some money. His baseball team had done very well; they had made it all the way to Regional, but they lost. He wasn't there for the last game. A few days before, his coach had bought him a bus ticket to Moses Lake. He didn't want him to leave, but my father had insisted on it so much that he let him go. And, without their star shortstop, they lost the championship game. But my father nonetheless celebrated his arrival, proud to see such a change in his young son: he had put on more muscle from working out, a good diet, and rest. I thought he looked like a different person, too. We'd go outside the barracks to hit him ground balls just to watch him field the ball. He scooped up everything. And he in turn would show us and others who came to watch him how baseball was really played. The change he had undergone from one year to the next was truly extraordinary. He fielded grounders, no matter how hard they were hit, with the grace of a professional. He barely moved; his hands and arms did everything. And he threw hard. That was why the coaches had argued with my father to let him keep playing back home.

It didn't take us long to organize a team. A few weeks after we started hoeing beets, happy and well-fed even if it meant we were working hard, we started playing in-between the barracks. The team grew, so we went to play in an old baseball field in town. Before long some passersby challenged us and our first game was on. We beat one, two, three teams handily. We played on Sunday afternoons. They even brought teams from out of town to play against us because the locals couldn't beat us.

One Sunday afternoon that summer, the local baseball park was filled to capacity with migrants and other folks who had come to watch us take on one of those teams from out of town. Somebody brought meat and a grill, other family members brought refreshments, and the support and cheerleading from the stands gave us the home field advantage. Judging from the appearance of the crowd and their animated chatter, our fans were mostly workers from the area labor camps. Pretty girls were all over the place; baseball players from some of those labor camps who had heard about the game came and asked if they could give us a hand. We welcomed a relief pitcher from The Valley and a catcher from one of the other migrant camps. Thus constituted, the whole team oozed confidence as we hit the field. Since I had just graduated from high school and spoke decent English, the players named me team manager. We ended up using three pitchers, including myself; we played around twelve or thirteen innings if I remember correctly. The game lasted more than four hours with only one brief intermission. The people from town and from the barracks had come to see my brother play. Family and friends had let it be known he was playing. And nobody left until the game ended. People cheered, whistled, and yelled to their hearts' content. We won that game by sheer force of will, and the numbers showed it: the final score was one to nothing. My uncles passed out freshly made beef tacos from meat grilled right on the premises, picante sauce, and drinks to all the players after it was all over. We celebrated the moment with friendly hugs and backslaps, and we thanked the players who had come in all the way from Toppenish to play against us.[1] That game was a jewel.

I didn't sleep that night; I stayed up doing my homework. I had registered at Big Bend Community College at the beginning of June as soon as the first summer session started. I took English, Philosophy, and Psychology: nine hours that first summer session. I had written to the Selective Service Board in Uvalde to let them know my new address, and I needed to confirm my new student draft status. Right away they sent me a postcard, Notice of Rights to Personal Appearance and Appeal. I could appeal if they re-classified me 1-A. That told me that they were considering it but had not yet done it. The 1-A status meant you were available for immediate conscription. That was what I wanted to avoid. But first I had to pass all my classes at Big Bend.

Psychology already interested me somewhat. I had filled out a college questionnaire in Uvalde, where I had stated I wanted to be a Psychology Major, though I don't remember why I selected it. Philosophy was tough. As far as I was concerned, the class was thoroughly disorganized. When the professor arrived in the morning the first thing he did was to place his foot on the chair, then he slowly and self-consciously began raising his dressy slacks up his leg until we could see the silken socks he was wearing. No, they were not like the ones we wore. I don't even know why I remember that. He would divide the class into those who believed in God and those who didn't. What position was I going to take on a topic like that? The first time I tried to say something, they shut me up right away. There was one gringo, older than the rest of us, whom we respected because it was obvious he knew what he was talking about. Or at least it seemed so to us. He assured everybody there was no God, that Nietzsche and Schopenhauer and the Nihilists were right, that happiness was simply the absence of pain, and he would go on and on like that in class. What did I, a simple migrant sugar-beet worker from Texas, know about such things?

We had been indoctrinated by the Catholic Church from the time we were little kids and taught not to argue about religion but to be obedient. Now I was learning there were other ways people interpreted things, even religion. I spent nights on end pouring over my books. In English class I had a very attractive young woman for an instructor. Professors didn't all have to be old, ugly, and pale-faced. I won her over with a short story about one of my aunts, "My Aunt Lupe." I wrote that I did not know the word *divorce* until someone mentioned that my aunt Lupe was a divorcée. I explained that, when I found that out, I was expecting to see some odd-looking creature walk through the door when my aunt came to visit. But it hadn't turned out that way. When I saw her she looked like any other normal woman. Little by little, I wrote in the paper, I had begun to learn that there were other divorced women in town, but that one never heard of there being any divorced men. It was my way of telling her that I came from a traditionalist society, that divorce was something unknown to me, and that I lacked cultural sophistication. She wrote some commentary on the margins and gave me a grade of B. I had traded family secrets for an academic grade. I was getting my ego stroked, and I liked it. I was also learning how to be a pretty good hypocrite.

I made three B's that summer. I don't know how I did it. When everybody took off in the morning to go work in the beets, I headed off to college. I was done with my classes by noon. Sometimes my mother picked me up at the campus, sometimes I walked back to the barracks. If the family was working nearby, I drove her back to the barracks, ate something, changed clothes, and headed to the field. If the crew was getting paid by the hour, the contractor allowed me to start at one o'clock, right after lunch, and I'd work until six. As soon as I got back in the evenings, I showered, ate, and hit the books. That's how I survived. On weekends I'd see V. for a little while, and I'd go back to study. I knew why I was doing it: by then I was convinced that I was going to stick with school, that I wasn't going to get married like my friend, that everything was for real this time. I was not about to go through another humiliating experience like what I had lived through in California. And neither was I going to let myself be influenced by my companions' decisions as I had done up until then.

I had gotten some valuable things out of the three subjects I took, not so much from what I learned in class, but rather because of my increased self-esteem. I had competed with the gringos, I went to hoe sugar beets every day after class, I played baseball on weekends with the guys from the labor camp, and I had gotten three B's. Not a single one of the other students kept a schedule like mine, not even the smart guy from philosophy class.

According to the map, Muscatine, Iowa, is 1,828 miles from Moses Lake, Washington. My parents and my sisters had been in Washington since late March or early April. I had arrived soon after from California by train with what remained of my last check from Square D with my tail between my legs. I had started college in Texas the previous fall only to drop out at the end of the first semester. After falling flat on my face at my aunt's and uncle's in East L.A. and with the Selective Service System after me, I returned to those habits of the mind that lie buried deep inside one's brain: the life of a migrant worker in my case. But it had been necessary for me to stumble for a bit in order to re-start my life. Once I had made contact with my people and my original lifestyle I found my way again. Not the same way back, but the way, or a way. I had learned that I needed the two communities, my family and academia, in order to succeed in both. If I abandoned the fields and moved away from my people too hastily, I'd get psychological indigestion. If I buried myself in the books, my nerves would get shot, I couldn't get along with anybody, and I ended up like a zombie. I could now see that going back to hoeing sugar beets, working hard in the fields, and taking in the energy and excitement of the crowds on weekends had helped revitalize me. At that stage of my life it would not have been a good idea to profess myself a Nietzschean individualist or a faithless Nihilist while wielding a short-handled hoe. I wasn't ready yet. First and foremost what I needed to do was learn to be pragmatic, which meant thinking of myself first rather than of the others. But that meant exile, loss of contact with members of my own family. That was not the way I had been brought up. I only knew how to function as a member of a group, and that meant suppressing the selfish urge to ignore the welfare of loved ones. I didn't know how to tackle the dilemma eating me inside. The individual in me had clearly emerged, nonetheless. I didn't realize it at the time, but that meant a gradual reconfiguration of my psychic identity.

CHAPTER 17

It was the beginning of July. Another season thinning and weeding sugar beets was almost over and the tomato harvest was about to start in Iowa. The other families living in the barracks also began to thin themselves out. All the male cousins found jobs in the spud warehouses, others found work in irrigation, and a few went back to the fields cutting asparagus. There was lots of work. In our case, each year as the harvests grew promising, we were followed by different members of the extended family who wanted to take advantage of the work we had dug up. They had heard that we made good money picking tomatoes. True, but we did well because we worked really hard at it and because we stayed until the end of the harvest. More than once we were accompanied by some of those members of our extended family who had been dreaming of making loads of dollars in a rather short picking season. But when the first scattershot pickings came in the early part of the season they would start scratching their heads asking, "Where are all the tomatoes?" Then, when we got to the really heavy part of the harvest, they complained because they had to pick on Sundays. There was just no pleasing them.

Still the caravan left for Iowa once again. We crossed four states: after driving through half of Washington State, we crossed all of Montana, South Dakota, parts of North Dakota and Minnesota before reaching Iowa. When we got to the ranch the people who had tagged along with us not only wanted help finding work, they also wanted my father to help them find housing. The burden fell on my parents. On my father because they were his family, and on my mother because she was the one who cooked and washed for the single males. Our lifestyle was also cramped: the more people there were at the camp, the less room left for us.

There's a story I have to tell not only because it really happened but because it's a bit hard to believe. It was that year, one of the last ones I went up north, when the tomato harvest turned out to be one of the best ever. The grower hired people wherever he could find them to help harvest the tomatoes. He had also asked my father to get help wherever he could find it. And he did. But there was no more room for one of the young men he had recruited. He had no car either. What they did, and I helped out, was to get the tractor and pull a big old doghouse from where it had been sitting out back. We brought it out and set it under some of the big trees away from the foot traffic in the front yard. People lent the guy some bedding materials and he slept there in the doghouse. At night he squeezed in feet first to go to sleep, and as he did he chuckled that things were a little tight, but he kept an upbeat and gregarious attitude about it all. He slept with part of his head sticking out of the front of the doghouse even though he was a short man. I saw him through the ordeal the first day and several times after that. I can't recall if he was a good picker or not. But those were his sleeping quarters. He actually lived there throughout the tomato harvest.

The best part of the harvest usually lasted no more than a few weeks, from the end of August through September and sometimes into early October. My brother and sisters, those who were left, already knew the ritual: pick every day from morning 'til evening, rest on Saturdays, pick Sundays half of the day so haulers had a load to take to the factory early Monday morning. My job was the same: help load the trailers, pass out empty baskets to the pickers, do some of the hauling. One of my best friends and I had gotten together that time to help with both the loading and the hauling. By then we were veterans at it. We were inseparable, and what we had in common more than anything else was school. The two of us would be heading back to Texas at the beginning of September (figure 10).

By then I had heard that my former friend L. had gotten married or was going to get married. There was nothing left of those Sunday chats under the trees except the memories. From time to time I heard rumors that she was living in town, that someone had seen her, that she would ask about me. Whether it was true or not I had no idea. Two of my best friends were already married. I had taken their decision to marry personally. After that I did not feel like my old self anymore. Now, having been burned more than once, I relied more on my own instincts. As the time to leave for Texas got closer I thought things through more carefully. This time I talked with my father face to face. We had worked out who was going to take my place loading and hauling, and we had decided how and with whom I'd be going back to school.

My best friend and I left family and friends picking tomatoes in the field and headed home in a 1953 Ford. We drove nonstop all the way to Crystal City. One or two days later we went to register at the community college in Uvalde. This time matriculation took no more than an hour, and it hadn't turned into a disaster like on the previous occasion. The two of us were different people now; we had matured thanks to the mistakes and humili-

10

The author's father and uncles loading tomatoes in a field in Iowa during the decade of the sixties. Here the workers empty the baskets directly into crates. Previously the tomato baskets were transported on trucks or wagons, depending on the distance to be covered, directly from the fields to the processing plant in town. These tomatoes have been genetically modified. They are more durable. The taste, however, is different. Courtesy of Mrs. Gloria S. Casas.

ations we had lived through the first year. No more taking thirty-six hours in one semester, no more going to class nonstop from eight to five. No more schedule conflicts, either. We chose our classes, filled out the paper work, and paid. I walked out of the Registrar's Office that day with eighteen hours plus three more Advanced Credit hours in Spanish. It cost the same for fifteen or twenty or more credits, so I signed up for twenty-one. Since I was still living my superman fantasy, I also decided to try out for college baseball as a pitcher and earned a spot on the team.

In my student record from Uvalde Jr. College dated May 27, 1965, it also shows that I was the president of the Newman Club and a parliamentarian of the TSEA Club.[2] There's a slot in the Athletic Activities section where it asks for my record in baseball, and I wrote in "3–0." My ego had clearly awakened to the world.

That academic year had its ups and downs as well, but I was better prepared to survive now. During the month of November, I lost a week and a half of classes. My appendix had ruptured, and I underwent an operation. I returned to class, caught up with my work, and picked up where I had left off. The added stress brought back my acne troubles, which had never totally gone away. The pustules came and went; the higher the stress level, the more serious the outbreaks. My treatments and medication helped alleviate the infections. But I did not suffer a relapse of that psychological breakdown I'd had the year before when I had wanted to smash everything against the wall. This time, instead of having a passive reaction, I sought ways out of personal dilemmas. I would remember my readings and discussions over Nietzsche and Schopenhauer, about an individual's personal will in confrontation with the world. I had learned something in my classes at Big Bend, especially in Philosophy. And I also remembered a particular word that seemed to summarize it all for me when I felt I was in a hole: stoicism. One had to learn to be a stoic instead of throwing up one's arms and giving up. Was that an active or a passive attitude? I don't know, but it helped. I ended the semester with my name on the Dean's List.

My '53 Ford quit on me the following spring. One morning my best friend and I were headed to college when the car's radiator exploded. We left the car by the side of the road and waited for the bus, which didn't take long to pick us up. We had been using my car to come and go to school so as not to depend on the bus. That way we could stay at the library after everyone had left, and we'd return home whenever we wanted. Staying after school to play baseball was also going to get a little complicated. Practice was in the afternoons after classes were over. Sometimes we'd stay out in the field until six or even later. That semester, I was the only one from Crystal City left in the baseball team. One afternoon, after pitching (and winning) a game against a Del Rio Air Force Base team, we stayed 'til seven. I couldn't find anybody who was going home that evening. I decided to walk the forty miles from Uvalde to Crystal City. I walked all along the road from the college until I reached town. From there a nice old man offered me a ride. "Where are you headed?" he asked without opening the door. "Crystal City," I answered. He was going as far as La Pryor, he told me, and he'd drop me off there. I jumped on the old jalopy floorboard, grabbed hold of the door post, and along we went at thirty-five miles per hour with the nice cool breeze whooshing against my face. Just past La Pryor he dropped me off, turned left onto a dirt road, and got lost in a cloud of dust at that late hour. I was still eighteen miles from home. I kept walking along State Highway 83, the same highway that passed right in front of our house next to the gin. It was a beautiful starry night with a gentle breeze. It must have been around midnight as I walked along, sleepily stepping on the white line in the middle of the road when right in front of me I saw the biggest reptile I had ever seen in my life slithering past me! It was a gigantic rattlesnake! I jumped back, unable to take my eyes off it. The fear of snakes must be innate in humans: my instinct had taken over and made me react without thinking. I started walking faster and got home around two in the morning. By seven o'clock I was riding the bus on my way back to school.

||||||||||||||||||||||||||||||||||||||||||||||||||||||||||||||||||||||||

CHAPTER 18

Using the Long Hoe in North Dakota

The certificate, an 8" × 10½" parchment printed in elegant French script, says in bold black letters, "The American Legion Certificate of School Award." A round blue and gold seal is stamped on one side, then follows this text: "This certificate of Distinguished Achievement is awarded Saul Sanchez of Southwest Texas Junior College School in recognition of attainment acquired as winner of The American Legion School Award. The Further Recognition of the possession of those high qualities of Courage, Honor, Leadership, Patriotism, Scholarship and Service which are necessary to the preservation and protection of the fundamental institutions of our government and the advancement of society. This award is made by Uvalde Post No. 26 The Department of Texas of the American Legion. May 27th 1965." It was accompanied by a heavy bronze medal attached to a bright-blue ribbon. It was presented to me at the graduation ceremony that evening. The announcement was so unexpected that I did not hear my name when it was pronounced the first time. My friend and I were kidding around about something or other when they called me. For us the simple fact of sitting in the auditorium was a rare event, something solemn and theatrical at the same time. We looked behind us and to either side: the place was full of strangers. Our families were not there; they had gone up north. Just the two of us had gone to the ceremony that night. We were surrounded by classmates that we had seen in the hallways every day, who read and scribbled with us in the library, who took exams and spoke perfect English. We had spent two long years rubbing shoulders in that setting. For me, to see them sitting at that moment while people were applauding and congratulating me did not seem logical, as if it were another me who was being recognized. I recall an elbow to the ribs: "They called your name!" When they repeated it I turned serious, stood up, and walked up to the stage. After the award was conferred on me with great solemnity I walked back and sat down. My classmates smiled at me; they seemed as surprised as I was. I carried the certificate and medal as if I were holding a symbol of authority: my expression remained fixed as I stared back at the crowd.

I had just sat down when they announced another familiar name: my friend's. "And the award for the highest average in mathematics goes to . . . Oscar Pérez." It was him, my inseparable companion whom they were recognizing now. We had been through so much together, from the fields to the classroom, the old hot rods we raced, the double dates, the trips up north and back, both of us from humble working families. That night, by the time we arrived at the auditorium, we knew very well that we were two of the very few migrants who had completed the degree. What we did not know or expect was what had just taken place: being publicly recognized at the same ceremony, one after the other, for having come out ahead of everyone else, he in mathematics and I in academic achievement.

In the United States, that degree is known as the Associate in Arts. It is granted by community colleges, academic institutions where they offer courses that are the equivalent of the first two years of a university degree program. For those who were pursuing two-year technical degrees such as Automotive Technology, Refrigeration, or Stenography that was the end of the road. But not for us. For us it was just another step along the road, another field we had just finished hoeing. And after that, there was another then another. I think that was the reason we didn't celebrate after we left the auditorium. We didn't go out for a beer, no one took our pictures, nor were we invited to any parties. We were still migrants. The truck taking us up north would be leaving early the next day. This time it was headed for North Dakota.

We did not return to Washington. By the time we graduated in May, it was too late to go do sugar beets in that state. My parents had found us a place where we would do only thinning and weeding somewhere near the Canadian border in a small town by the name of Drayton, North Dakota. Sugar beets were just beginning to come up when we arrived. This time we would not be using short hoes. By then, in the year 1964 or 1965, sugar-beet companies had stopped requiring them. In some states they had even been outlawed. For us to do sugar beets with a long hoe was a treat. From day one, my brother and I set a torrid pace. With the short hoe we had become accustomed to hoeing an acre and a half and calling it a good day. We were doing upwards of three, three and a half now! Unheard of before. The difference, of course, was that now we were taking long versus short steps as we went along the rows blocking and thinning the plants. That was one obvious difference. But from our vantage point as old school, short hoe sugar-beet thinners, this change in work implements signaled other, deeper realignments in our thinking.

It was not just that we were covering more territory now. A more psychologically meaningful change, as far as we were concerned, was that now we could stand straight up as we worked. To us that meant leaving behind the stooped, bent-over-at-the-waist position we had always been required to adopt in the past when thinning sugar beets. To say that it had been a humiliating way to earn our daily bread is to understate the brutality of its effect on our character, the toll it took on our subtracted self-esteem. Working year in and year out in such an awkward, dehumanizing position required not just superhuman endurance but also a hardening of one's psyche. It seared one's soul to see one's self, and one's entire family, forced to adopt such a servile position. So, to say that, from our vantage point at least, a new era in the storied history of sugar-beet thinning had begun with the introduction of the long-handled hoe is not overstating the case. Technology had invaded one more domain of American agriculture, and migrants like us were simply adapting to its all-pervasive influence, its encroachment upon people's lives.

We eventually heard through the grapevine what had brought about such a momentous change: the sugar-beet industry was undergoing its own version of the genetically modified tomatoes. It seems that cries to ban the short hoe had started in California or, if not there, in some other western state. Certain influential voices had claimed that hoeing sugar beets with a short hoe, aside from the severe pain induced by the stooped position, led workers to suffer long-term damage to some of their body parts. Carpal tunnel syndrome, they called it. Why not, claimed a group of scientists, use a long hoe instead and modify the seeds so they don't come out clumped together? That'll make it easier to thin the tender, new beet shoots as they begin to make their way up out of the ground. And so they did. Instead of planting whole seeds the growers began planting seed granules and, *voilà!* Henceforth, blocking and thinning with the long hoe was possible because the shoots came up, not clumped together as before, but rather as individual plants separated from each other. And the grower himself could determine, by adjusting the dial or the setting on his machine, how thickly or lightly he wanted to plant his sugar beets.[1] Just as with the tomato seeds in Iowa, scientists working with sugar beets had supposedly perfected the seeds. The machines did the rest.

With the long hoe as the new implement of choice, my father, my brother, and I hit the North Dakota beet fields at a clip just short of a jog that year. We had never covered so much territory in a single day. And, in accordance with the new scheme of things brought about by the change in tools, a new hierarchy based on hoeing prowess also had to be worked out. My younger brother, the athlete who would start college at the end of that harvest season, led the way. He was the fastest of the three. I followed and then came my father. We were now leaving him behind, not because he had slowed down but because we were in our prime. We just went at it all day, perhaps in much the same way he himself had done just a few short years before, when he was trying to impress my mother with his manly endurance. We were doing it because we wanted to finish and get out of there. My sisters went at their own pace, but at least now that they were using long hoes, they were able to avoid the indignity of being stooped over the rows with their behinds up in the air like the men. In no time we had completed close to 180 acres that year.

We lived in beet country, surrounded by miles of nothing but fields on every side. Even the grower lived far away. He had put us up in an old abandoned house close to some trees. There was no money and so no point in going to town. As long as the fields were being readied for hoeing and the weather permitted, we did nothing else but stay on top of the thinning. As always, we followed a strict regimen. Even though we worked by the piece rate, my father did not allow us more than an hour for lunch. The grower could have cared less if we worked ten or twelve hours per day, if we took exactly one hour for lunch or not. He was a nice guy and didn't pay attention to those details. But at home he was not the authority; my father was. And that meant we had to work hard and steady in order to impress our new host, to show him we were responsible workers. That way we would be assured of a place to work sugar beets the following year. And, knowing my father, he wanted to finish so we could get paid and that meant he, in turn, would be able to go to town and pay off the food bill he was constantly worried about. Just like in Montana, the growers made arrangements with merchants in town so workers could get their groceries on credit during the sugar-beet harvest. When that was over, we got paid, they got paid, and then we could leave.

While work was coming to an end, my resentment was not. What tormented me more than anything else that season was not being able to see my girlfriend. V. kept writing to me, and I would pour out my soul to her. We were so far from each other. Here I was with two years of college, had graduated with distinction and gotten awards, and I was still hoeing sugar beets. I had no friends to talk to. Some of them had gotten married, others had dropped out of school. Everyone had taken off in different directions. I had begun to lose any hope of seeing her again. At first her letters were nice and thick, filled with amorous details and fantasies of what we'd do once we were together again. I fantasized right back. I told her I was worried that she was living in a large city with a military base, that she was very attractive, and that she spoke flawless English. I didn't stand a chance. I was stuck in some farm surrounded by fields of sugar beets. We saw no one, we worked in the fields all day, and I spoke poor English. How could I overcome so many disadvantages? I was truly desperate, but I went on suffering in silence. I was not a college student; I was still a migrant.

But, as it turned out, Drayton, North Dakota, was the last place I hoed sugar beets in. We finished around mid-July, got paid, and took off for Iowa to work in the tomato harvest. Before we left, though, there was one more chore we had to take care of. I'm not sure if it had been part of the deal my father and the grower had worked out before I got there, but my brother and I were asked to clean out the water cistern before we left. The grower had left us a big truck with a water tank on top so we could bring in water during our stay there. That was how we kept ourselves supplied with water. But since we were good Mexicans, we were going to clean the old cistern out before leaving. After a good cleaning we would haul in fresh water and refill it so as to leave it just as we had found it when we got there. We wore some old rubber boots he lent us for the job. My brother and I climbed down into the cistern, a cavernous cement hole, with hoses and water buckets. There were live worms and other insects swimming around at the bottom where pools of water remained. It was from there that we had drawn our drinking water all season. Good thing we had not known what was down there until the end. No one had gotten sick. We were not squeamish at all, thank God. It seemed we were used to those impurities, our bodies immune to poisons, as if our daily contact with the earth made us resistant to whatever crud we consumed. After all, ingesting some worms and other critters, even on a daily basis, was not going to keep us from working. At least not at the time. We kept quiet and obeyed . . . that was the idea.

We made the trip from Drayton, North Dakota, to Muscatine, Iowa, from one day to the next. We crossed one other state besides those two, Minnesota. There was no comparison between this trip and the earlier ones from Washington. By the time we arrived, the old pigsty where we always stayed was empty and waiting for us to move into. Since to my mother's way of thinking nothing was ever clean enough, she had us wash the floor and walls with bleach. We then hosed the whole place off and waited for things to dry. Then it was time to bring in our old bags of clothes, boxes, utensils, and my father's religious icons and his guitar. My sisters helped my mother put things away. They hung bed sheets for partitions as they always did, and at the end came the crowning jewel: my mother's twin-burner kerosene stove. Her rolling pin and board for the tortillas were wrapped in their pillowcase. I still have that board; one of my sisters has the rolling pin. But that little stove, left by the wayside after so many years, should be recognized for the service it provided all those years, thanks to my mother.

With that little stove and on that kneading board my mother satisfied the family's huge demand for tortillas. In the morning, before we left for work, she made us oatmeal and maize biscuits. Our main breakfast, which she took to us at the field, consisted of tacos (they call them breakfast tacos now): flour tortillas filled with small chunks of meat, beans, egg, and picante sauce. At noon, for lunch, we all sat around a big table set in the middle of the pigsty. At the center of the table there was a large bowl lined with dish towels and from there we each drew however many tortillas we wanted. The usual number of men eating was four or five and each ate easily three or four tortillas. Four tortillas per male makes twenty. The three girls ate no more than two each. Twenty-six tortillas for lunch. Same thing at supper time. That makes fifty-two, plus fifteen or twenty for our regular breakfast, which adds up to seventy tortillas per day without counting the ones she and the grandkids had. We ate like that every day, except on Saturdays. Everybody, except my mother, went downtown after lunch and spent the rest of the day there. Let's say she made seventy-some odd tortillas per day six days a week. That adds up to over four hundred tortillas per week, every single one of them made from scratch! Actually, that reliable little stove where she made tortillas by the hundreds was not the jewel. The real jewel was my mother.

By August people were already doing the first pickings. As usual, I started working as the stacker. My brothers-in-law did most of the hauling now. We were all familiar with the routine. The grower employed a full-time maintenance man at the farm, and he took care of the upkeep. When we started working, the tractors were ready for us to climb on board and take off. He also made sure that all the trailers were in good working order. He greased the wheels, changed the oil, and always warned us about what to look out for when we took the equipment out on the road. The fields where the tomato crop was planted varied little from year to year. They were the same gentle hills, the same valleys and meadows extending out from the edge of town. As the weeks went by and the pickers produced more, we all worked more and more hours to keep up. It was not unusual for us to be loading and hauling 'til late at night. We just turned the tractor lights on and kept going, whether in the fields or on the road.

As the tempo of the activity in and around the farm gradually intensified it signaled something else as well. The time for me to leave was fast approaching. It was never easy to bring up the topic. Beginning a few days before departure time, conversations would start to take a different turn. It was my father's responsibility to load all the tomato crop and haul it out of the fields no matter how much was picked. When just a single worker from the crew was missing, it complicated things for him. The crew had been working together from the beginning of the picking season to keep up with the pickers: load, haul, distribute empties, making sure it all went smoothly and people didn't waste their time. Nobody liked to sit around and wait for empty baskets while others were picking. When the picking was at its best, one could feel the tension between us and the pickers. And I couldn't help feeling that tension myself. My leaving just made it worse. First, what I would do was to find a way to talk about the importance of getting an education, of finding a better way to make a living, of a better future for us. From there I changed the subject to transportation. I'd mention how I had been keeping an eye out for an old car, how it was important to arrive back in Texas in time to register for classes, and how important it was for me not to fail to fulfill my obligations.

That was important: fulfilling one's obligations. I tried not to make it seem as if I were being selfish, but it wasn't easy. They stayed behind working while I left. How was I to avoid feeling guilty? The first thing that had to be decided was who would take my place stacking baskets on the wagons. Who would replace me and who would communicate with the grower when there were incidents like those of previous years? My father said nothing; that made it worse because it made me feel even guiltier. That September I used my brother as an ally to help me ease my conscience and also to help me make my getaway with a minimum of damage to the family. We convinced him to buy a used 1955 Chevy that we both would drive. That was the clincher: both of us could use it to go to college. It was not an elegant '55 or the classic kind; it was the cheap variety. But that was the car I used to drive back to Texas and start my first year at the university. It was the end of August or the beginning of September. The understanding was that, when they returned to Texas, I would hand the car over to my brother so he could use it. Since I was attending the university, I would be staying at one of the dormitories. I didn't need a car.

I left early by mistake. I could have stayed another week to help with the loading and the hauling. When I arrived at the university, the dorms were just being readied. Classes had not yet started. Unconsciously what I wanted to do was to abandon my life as a migrant worker forever, but I could not admit as much to myself. That was the same as saying I wanted to abandon my family, that I considered myself more important than they were. I didn't quite understand it at the time, but I sensed somehow that there was some validity to that way of thinking. I was facing a whole new future, and that meant having to adapt to a more modern way of life. To live as if in exile from my own family and at the same time divorced from the soil was a bit much to take in all at once, just like that. Best to do it like the gringos said, "First things first." I got in touch with the Selective Service Board in Uvalde to make sure I still had my 1-s classification. They were drafting plenty of young men my age to go to Vietnam, and I didn't want to be one of them.

CHAPTER 19

|||||||||||||||||||||||||||||||||||||||||||||||||||||||||||||||||||||||||||

Adjusting to Academic Life in San Marcos

The first year I went to the university at Southwest Texas State in San Marcos, I ended up at Arnold Hall. The dorm is still there. At the time, it was one of several where single males were housed, and that's where I spent a year with the new roommate that chance and the gringos assigned to me when I arrived. He was, of course, a Mexican like me, one of the few at the university at the time. He called himself a "Metsican" American but I understood what he meant. I don't remember his last name, but his first name was Carlos. He was a dude from San Antonio, rather short and with a compact build, my color or a bit darker. His hair was black and kinky and he had a heavy beard and thick lips. He could have been mistaken for an Arab or a Turk, except that he had the easygoing manner of someone who was socially well assimilated.

We had no problems. He went off to his classes, I went to mine, and it was rare for us to see anymore of each other during the day. Better for me; I noticed right away that he felt uncomfortable speaking Spanish even though he understood it. We had nothing in common. He never talked to me about his family. I never met any of his friends or even a girlfriend; he never asked me for anything nor did I ask him. He was courteous with me and I with him, and that was it. I knew no one; no one knew me. Carlos and I lived in the same room in a large dormitory, but it was as if I lived with an imaginary being. We didn't seek each other out for anything. Our lives were lived in total anonymity. It seemed to me that ours was the kind of impersonal relationship symptomatic of university life in general. That was okay with me, and I supposed it was the same for him. That empty space previously occupied by my family was now taken up by the institution: there was a schedule for lunch, a schedule for class, a schedule for turning out the lights, and a monitor to remind us when we were being too noisy. I adapted as best I could to the new regimen, and I buckled down with my new subjects: chemistry, French, English, Spanish-American literature, and Spanish conversation!

I did not do too badly the first semester, and when my first encounter with academia at the university level was over, my name even appeared in the local newspaper.[1] Yet from the very beginning my first disappointments were the professors. Or at least some of them. It's not that I wish to be critical: I'm simply being sincere. I had decided to attend Southwest Texas State in San Marcos because I wanted to study under a professor there who was well known in the field I was interested in. He had been my instructor at Uvalde Junior College when I first went there. I hadn't studied under him at the time. He had only been appointed by the administration to monitor my Advanced Placement work. But I had heard good things about him. I found his name on the class schedule, and I signed up for one of his classes. But after meeting him in class I was disillusioned. He was timid and monotonous. He had a gentle demeanor, but he didn't inspire me. He gave me the impression he did not want to call attention to himself. What was interesting to me was that he came from San Antonio, like my roommate. I even found similarities in their personalities. They were both introverted; they smiled a lot and spoke in a low, cautious tone of voice. But since there were no other Mexican American professors at the university, I sensed that that had something to do with it: he did not want to attract too much attention to himself because he was overly conscious of being the fly in the ointment at the institution.

There were two other professors who taught Spanish in the department, a gringo and a gringa. They were just the opposite of the Mexican. The gringo literature professor entertained us just by his ostentatious manner of speaking the language. Not only did he speak Spanish perfectly well, he seemed to savor using it. He pronounced every single word as if he were dictating some important document in public. He made faces and imitated the speech of characters in the novels and poems and added drama to the plays we read in class. He loved Tirso de Molina, the seventeenth-century Spanish dramatist, he recited with flair the gaucho poetry of José Hernández,[2] and he got all emotional with the short stories of Juan Rulfo.[3] It was he who got me seriously interested in Latin American Literature. From the time many years earlier when I had learned how to conjugate verbs with *Profesor* Rivera, until now this was the first time I had been taught something new and exciting in my own tongue. Everything else I had studied had come from within the perspective of Anglo American civilization. Another world was opening up to me now, one I had been searching for since I didn't know when but which I recognized once this professor introduced me to it. I had expected as much from the other professor, but it was not meant to be.

When he talked to us in class about his divorce and about some of the other personal disenchantments he was living through, my initial enthusiasm for him began to wane. I was not accustomed to listening to such intimate details about my professors' lives. But, in spite of it all, he was a good teacher, and I learned a lot from him. With the linguistics professor that was not the case. She had the big disadvantage, students complained, that she knew a lot but she could not communicate it very well. She confused herself, and her pronunciation was defective. I took a couple of her classes in literature, but by then I had gotten conveniently used to her uninspiring teaching style. For those of us who spoke the language well, we could easily count on getting an A with her even when we did not merit the grade. But I nevertheless took her classes more than once.

I finished the semester with a decent overall grade point average. My name began to appear in the local newspaper rather frequently.[4] I started receiving invitations. They came from Sigma Delta Pi, "Outstanding Students in American Colleges and Universities," and other such organizations. Of course, the extra attention made me feel special. Here and there, gringas from different honorary organizations would talk to me.[5] And that was how my name reached the ears of the Head of the Department, a short blond German with a crew cut who was very ambitious and who had a big heart. He was the professional administrator par excellence. He taught a single course every semester which we all had to take sooner or later. The rest of the time he was out soliciting funds for this or that new program. He was constantly on the move; like a hyperactive juvenile, he rarely slowed down. And he was as involved in academia as he was in the community. He was a full-fledged Baptist Minister at the local First Baptist Church. In the end, it was he who altered the course of my life at the university more than any other professor I had there.

It was during my second semester that he called me to visit him at his office. It was in the spring of 1966. He explained to me that the institution had received a federal grant for the summer. It had to do with training Peace Corps volunteers. These volunteers, about three dozen of them, would begin arriving at the university at the beginning of June when regular classes were already over. The university had committed to providing instruction in Spanish to prepare them to teach physical education in Costa Rica. They came from several states, all of them from the north: New York, New Jersey, Rhode Island, and Massachusetts. There was only one problem, and that was where our department came in: the Peace Corps volunteers knew very little or no Spanish. We had three months to prepare them. He wanted to know if I was interested in staying around that summer to work for the Department of Modern Languages as coordinator of the language lab.

The offer came as a complete surprise. What he was offering me was nothing less than the opportunity to work inside an air-conditioned building, sitting on a nice padded swivel chair, arranging and supervising language lessons for the students in the lab. It was the first time in my life someone was paying me for what I knew rather than for what I could do. The only other occasion that more or less got close to this was when I operated the projectors at the movie theater back in Crystal City. But I had gotten that job more as a bribe for helping someone get close to my sister than for what I knew. That had been when my future brother-in-law was courting my sister. Any other kid my age could have done the job. But now I was being offered a good salary plus room and board at the dorms. What was more, I would stay on campus and had no need of a car. I sat down to write my parents. That decision represented a drastic change for the family because I was the eldest male. And now that my younger brother was starting college he couldn't go up north until late May when classes ended. What were they going to do?

The truth was that they did the same thing they had done the previous year: instead of going to the sugar-beet harvest in Washington they went to Drayton, North Dakota. Sugar-beet work didn't start there until late May when classes were over. They would simply do what they had always done. And, as far as being short-handed one worker was concerned, that was easily remedied: my father recruited a baseball buddy of my brother's, and that was how he completed the crew. They were not migrants for nothing. They weren't going to drown in a puddle. I was not as indispensable as I thought I was.

That spring semester did not turn out as I would have wanted, but I got the courses that I needed for my teacher certification out of the way even though they bored me: Chemistry, Education and Methodology courses, along with a couple that were more to my liking: American Literature and Physical Ed. By the time I stepped out of my last exam toward the end of May, I already knew where and for whom I would be working, where I would be staying, and even how much I was going to get paid. It was something new to me, this business of knowing ahead of time how I was going to live my life. At home we were used to seeing the future as a big unknown where only one thing was certain: if you didn't work, you didn't eat. Thus, we were always searching. And it was precisely for that reason that we survived. Not knowing what to expect from life, we were prepared for anything and thus nothing was impossible. But that also meant we hid in our own world and not much light came in from the outside. Ours was a physical kind of labor, not an intellectual one. And now I was going to rub shoulders with professionals; I'd be working alongside other professors and students from different parts of the country, all of whom were coming together in one place to teach and learn.

The Department Head hired two part-time professors to teach Spanish to the Peace Corps volunteers. They were both working on a doctoral degree in Spanish at the University of Texas at Austin and they were brothers. They came from The Valley, like some of the sugar-beet workers we had run into in Washington. When I was introduced to them, I immediately noticed how different they were from the other professors at our university. They joked around and laughed with the rest of us, without putting on airs, just like normal people. They were completely different from the other Mexican American professor who taught there. By observing them closely I began to notice what those differences consisted of: they chatted and laughed with the students in the same good-natured way as they did with the other professors. And they talked about every subject imaginable: girlfriends, the War in Vietnam, the latest fads in literary criticism. They appeared to be intellectuals without being offensive or intrusive about it, and they knew how to listen. They called things by their exact names. They called pens *bolígrafos* instead of *plumas*, they said *cochera* (car garage) instead of *garaje* and *texto* instead of *libro*. I had never in my life known people like them.

The same thing was true for the volunteers. Fifty-five of them had arrived although only thirty–some odd were left by the end of the program. It seemed to me that they came from another world. To begin with, they did not keep the same distance as the Texas gringos did when speaking to people. They got close just as they did when they spoke amongst themselves, and they also listened with genuine interest. I'd get tongue-tied when trying to explain things to them because they looked at me earnestly, waiting for me to explain, and I was not used to that. In the Texas tradition when speaking to gringos we learned to listen quietly—or at least I did—but we were not expected to offer any explanations or rebuttals in return. And to make things even more unreal, they actually wanted my opinion on things. Little by little I was emerging from the cave.

The truth of the matter was that the laid-back, ivory tower world I was just becoming familiar with, that had appeared to me so sweet and tantalizing (as the Nicaraguan poet Rubén Darío puts it), suddenly showed that it also had an unpredictable and far more sinister side to it. August 1st, 1966 started out like any other normal day at the laboratory. I arrived early in the morning, opened the drawers where we kept the lab materials, took everything out and arranged the pieces in their usual place. By then I had had plenty of practice. I placed the cassettes with the day's lesson in the machines, I checked all the equipment and just made sure everything was in proper working order for when the the Peace Corps volunteers came in. We always started working between nine and nine thirty in the morning. They walked in, took their stations, and listened to the lesson. Once in a while a student (there were both males and females in the group) raised a hand. They wanted to know if I could replay some part of a lesson, if this or that was correct, stuff like that. Since it all had to do with Spanish, particularly with the pronunciation, I helped out and corrected simple errors.

We were in the thick of one such lesson when someone suddenly stuck their head through the door. I don't recall who it was, but they yelled at us excitedly to go and listen to what was happening. Some of the students understood and some did not; because of the momentary confusion, not all of us got up to leave at the same time. I didn't wait, though. Following the commotion, we ran directly to the classroom where one of the two brother professors taught his Spanish classes. He and a group of students gathered around him were listening to a radio that had the volume turned up unusually high, as when one listens to a baseball game. He was looking around, as if distraught, when we began crowding into the room. I had not seen that strange look on his face before. What he was telling the group already gathered there, when we were able to hear, was that they were killing people at the University of Texas, that someone had climbed up to the highest floor of the University Library Tower and was shooting from there with a high-powered rifle. I also remember he said, his voice breaking with emotion, "My girlfriend is there! She's on campus!" His brother was by his side. In the back of the room, shocked students could be heard muttering, speaking in unintelligible voices, as some others covered their mouths in disbelief. Then I began to hear the shots distinctly. After each shot rang out, people cringed or shook or trembled; tears were visible on the faces of Volunteers. The announcer's voice trembled too as he attempted to capture in terrified words the senseless carnage he was witnessing. Little by little we began to comprehend what was taking place as he presented listeners with the graphic details: an unknown number of people had been killed, the gunman was shooting victims in different parts of the campus, what we were witnessing was a massacre. We were paralyzed for I don't know how long, things became eerily quiet, and only the harsh piercing sounds coming from the radio could be heard. In a total stupor, some of us stared at no one in particular as if in a daze.

His name was Charles Whitman, ex-U.S. Marine, who had climbed to the top of the old Library Tower at the University of Texas and from up there was mowing down pedestrians on campus with a high-powered rifle. He chose his victims arbitrarily; he shot men as well as women, young and old regardless. Many, probably most of them, had no idea what was happening when the shots rang out. His gun had a high-definition scope; he could hit people several blocks away. Others were slain close by, as they walked out of class or out of their offices. It was close to noon. But even with all the commotion going on, the City of Austin Police Department didn't take long to respond as soon as they got the word. Four of them, amongst them Ramiro Martínez, went directly to the Tower and climbed all the way up to where Whitman was. When they finally got to him, after more than an hour of his raining down death on the people below, Martínez and McCoy shot him to death with a gun and a rifle. He had killed sixteen people and wounded thirty-two.[6] He wrote these brief words before embarking on his campaign of terror (his first victims were his wife and his mother): "I truly do not believe this world to be worth living in . . ."[7]

CHAPTER 20

||||||||||||||||||||||||||||||||||||||||||||||||||||||||||||||||||||||||||||||||

Leaving the Migrant Trail

There was no denying I missed my family. I hadn't seen them in months. The Whitman massacre, with all its depravity and as traumatic as it turned out to be, was but a single instance of the violence that assailed Americans of all stripes at the time, rich and poor alike. It was therefore not unusual to seek solace in some form of escape or another. One began to hear students talk about LSD, about getting high, about all kinds of psychedelic trips. It was all Greek to me. If the young people were seeking relief from their suffering in drugs, I was suffering from bouts of severe nostalgia. Next to the images of railroad flatcars loaded with the caskets of the latest Vietnam casualties traversing the country, in my everyday thoughts I found myself juxtaposing events of my recent and more innocent past. The explosions and bombing runs we saw on television clashed in my own consciousness with longings for the words and sounds of my own people, for the familiar aromas of our kitchen, for the noises and laughter of our after-dinner chatter. How to understand such anomalies, these brutal explosions of violence, coming from the very heart of academia? Whether attending a prestigious university or working in the sugar-beet and tomato fields, it seemed to me no one in the country was immune from wholesale violence anymore. And no, it was not just happening on the other side of world either. It was also coming at us from a major American university just a few short miles up the road from where I was a student that summer.

The fact of the matter was that the shadow of Vietnam followed us no matter where we went, and that was true not only for me but for all the normal young males of my generation. When I turned eighteen we were hoeing sugar beets in Moses Lake, Washington. Up there I received a letter from the Selective Service System. I had to show up at Spokane, Washington, for two exams, a physical and a written one. Several kids and I from the barracks took off a couple of days from work. Those dudes were more on the ball than I was. They failed one or in some instances both of the tests. They took some crap so that their urine came out positive; on the written test they wrote nonsense. But I thought of myself above all that. For me it was a matter of pride to show the gringos that I knew how to read and write, that I had a healthy mind in a healthy body. It didn't take long before I received my new classification in the mail: 1-s (Student Grade 1). I was still in school then. I would keep that classification until I finished my baccalaureate degree four years later. If I dropped out of school, I was required to inform the government or risk jail and a fine.

That had been when I was eighteen years old. Now there were new rumors flying around. Casualties in Vietnam kept climbing and there was no end in sight to the carnage. Secretary of Defense McNamara was now recruiting holdouts, illiterates, and dropouts. He had just come out with the brand new idea of retesting 100,000 more young men from those who had failed the Selective Service exams the first time around. The passing grade had been lowered to assure they didn't fail. It was called the Armed Forces Qualification Test.[1] The exam was ridiculously easy. Anybody could pass it. That was the idea.

There was another exam for those of us already enrolled in college. One morning when I was still enrolled, I went to take it. By coincidence we were sent to the same room where I had taken an advanced English Grammar course the year before. Evidently the university and the professors—some of them at least—were in cahoots with the federal government to recruit enlistees. I recognized the professor who was to administer the test.

When I first registered for her class the year before, I had heard she had a reputation for being quite demanding. I had taken the class anyway. I didn't do so badly. I remember walking out of her midterm exam with a smile on my face. She had loaded the exam with all kinds of clauses: noun, adjective, adverbial, appositives. That was my forte. Thanks to my old high-school teacher, Mrs. Lunz, we had practiced just such grammatical constructions backwards and forwards for a whole semester. I finished in twenty minutes. "I'm finished," I said to her. She didn't believe me. "Check your work." I went over it once more. I looked around; the students were all gringos with maybe one or two exceptions, and they all appeared lost in concentration. I let her know again, and this time she came over. A week later she returned the exams. I had gotten an A. I was expecting it.

But things were different now because it was not just a case of taking some ordinary exam. We were actually putting our lives on the line. If you failed the exam, you had no more choices: the university was obligated to kick you out. You would then be at the mercy of the Selective Service System. Everybody knew that kids were signing up for college and university classes to avoid the draft. According to calculations making the rounds then, the military estimated that by retesting single men between the ages of eighteen and twenty-four, a goodly number would fail. From there a draft-eligible pool of recruits would become available. And it would not take long to assemble: you failed, you walked.[2] A few weeks later, when we went to pick up the results, I witnessed a scene I've never forgotten. Some of us were going up the stairs and others coming back down after having picked up the official-looking letter with the grade inside. I had no doubt I had passed. So I just walked leisurely up the stairs. Amidst all of the commotion I noticed a student who was coming down the stairs, a fair-haired gringo dressed in informal, after-school attire, an empty, painful expression on his face. He dabbed at his eyes with one hand as he stared at an open letter he held in front of him on the other hand. He was one of those who, with the complicity of the institution, had been snared in the net set up by the State to trap victims.

The 1966–1967 academic year was beginning. I had not spent that summer that had just ended working in the fields up north, but rather running a language laboratory for the university's Peace Corps program. It was something new for me to stay behind in Texas during the summer. I had not realized how boring life was without working or studying. For me the job running the lab was not work. I rarely went out, but my room and board were covered, and I got paid regularly. I managed to save some money. I started looking around for a used car so I didn't have to walk everywhere. There was a red and white four-door 1956 Chevy v8 I was interested in. It belonged to a guy from Crystal City who had used it to go to college himself. He was a teacher now and was getting rid of it. We talked, and when I brought him the money he had it ready. Then I got lucky again. As we were matriculating, one of my former baseball teammates from Crystal City came up behind me and called my name. "Come and stay with me," he said in Spanish. "I just rented a small house." He didn't have to tell me twice. I had gotten tired of the regimented existence in the dorms. The first thing I did was to go to Student Housing to ask for my deposit back. I still remember the man's answer because he said it to me in a loud, rude voice, "You ain't gettin' no deposit back. You don't know the trouble you just put us through." We were in Texas all right. It didn't surprise me. I went back to the dorm, picked up my stuff and set off to look for my ex-teammate who had invited me to share the rental house. It was a couple of blocks from the University.

I had not seen my family in over six months. In May, after my brother graduated from high school, they had gone to work in the sugar beets in North Dakota. I was just finishing the second semester at the university, and my new job at the language lab was waiting. We had agreed that I would stay behind in Texas. They finished doing the thinning and weeding with help from my brother's companion, and when that was over they went to Iowa for the tomato harvest following the same cycle we had been following since 1958. By then only three of my sisters, my brother, and my parents were living together. To help him with the loading and hauling, my father had recruited another of his brothers and a nephew. That was the year that the young man whose family had been living at the farm when we first arrived came back from Vietnam. He had finished high school there, he knew English, and he had not wanted to be a migrant all his life. But he did not go to college either. We did not find out until much later, because he himself told us, that he had volunteered for Vietnam. He preferred that to working in the fields. He was back now, alive though with several scars on his body and in his psyche, to elope with another one of my sisters. Who was left?

I went to see them in November when they returned. I walked in the house and went straight to the kitchen. My brother was not there. My sisters —the two who were left—were shut up in their room doing their thing. My father was sipping coffee at the old table with aluminum legs. My mother, her arms crossed over her breast, stood by the stove. They knew I was coming, and they were happy to see me, but there wasn't much commotion to speak of inside. In town, school was out; it was Thanksgiving. As far as they were concerned, though, it didn't matter. If it wasn't the Day of the Virgin of Guadalupe or the Feast of St. John's, they were not in any mood to celebrate anything else. And Christmas meant Christmas Eve only. It had always been like that. Their customs, when we were not up north working, did not include celebrating events outside their own tradition. There they stood now, symbols of domestic authority, settled comfortably in their home and hearth and totally at peace within their own space. In figurative terms, they had guided me through the labyrinth of adolescence and led me to the exit from the cave. And they had done it in their own way, following their own instincts and family traditions that went back for at least three generations. I had now matured and could fend for myself.

At that time, final exams at the universities were administered after Christmas, not before, like it's done today. We celebrated, or those who were in the habit of celebrating did, and then we went back to prepare for finals. I had registered for five classes in the fall of 1966. The following year, around the end of February or the beginning of March when I arrived at our rental house one day, I found a letter from the Dean of the University addressed to me. In it he expressed his congratulations to me for having received five A's in the semester that had just ended. The letter also said I had been awarded a $1,000 scholarship and for me to come by his office to pick up the check!

I went by the Dean's Office the next day. A receptionist quietly handed me an official-looking envelope, congratulated me with a very formal smile, and saw me out the door. The award was an acknowledgment by the university, I thought, that I had achieved my goal, that I had finally arrived at my destination. I didn't have anyone to share the excitement with, so my thoughts turned to money. As I walked back to our little rental house I began crunching numbers in my head. My tuition for the last semester was covered and I had money left over. Back then tuition and fees did not set you back more than $150 per semester. You could buy all of your books for $50. Our rent was $120 per month divided by two. I even had my own bank account in town. I paid for my purchases with a check now. Before, I scrambled for money every month and paid everything in cash.

In April recruiters representing school districts from various parts of the country came to interview prospective teachers. I interviewed at several places. Texas public school salaries were ridiculously low. When I went to

11

Young sugar-beet workers during a day of rest. The
author at 15 years of age (on the right) with a cousin in
the state of Washington during the decade of the fifties.
Courtesy of Mrs. Gloria S. Casas.

speak with the people from the Bakersfield Independent School District, they offered me a contract for twice as much. I signed right then and there, and after that, I stepped onto a sugar-beet field only once more in my life. But it was not as a migrant. It was just to show off to some colleagues in California that I still had what it took. I got paid at the end of the day and never returned.

I still have family on my father's side who go work in the sugar-beet harvest. They are the sons and daughters of those ancestors who first went up to Mason City, Iowa, to hoe sugar beets in the thirties and the forties. They didn't go to any schools, and they didn't fight in any of the wars. But just like our ancestors in the past, they can't wait for the month of May to come around so they can go to *el norte*. They still do the thinning and weeding by hoe. They finish, get paid, and come back to Texas. They don't have to go. They are retired; some have a pension. But it is their way of remaining tied to the soil, of reinvigorating their masculinity by thumping the dirt or chopping away at the weeds with a hoe. But I think there is a deeper, more instinctive motive for maintaining their traditional way of life. The family is their point of reference, and by following the migrant stream, they retain their tribal affiliation. At that stage in their lives, *being* a migrant is not important. What is important is to live out the migrant experience, and the only way to do that is to be a member of a group, to be part of a family. If you ask them why they keep following the migrant stream year in and year out, they'll just shrug their shoulders and answer the same way they always have, with a question: "*¿Pos qué más hace uno?*" ("What else is there to do?"). They'll say in their colloquial Spanish. "*¿Quedarse de flojo?*" ("Become a lazy bum?"). "Like you?" is understood. Flojo is "lazy" in informal Spanish, but its formal meaning is to be "loose" or "unattached." In other words, to be separated from the group, to be an individual. If you knew them as I do, you'd understand exactly what they mean. They are just like our ancestors (figure 11).

Notes

Introduction

1. David Lowenthal, *Possessed by the Past*, p. 106.

2. Gringos = Euroamericans in the informal parlance of Spanish Speakers. See the Glossary for additional details relating to the use of the term.

3. The Lower Rio Grande Valley in South Texas. The term *The Valley* is used in state signs and maps to designate the southern most tip of Texas. Natives consider it a culturally distinct area of the state. Within the migrant community, during this era, one could easily recognize people from *El Valle*. Their use of a more traditional Spanish, the music they listened to, and their attire all set them apart from other migrants.

4. A colloquialism used by working-class Spanish Speakers in reference to themselves.

5. Literally the term *Mexican* refers to persons born in Mexico. Figuratively, the term is loaded with stereotypical connotations. See Glossary for further details.

6. All these terms are Spanish colloquialisms for poor, working-class Mexican Americans. See Glossary for further details.

7. Both terms refer to legal workers from Mexico. See Glossary for extended definitions.

8. *Raza* is a generic term that means "Mexican American descent" in colloquial Spanish.

9. Both terms are akin to "lazybones."

10. Güevón, güevona = Masculine and feminine forms. "Loafers," but with a sting added.

Chapter 1

1. Zavala County Historical Commission, *Now and Then in Zavala County*, p. 61.

2. Zavala County Historical Commission, *Now and Then in Zavala County*, p. 15.

3. Zavala County Historical Commission, *Now and Then in Zavala County*, p. 17.

Chapter 2

1. There is a rhymed letter that a first cousin of my father's writes from Elmore, Minnesota, to his brother in Crystal City dated May 15, 1935. This is what it says: "Life in Crystal City is hell / Though it really hurts to tell / Without Uncle Sam's help / You are sure to starve to death." And a little further on: "Not here; we all eat now / And have a place to sleep / Though we're not fat / We do have our bellies full." (Author's translation).

2. Dennis Nodín Valdés, *Settlers, Sojourners, and Proletarians: Social Formation in the Great Plains Sugar Beet Industry, 1890–1940* (DigitalCommons@University of Nebraska-Lincoln, 1990), http://digitalcommons.unl.edu/greatplainsquarterly/418.

3. The term has a storied history in sugar-beet worker tradition. See Glossary.

4. Valdés, *Settlers, Sojourners, and Proletarians*, pp. 116–17.

5. Harvesting onions means to cut off the root or stem or both from each onion before sacking them.

6. This comes from conversations that I remember. The reference is to the time and places where my father's family worked.

7. Two generations later, a great nephew of theirs, Santiago "Jimmy" Casas Sánchez, was named High School Principal of the Year for the state of Iowa for the year 2012. He lives and works in Bettendorf, Iowa. He was informed at the end of June, 2012, that he was one of three finalists left in the competition for the 2013 NASSP/ Metlife National High School Principal of the Year.

Chapter 3

1. "Historical Timeline: A Story of Progress," *American Crystal Sugar Company*, http://www.crystalsugar.com/coopprofile/history.aspx.

2. Valdés, *Settlers, Sojourners, and Proletarians*, p. 116.

3. Mariachis = Groups of musicians who play traditional Mexican ballads. Their folk music is popular in the Mexican American communities both in Mexico and in the United States.

Chapter 4

1. My guess is that this dates to 1946 or 1947.

2. It was 1945 or 1946 according to what I've been told by an older sister.

3. Gabriel García Márquez, *Los funerales de la Mamá Grande*, a collection of short stories published in 1962.

4. We called them *pichilacos* in Spanish. They were probably yellow-breasted winter warblers.

5. El Avispero = "The Hornet's Nest" or also "The Beehive."

6. "The American School."

Chapter 5

1. Mexicanitos is the diminutive of mexicano.

2. Saúl Sánchez, *Hay Plesha Lichans Tu Di Flac* (Berkeley: Quinto Sol Publications, 1976). The title is a phonetic rendition in Spanish of "I pledge allegiance to the flag."

Chapter 6

1. "Migrant worker" and not *obrero migratorio.* The Spanish translation was considered too formal; thus, the English expression was preferred.

2. Bonus money = growers normally deducted a few cents per hour or unit (basket, hamper, sack) from a worker's pay to guarantee they would stay until all the work had been completed. It was separate from Social Security.

Chapter 7

1. *Teatro Campesino* was the famous California-based people's theater group founded by Luis Valdez. It grew out of, and was associated with, the César Chávez grape-strike workers in Delano, California in the mid-1960s.

2. The phrase rhymes in Spanish, *"Ya vete, Kenete,"* and being kids, we'd delight in repeating it to him. He'd just laugh good-naturedly.

3. NAACP = National Association for the Advancement of Colored People.

Chapter 8

1. Considered the poorest working-class barrio in Crystal City at the time.

Chapter 9

1. Bushels were for packing spinach; twine was for tying set onion plants in bunches before chopping off stems and packing them in crates.

2. Sugar-company agents rented El Teatro Nacional for a few weeks in the spring and used it as a gathering place to sign up migrants interested in going north to hoe sugar beets.

3. In formal Spanish, *calavera* means "skull." The colloquial version refers to the work implement as well.

4. In this context *machitos* means "little he-men."

5. The literal meaning is given here. See Glossary for an extended explanation.

6. I am guessing here. All I remember for certain is that there were three large beet fields. This was the third. We hoed between 150 and 200 acres of sugar beets that season with that particular grower. A third of that would come out to between fifty and seventy-five acres.

Chapter 10

1. The rhythmic beat of "Dos arbolitos" and "Canción huasteca" is called *huapango* in Spanish. It is complicated to do, and I've known very few non-professional musi-

cians who master it. My father learned it as a young aspiring guitarist from the *Trío Tariácuri*, who were considered the premier huapango players of their time, when they came to perform at the Luna Theater in Crystal City in the 1940s. "Usted" is a classical Mexican *bolero*.

2. In sugar-beet work each shoot must be between twelve and fourteen inches from the other so that plants, as they grow, have enough space to produce adequate tubers for harvesting. At this stage (weeding), they are no longer shoots, they are plants.

Chapter 11

1. There was one year, when I was a sophomore, that an English teacher scolded me in front of the class for coming in during the month of November, a week before Thanksgiving. We had been picking cotton in west Texas. They were reading *Othello* in class.

2. The Civil Rights Act that officially desegregated schools in Texas and put an end to the legacy of Jim Crow was not passed by Congress until the Johnson Administration in 1967: four years after I graduated from high school.

3. Here, Mexican refers to "group identity" in a linguistic sense: our Mexican-accented English identified us as members of the same group regardless of where we were born. See Glossary for additional comments on the word.

4. See Michael Lind, *The Next American Nation: The New Nationalism and the Fourth American Revolution* (New York: The Free Press, 1995).

5. Laissez faire = To "let do" in French, a nineteenth-century capitalist version of no government regulations.

Chapter 12

1. According to one family source, it was Kalona; according to another, it was Columbus Junction. "There were lots of Mennonites" the first sources recalled. But, according to my second family source, there are also Amish communities in the area. The fact remains that it was tomato country, and it lies due west not far from the Mississippi River.

2. I base this observation on subsequent conversations with pickers who continued to go there over a span of many years. Things deteriorated soon after this episode with the arrival of ever-greater numbers of pickers.

3. *Pepena* = the Spanish term as used here means "to pick off" or "to pull off" the vines what few ripe tomatoes there are without molesting the plants.

Chapter 13

1. *Raza* = The term means "race" in formal Spanish, but in the colloquial sense it means "Mexican Americans." See Glossary for an extended explanation.

2. Matt S. Meir and Feliciano Rivera, *Mexican Americans/American Mexicans: From*

Conquistadores to Chicanos (New York: Hill and Wang, 1993), p. 208. See also Mario T. García, Mexican Americans: Leadership, Ideology and Identity, 1930–1960 (New Haven: Yale University Press, 1989), for a comprehensive view of the subject.

3. passo = Political Association of Spanish-Speaking Organizations. mapa = Mexican-American Political Association.

4. Ellwyn R. Stoddard, *Mexican Americans* (New York: Random House, 1973), pp. 190–91.

5. I have surveyed all of the *Mexicano* students who graduated from high school with me that year and went on to college. Not a single one of them received orientation from the school counselor.

6. This is not official; rather, it is based on my own calculations which I obtained by finding out how my companions were ranked. I extrapolated from there.

7. If we were doing the thinning at sixteen dollars an acre, for example, they offered to do it for twelve.

Chapter 14

1. Translation of figurative, poetic language does not do justice to these titles. Suffice it to say that these folk songs are old, traditional lover's ballads sung and played in a slow, mournful nostalgic tone. People of the barrio knew them by heart back in those times.

Chapter 16

1. *Cholo* = What we call *pachucos* in some parts of the country, and in Texas particularly, are known as *cholos* in California.

Chapter 17

1. I am no longer sure about their city of origin. They could also have been from Sunnyside, where we went to play a game on another occasion. What I am certain about is that they were from out-of-town.

2. tsea = Texas State Education Association.

Chapter 18

1. This is an abbreviated version of the stories we heard heading into the last years of working in the sugar beets. It is obviously told from the workers' point of view, not from the point of view of professional scientists or agricultural experts.

Chapter 19

1. The article appeared in the *Zavala County Sentinel* in May, 1965, under the heading "Three Students Named to Dean's List," and it has the names of three students from Zavala County who received academic distinction that year. My name appears there along with that of two Anglo American females.

2. José Hernández = Nineteenth-century Argentine poet.

3. Juan Rulfo = Twentieth-century Mexican short story writer.

4. My mother kept copies of the newspaper clippings until the end of her life.

5. The president of the Chemistry Club, for instance, invited me to join their ranks.

6. According to one of the reports, he wounded thirty people; according to another, 32.

7. Marlee McLeod, "Charles Whitman: The Texas Tower Sniper," *Crime Library: Criminal Minds and Methods*, http://www.trutv.com/library/crime/notorious _murders/mass/whitman/index_1.html.

Chapter 20

1. For additional background information on the topic see George Mariscal, *Aztlán and Viet Nam: Chicano and Chicana Experiences of the War* (University of California Press, 1999).

2. See introduction of George Mariscal, *Aztlán and Viet Nam*, pp. 15–46.

Glossary

Adjectives in Spanish use a variety of forms. They are not limited to singular and plural (i.e., *pachuco/pachucos*). Standard adjectives frequently use four forms: two for gender (masculine and feminine [i.e., *pachuco/pachuca*] and two for number, singular and plural [*pachucos/pachucas*]). Additional descriptive forms come from diminutives (i.e., *pachuquito/pachuquita*) or augmentatives (i.e., *pachucón/pachucona*). Written accents are required in Spanish for correct grammatical usage and for proper pronunciation. Accent marks indicate either a stressed syllable (i.e., *cámara*), a change in meaning (i.e., *él = he; el = the*) or a change in pronunciation of a letter (i.e., *cañón/canón*).

Arrastrado = lazybones or lazy bum; litererally one who "drags" himself from place to place or shuffles around. Also one who looks for ways to avoid hard work.

(El) Avispero = one of the segregated Mexican-American *barrios* in Crystal City. The word means "Wasp's Nest" or "Beehive" and referred to the congested quarters.

Betabeleros = literally "those who work in beets" or "who do beets." The term is loaded with semantic shades in the migrant community. As used here, it refers to the people who earned their living hoeing sugar beets, either with short or long hoes.

Braceros = guest workers from Mexico who came to the U.S. between 1942 and 1964 "as a wartime labor emergency measure to provide contract labor for agribusiness." (From Mario T. García, *Mexican Americans*, p. 52.)

Calavera = a neologism derived from the English "cultivator" that refers principally to the farm implement sugar-beet growers used to prepare crops for thinning and hoeing.

Chambón/a = in migrant informal speech it refers to a person who does sloppy work.

Chaparral = from the Spanish word *chaparro* meaning "short" or "low," as with shrubs and bushes.

Chicaspatas = a colloquialism derived from *chicas* (small or smallish) and *patas* (hooves or feet). In migrant informal Spanish its meaning is akin to "poor Mexicans" or "poor Mexican Americans."

Cholo = a variant form of *pachuco*. The term refers to marginalized Mexican or Mexican American youth. It is more commonly heard in California than in Texas.

Chorizo = Mexican-style sausage (i.e., ground pork meat) typically very greasy. A favorite (and inexpensive) food in the migrant and working class communities.

Chuco = also used to refer to marginalized Mexican or Mexican American youth; it is a shortened form of *pachuco*.

Chusma = as used in migrant communities, it means "lower class people" or "working class people" particularly when crowded into a relatively small space.

Compadre = Godfather; also bosom buddies.

Cuatas = literally "twins" or "doubles," but in sugar-beet parlance, it means leaving behind "twin-plants" (a no-no when thinning sugar beets).

Curandera = a faith healer. In the barrios and migrant communities *curanderos* and *curanderas* employed folk remedies to heal physical and psychological ailments.

Flojo/a = a milder equivalent of the term *lazy* which is used in mixed company without giving offense.

Gringo = the traditional Spanish meaning of the term is "foreigner," but in the Mexican and Mexican American communities, it is the equivalent in meaning to "Euro American." Figuratively the term denotes (in the older generations) a "them vs. us" relationship between the two prominent social groups of Americans in the Southwest, Anglo Americans and Mexican Americans. As used in this memoir, the term is meant to convey the linguistic authenticity appropriate to the times, not to give offense, and no such intent should be inferred.

Güevón/Güevona = masculine and feminine term employed to give offense to those who refuse to work.

Hoja = it means "leaf," but for spinach cutters or harvesters it referred to the practice of slicing the plant with a special knife just above the stem to collect only the leaves.

Mantenido(a) = a normal or healthy person who is averse to work and depends or relies upon his/her spouse for financial support.

Melga = in fieldwork, the section of a field comprised of a specific number of rows. In the tomato fields, one melga consisted of fourteen rows. Melgas in turn were separated from each other by narrow paths that served as roads in the confines of the field.

Mexican = the term as commonly used in popular language, especially in South Texas, is loaded with figurative and stereotypical connotations. Literally it refers to a person born in Mexico. Beyond that all other uses have historical and traditional biases attached to them. In this memoir I apply the meanings of the word that I learned growing up in South Texas.

Mexicano = the usage of the term among Spanish speakers in the U.S. Southwest mirrors the English speakers' use of "Mexican," not necessarily to denote citizenship as much as to suggest ethnicity. Beyond that, as in the word *mexicanitos*, the rules of Spanish apply. Thus, while an English speaker might prefer more commonly used circumlocutions, such as "little Mexican children," a Spanish speaker would simply apply the appropriate diminutive to the word *mexicano* (minus the final *o*): -ito, -ita, -itos, or -itas.

Mojados = wetbacks.

Pachón = as used by migrants in fieldwork, the term referred to rows of field crops that were thick with weeds.

Pachuco(a) = a marginalized Mexican or Mexican American youth, especially one who marks his/her status as an outsider with outlandish or colorful attire. The zootsuiters of California supposedly initiated the trend in style during the 1940s. From there it spread to Texas, where Pachucos cultivated their own version of the zootsuiter attire and behavioral traits.

Palomilla = a colloquialism used to denote "the (working class) people" or "people like us." Derived from *paloma* (dove) and the diminutive *illa* (small).

Peluza = also a colloquialism used to refer to an aggregate of common people, especially of working class status.

Pepena = literally "orphan" or "one abandoned." As used in migrant-worker parlance it refers to the "slim pickings" or scarce ripe tomatoes typically encountered in tomato plants during the first go-around.

Poll Tax = in Texas and elsewhere in the Southwest, a special tax levied on voters before voting. Failure to pay the fee disqualified otherwise qualified voters from voting. It was one of the Jim Crow segregationist practices, along with segregated schools, that was not ended until the passage of the Civil Rights Act of the 1960s.

Rastra = a shortened form of *arrastrado*. See entry above.

Raza = another semantically-loaded term whose literal meaning, "race," is rarely invoked. Rather, it is more commonly used in its figurative sense to express abstract notions of "ethnic solidarity" or "camaraderie."

Sinvergüenza = literally "one without shame"; i.e., a member of a social group. In this case it refers to migrants whose behavior shames the group.

Thinners = short for "beet thinners." Migrant workers who made a living harvesting sugar beets with a long- or short-handled hoe.

Topping = Spanish speakers coined the term *tapeo* from *topping* to refer to fieldwork where removing the top off of a crop (onions or sugar beets) was necessary before packing, crating, or loading.

Tronco = literally the "trunk" of a tree or "stem" of a plant. In cutting spinach, workers used the term to refer to the task of slicing the plant at an angle to bring the plant up whole, including a portion of the root (cf. *hoja*).

Wetbacks = a derogatory term that was, and is, used in Texas to refer to Spanish speakers whose ethnic profile is Hispanic. Bilinguals simply translate the word when referring to people from Mexico: "wetback" is "mojado" in Spanish. Whether true or not, the implication is that a mojado swam across the border and is thus in the U.S. illegally. The formal term in Spanish and English for government-approved Mexican agricultural workers was *Braceros*.

Bibliography

Cook, Georgina A. "Fact and Fiction: German-Russian Sugar Beet Workers in Colorado." In Sidney Heitman, ed. *Germans from Russia in Colorado*. Fort Collins, Colorado: Western Social Science Association, 1978.

García, Mario T. *Mexican Americans: Leadership, Ideology and Identity, 1930–1960*. New Haven: Yale University Press, 1989.

Lind, Michael. *The Next American Nation: The New Nationalism and the Fourth American Revolution*. New York: Free Press, 1995.

Lowenthal, David. *Possessed by the Past: The Heritage Crusade and the Spoils of History*. New York: Free Press, 1996.

Mariscal, George. *Aztlán and Viet Nam: Chicano and Chicana Experiences of the War*. Berkeley: University of California Press, 1999.

McLeod, Marlee. "Charles Whitman: The Texas Tower Sniper." *Crime Library: Criminal Minds and Methods*. <http://www.trutv.com/library/crime/notorious _murders/mass/whitman/index_1.html>.

Meir, Matt S. and Feliciano Rivera. *Mexican Americans/American Mexicans: From Conquistadores to Chicanos*. New York: Hill and Wang, 1993.

Montemayor Guerrero, Ramón. "Carta a mi hermano." *Inspiraciones Originales*. Crystal City, Texas, 1935.

Norris, Jim. "Betabeleros and Sugar Beet Growers in the Red River Valley, 1919–1973." Bismarck: North Dakota Humanities Council, 2002.

Sabin, Dana Markoff. *How Sweet It Was! The Sugar Beet Industry in Microcosm: The National Sugar Manufacturing Co., 1899–1967*. New York: Garland Publishing, 1986.

Stoddard, Ellwyn R. *Mexican Americans*. New York: Random House, 1973.

Sykes, Hope Williams. *Second Hoeing*. 1935. Lincoln: University of Nebraska Press, 1982.

Valdés, Denis N. *Settlers, Sojourners and Proletarians: Social Formation in the Great Plains Sugar Beet Industry, 1890–1940*. DigitalCommons@University of Nebraska-Lincoln, 1990. <http://digitalcommons.unl.edu/greatplainsquarterly/418>.

Zavala County Historical Commission. *Now and Then in Zavala County*. Crystal City, Texas: Zavala County Historical Commission, 1985.

Index

boxcar residence of family, 29–30

Bracero Program, xxii–xxiii, xxviii (n30)

braceros (guest workers), 3, xxviii (n30)

Breaking Through (Jiménez), xii

Brown v. the Board of Education, xx, 57–58

Buenaventura, Coahuila, Mexico, 6

Burlington, Wisconsin, 58

bushels, 189 (n1)

cabbage crops, 58, 60

calaveras (cultivators), 74

California: birth of author in, xi; cotton harvest in, 3; and internment camps, 36; labor demand in, 24; memories associated with, 28–29; nonagricultural jobs in, 5; relocations to, xxii, 24, 39–40, 51, 52, 54, 144; return to, in later life, 53–54; sugar-beet processing plants in, 16; time with aunt and uncle in, 144–48; winters in, 31

cantinas (beer joints), 38–39, 71

carpal tunnel syndrome, 164

carrots, 28

cars. *See* automobiles

car wash job, 145, 150

categories and subcategories of laborers, 2–5

Catholic nuns, 37

chain migration, xv

Chávez, César, 54, 189n1

cheaters and cheating, 2–3, 92, 122–23

children: and child labor laws, xx–xxi; income contributed by, xx; segregation of, xix–xx; translation skills of, xii–xiii, 102. *See also* education and schools

Cholo, 191 (n5)

chucos (*pachucos*), 62–64

circular migration, xiv, xviii

civil rights activism, xxiii

Coahuila, Mexico, xv, xvi, 6

collective memory, 1, 7, 22, 30

college and university studies: and academic counselor, 139–40; academic performance, 141, 155, 156, 173, 183; academic preparation for, 138–39, 180–81; ambitions for, 116–18, 152; and appendix surgery, 160; baseball team, 160; Big Bend Community College, 149, 152, 154–56, 160; buying supplies for, 136–37; college orientation, 112; competitive spirit in, 140; confidence in academic abilities, 116–17, 140; course load, 140; and dating, 135–36; and dormitories, 169, 171–72, 174, 182; final exams at, 183; graduation, 54, 162–63; guilt associated with, xiii, 169; language lab job, 174, 175–76, 181; leaving the fields for, 135, 158–59, 168–69, 174; Mexican American professors, 172; money for, 135, 136–37; nervous breakdown in, 141–44; and responsibilities to family, 169; scholarship for, 183; and self-esteem, 156; stability in, 175; typewriter for, 141; UT sniper incident, 177–78, 179; Uvalde Jr. College, 135, 139–44, 156, 159–61; working the fields while attending, 155, 156

Colorado, 16

Columbia Basin, 82

communal existence of migrants, 22

company agents, 72

company stores, xix, 17

company towns, xviii–xix

competition: among laborers, 90–91; for work, xvi, 3, 102, 117

contractors: and categories of laborers, 3; for Dick's Ranch, 41–43, 42, 49; good vs. bad contractors, 4; and interpreter skills, 102; and lodging for laborers, 43; transporting laborers, xxi–xxii, 41–43, *42*, 81; treatment of laborers, 9; working without, 54

Cook's Point settlement, xviii, xix

corn crops, 55, 66

Corpus Christi, Texas, 9, 10

cotton: *algodonales* (cotton laden), 10; and categories of laborers, 3; and generational cycle, 5; mechanical pickers for, 5; and migratory cycles, 9–10; wages for, 9; weeding of, 9; and weighers, 3

Cotulla, Texas, 43

courtships, 70–71

credit, buying supplies on, 75, 166

crops, xvi. *See also specific crops, including* tomatoes *and* sugar beets

Crystal City, Texas: and college studies, 136, 158; economic boom of, 7–8; education in, 35–38, 61–66, 94–101, 109–18; elections in, xxiii, 110–12; feminine atmosphere of, 33; home in, 70; and internment camps, 36; Mexican population of, xxiii–xxiv; poetic depiction of, 188 (n1); as population hub, xvi; recruitment of laborers from, 12, 21; schools of, xx, xxiii–xxiv; and seasonal migration, 19; as Spinach Capital of the World, 7–8; summers in, 40; white population of, 33. *See also* Uvalde Jr. College

Crystal Sugar Company, 12, 16

cucumber crops: and categories of laborers, 3; at El Clifa's farm in Wisconsin, 55; father's overheating incident, 30; harvesting of, 47; of La Radke's farm in Wisconsin, 58; in Michigan, xvii; wages for, 47–48

cultural interests of migrant families, xv, 19

curanderas (faith healers), 63

'cutters' category of laborers, 3

dairy farm of family, 7

danger associated with working conditions, xxiv

dates and girlfriends: and college ambitions, 116–17; and confidence, 116–17, 133–34; with field workers, 122; L. (university student), 128–30, 133, 135–36, 137, 158; V., 116–17, 149, 150–51, 152, 155, 166

Davenport, Iowa, xviii

decision-making process of migrant families, 12–13, 82

Delano, California, 51

Delgado v. Bastrop Independent School District, xx

dermatologist appointment, 142–43

Des Plains, Illinois, 68–69

Díaz, Porfirio, xiv

Dick's Ranch, 41, 43–46, 49

diet and nutrition, 133–34

discrimination, xxiv, 57, 190 (n2)

divorce, 155

doghouse sleeping quarters, 157–58

domestic routines, 33

Drayton, North Dakota, 163–67, 174

drinking water, 166–67

Durango, Mexico, xv

Dust Bowl migrants, xvi

economic opportunities as immigration motive, xiv, xv

education and schools: academic success of author, xi; active participation in, xxiv; additive vs. subtractive model in, xix; ambition in, 100–101, 117–18; in the barrio, 38; and *Brown v. the Board of Education*, 57–58; chucos (*pachucos*) in, 62–64; in Crystal City,

35–38, 61–66, 94–101, 109–18; de-
segregation attempts, xxiii; disadvantages faced in, xiii, xix, 95; discrimination in, xxiv, 110; and elections,
112; and English language, 35, 96; and
family responsibilities, xii, 72, 169; as
foundation for college studies, 138–
39, 180–81; and generational cycle,
5; graduation, 109, 113; grammar
school, 61–66; guilt associated with,
xiii, 169; harrassment in, 63–64; high
school, 94–101, 109–18, 139; humiliation of migrant children in, xix, 37,
58, 97–98; in Illinois, 68–69; interruptions in, xx, 65–66, 95, 109; low
expectations for Mexican students
in, xx, xxiii; middle school, 61; and
migration patterns, 35, 95; obedience/
disobedience in, 112–13; opposition
to Mexican students, xxi; private
preschools, xxiii; and prom night,
109–10; race relations in, 110; report
cards, 65–66, 68–69; and school
counselors, xx, 113, 139, 191 (n5); and
Spanish language, 36, 37; strategies
for, 97; and summer vacation, 114;
in Texas, 35–38, 61–66; traumas
experienced in, 97–99; in Wind Lake,
Wisconsin, 56–57. *See also* college
and university studies
eggs, consumption of, 92
El Avispero (The Hornet's Nest) neighborhood, 32, 35
El Campo (The Camp), 35–36
El Clifa's farm in Wisconsin, 55–56
elections, 110–12
El Gin barrio, 70
El Paso, Texas, 17, 21
El Teatro Nacional (National Theater),
72, 189n2
el viejo (the old man), 4

El voladero del diablo (Devil's Canyon), 81
Elk Grove Consolidated #59, 68
emigration from Mexico, early history
of, xiv
employers, xix. *See also* company stores;
company towns
English language: categories of laborers,
1–2; difficulty of learning, 96; English-only instruction, xix; English-
only speakers, 24; as foundation for
college studies, 138–39; as means to
escape poverty, 114; in schools, 35,
96; and segregation, xix–xx; and suc-
cesses experienced by migrant families, 53; teaching experience of author, 53; translation skills of children,
xii–xiii, 102; and truck drivers, 3
ethnic differences, xix
European immigrants: in company
towns, xix; and farming lands, xvi;
and quota laws, xvii–xviii; recruitment of, xvii, 16; transition to growers, 16, 17
E-Z Way Potato Picking Belt, 48

faith healers (*curanderas*), 63
"false consciousness," 57
families of migrants: arrival in Winter
Garden, 6; courtships in, 70–71;
decision-making process of, 12–13, 82;
earnings of members, xx, 14; and education, xii; living conditions for, 14–
15; longevity in, 6; pride and respect
in, 14; and recruitment of laborers,
xvii, xviii; responsibilities to, xii, 72,
169; sacrifices made for, 1; separation
of, 39–40, 102–3; varying citizenship
in, xvi; working as a unit, 49–50
fantasizing, 87–88
farming lands, xiv, xvi
field agents, 15

Filipinos, 53

financial status of immigrants: and annual migration, xxiii; and author's family, 19, 22–23; and credit at stores, 75, 166; and delays in payment, 75; inability to purchase farms, xviii, 17; indebtedness of families, xxii; and struggles endured by families, 147, 148, 151, 152, 165. *See also* wages

"The First Day of School" (Sanchez), 37

flojo (lazy bum), 4

following crops, 15, 182

Fort Madison, Iowa, xviii

Freedom Riders, 110

friends: in Texas, 64–65; in Wisconsin, 43–45, 56–57, 66–67

fruit, 3

García, Mario, xiii

generational cycle, 4–5

genetically modified crops: sugar beets, 164–65; tomatoes, 131–33, 134, *159*

Gilroy, California, 28

girlfriends. *See* dates and girlfriends

gloves, 47

grape crops, 52–53, 54

Great Depression, xxii, 11, 15, 19, 20, 23

Great Western Sugar Company, xviii, 5, 72

gringos, 2

groceries on credit, 75, 166

growers: European immigrants' transition to, 16, 17; farming practices of, 9; and mechanization, 133; pursuing extra work from, 78–79; recruitment of laborers, 72–73, 103; treatment of laborers, 55–56; working directly for, 54–55

guest-worker program, xxii–xxiii, xxv

güevón or *güevona* (loafer), 4

Haley, Alex, 92

hands disfigured from labors, 14

Hay Plesha Lichans Tu Di Flac (Sanchez), 37, 77

hazards associated with agricultural labor, xxiv

high school. *See* education and schools

H. J. Heinz Tomato Company, 104, 105, 106, 120–22

hoes: long-handled hoes, 164–65; posture associated with, 17, *18*, 75, 164; short-handled hoes, 17, *18*, 20, 75, 163–65

Hollandale, Minnesota, 12, 19

Holy City, Iowa, xviii

home purchases of migrant families, 19–20, 23, 70

Horner's Ranch, 41

Hot Rod Magazine, 86

Hunger of Memory (Rodriguez), xiii

hunting, 31

hygiene, 98, 120–22, 140

Hysham, Montana, 31

identities, xiii, 1–2

Illinois, xviii, 68–69

immigration quota laws of 1921 and 1924, xvii–xviii

Infante, Pedro, 25

In Search of Lost Time (Proust), 27

involuntary memories, 27–28

Iowa, 102–8; arrival of family in, 12, 13; dating in, 128–30; experimental crops in, 131–33; labor camps in, 103–4; laborers at tomato farm, 105; lodging for laborers in, 104–5; Mexican population of, xviii; and migratory cycles, 5; and seasonal migration, 19; sugar-beet crops in, xvii, 16; tomato crops in, 103, 105–8, 119–27, 132, 157–58, *159*, 168–69; tractor

incident in, 124–27; and watermelon
party, 106
Iowa State University in Ames, 131

Japanese Internment Camp, 36
Japanese laborers, 16–17, 21
Jiménez, Francisco, xii
jobs (nonagricultural): car wash job, 145,
150; language lab job, 174, 175–76, 181;
shoeshine work, 38–39; at Square D
Company, 146, 147–48, 149, 150. *See
also* wages

Kansas, xviii
ketchup, 133
King, Martin Luther, Jr., 110–11
Knippa, Texas, 6
Korean War, xxiii, 5

labor agents, recruiting practices of, xvii
labor camps: and baseball games, 153; in
Iowa, 103–4; and Japanese laborers,
16; living conditions in, xxi; in Moses
Lake, Washington, 83; and parents
of author, 18–19; and segregation,
17, 22; tents associated with, 10; in
Wisconsin, 41
laborers: categories and subcategories
of, 2–5; and child labor laws, xx–xxi;
competition among, 90–91; contracts
with, xxii; decline in number of, xxiv;
demographics of, xxiv; following
crops, xxiv–xxv, 182; ideal qualities
of, 21; marital status of, xvii, xviii;
treatment of, 9, 55–56; willpower of,
20, 85, 96; work ethic of, 20, 21, 46,
96. *See also* lodging for laborers; physical demands of labor recruitment,
transporting laborers; wages
labor shortages, xxii, xxiii
la chusma (poor masses), 2–3

la palomilla (working class), 2
La Radke's farm in Wisconsin, 58–60
law enforcement officials, hostility of,
xxi
lazybones (*Arrastrado* or *rastra*), 4
lazy bums (*flojo*), 4
Lehigh Portland Company, xviii
Lehigh Row settlement, xix
leisure time, 49, 59
Levelland, Texas, 10
living conditions, 1; in barracks, 84–85;
in company towns, xviii–xix; crowded
residences, 32; and drinking water,
166–67; and guest-worker program,
xxiii; and multi-generational families,
14–15
loafers (*güevón* or *güevona*), 4
lodging for laborers: in Billings, Montana, 73; in company towns, xviii; in
Delano, California, 51; in Des Plains,
Illinois, 67; at Dick's Ranch in Wisconsin, 43; in Drayton, North Dakota,
165–66; at El Clifa's farm in Wisconsin, 54; at La Radke's farm in Wisconsin, 58–59; in labor camps, xxi; living
conditions in, xviii–xix, xxi; in Moses
Lake, Washington, 83, 84–85, 151; in
Muscatine, Iowa, 104–5, 157–58, 167
Los Angeles, California, 144–48
los chicaspatas (unwashed masses), 2–3
low class (*peluza*), 2
Lowenthal, David, 1
Lubbock, Texas, 10

Manly, Iowa, xviii
mantenido (welfare bum), 4
MAPA (political party), 111
mariachis, 25, 188n3
marijuana, 92–93
Márquez, Gabriel García, 29
marriages: of former girlfriend, 158;

modified crops, 164–65; Great Western Sugar Company, xviii, 5, 72; in Iowa, xvii, 16; loading of, *101*; in North Dakota, 163–67, 174, 182; planting of, 165; processing plants in, 16; rebellion in, 77–78; and recruitment of laborers, xvii, 12, 15, 19, 20, 72–73, 189 (n2); return to, in later life, 184; thinning of, 16–18, *18*, 74–78, 84, 117, 164, 165; tools for, 16–17, 20, 74, 163–65; transition of family to, 11, 12, *13*; wages for, 19; in Washington, 82, 83, 84, 85–86; weeding of, 78, 86, 117, 157. *See also* hoes

Taft, Texas, 9
Tamaulipas, Mexico, xvi
teacher position, 183–84
Teatro Campesino (farm workers' theatre), 54, 189n1
tents of migratory families, 10
Texas: arrival of grandparents in, xiii; categories of laborers in, 2; college experience in, 135, 139–44, 156, 158–61, 171–78; communication styles in, 176; cotton crop in, 3, 5; discrimination faced in, 57, 190 (n2); family homes in, 19–20, 70; friends made in, 64–65; and generational cycle, 5; lack of economic opportunities in, 23; management practices in, 50; recruitment of laborers from, 5, 17; returning to, 94–95; and seasonal migration, 19; segregation in, xx, 43, 58, 111–12; summers in, 40; winters in, 31, 49
Texas Rangers, 111
thinners and thinning, 74–78; as category of laborer, 3; difficulty of work, 16–18, *18*. *See also* hoes
tomatoes: and categories of laborers,

3; and cheaters, 122–23; experimental crops, 131–33; fertilized crops, 130–31; genetically modified crops, 131–33, 134, *159*; harvesting of, 66, 106–8, 119–27, *132*, 133; hauling of, 119–22, 158; and H. J. Heinz Tomato Company, 104, 105, 106, 120–22; in Iowa, 103, 105–8, 119–27, *132*, 157–58, *159*, 168–69; of La Radke's farm in Wisconsin, 58; loading of, 119–21, 158, *159*; planting of, 130; roma tomatoes, 131–33; wages for, 47–48, 108; weeding of, 105
tools: for onion crops, 47; for potato crops, 48; purchase of, from company store, 17; for spinach crops, 8; for sugar beet crops, 16–17, *18*, 20, 74. *See also* hoes
Topeka, Kansas, 57
tortillas made by mother, 75, 167–68
tractors, 66, 120–21, 124–27
translation skills of children, xii–xiii, 102
transporting laborers: difficulties endured, 83; fees associated with, 3; in migrant trucks, xxi–xxii, 41–43, *42*, 81–82
Treviño Hart, Elva, xii
troquero system, xxi
truck drivers, 3
truck farming, 41
trucks, 41–43, *42*
typewriter for college work, 141
Tywoniak, Frances Esquibel, xiii

underemployment, xvi
United States immigrant population, xiv, xviii
University of California, Los Angeles, 146

University of Texas, Tower sniper incident, 177–78, 179

unwashed masses (*los chicaspatas*), 2–3

urine incident, 31

Utah, 115

Uvalde County, Texas, xiv

Uvalde Jr. College: first semester, 135, 139–44, 156; graduation, 162–63; second semester, 159–61

Valdés, Dennis Nodín, xvii, xxi, 15–16, 21

Valdez, Luis, 189n1

The Valley, 2, 4, 187 (n3)

Vietnam War: and draft, 113; increasing seriousness of, 107; and Selective Service exams, 179–80; and social activism, 110; and student status, 137, 170; volunteering for, 134, 135, 182

voter intimidation, 111

wages: and advances, 73, 85; bonus money, 108, 124, 189 (n2); from car wash work, 145; and company store credit, 17; for corn crops, 66; for cucumber crops, 47–48; delayed payment of, 75; at Dick's Ranch, 46; drops in, xviii; from extra work from other growers, 75; and family responsibilities, 14; and guest-worker program, xxiii, xxv; inconsistency in, 47–48; low wages, xxiv; and marital status of laborers, xvii; from midwest work, 22–23; for onion crops, 46, 47; refusal of growers to pay, 88; from shoeshine work, 38–39; from Square D Company, 148; for sugar beet crops, 19, 152; suppression of, xxiii; for tomato crops, 47–48; for weeding, 88

Washington: attending college in, 153; dating in, 116–17; financial struggles in, 151–52; maturation in, 102; return to, 148, 149–51; and Selective Service exams, 180; travels to, 114, 115–16

water cistern, 166–67

watermelon party, 106

Watsonville, California, 28

weeding: of bean fields, 46–47; of cotton fields, 9; at El Clifa's farm in Wisconsin, 55; of La Radke's farm in Wisconsin, 58; of onion fields, 12, 45, 46–47; of sugar beet fields, 78, 86, 117, 157; of tomato fields, 105; wages for, 88

weighers, 3–4

welfare bum (*mantenido*), 4

West Liberty, Iowa, xv

wetbacks (*mojados*), 3, 51

Whitman, Charles, 177–78, 179

willpower of migrant laborers, 20, 85, 96

Wind Lake, Wisconsin, 41, 54, 56–57

Winter Garden Valley of Texas: civil rights activism in, xxiii; development of commercial farming in, xvi; family's arrival in, 6; recruitment of laborers from, 21; schools of, xx; segregation in, xxiii; spinach harvests in, 8

Wisconsin, 41–50, 54–60; and contractors, 41–43, 42, 45, 47, 49, 50; Dick's Ranch, 41, 43–46, 49; friends made in, 43–45, 56–57, 66–67; lodging for laborers in, 43; potato crops of, xvii; relocations to, 66

women and girls: and author's youthful relationships, 79–80; domestic routines of, 33; societal expectations of, 116. *See also* dates and girlfriends

work ethic of migrant laborers, 20, 21, 46, 96
working class (*la palomilla*), 2
working conditions, xxiii, xxv
World War I, 16
World War II: and effect of rationing on travel, 31; and internment camps, xxvii (n22), 36; and labor shortages, xxii; service in, 5, 24

Zavala County, xvi
Zavala Elementary School, 37